T0305497

The Bulgarian Economy in Transition

For Magdalen

STUDIES OF COMMUNISM IN TRANSITION

General Editor: **Ronald J. Hill**
*Professor of Comparative Government
and Fellow of Trinity College,
Dublin, Ireland*

Studies of Communism in Transition is an important series which applies academic analysis and clarity of thought to the recent traumatic events in Eastern and Central Europe. As many of the preconceptions of the past half century are cast aside, newly independent and autonomous sovereign states are being forced to address long-term, organic problems which had been suppressed by, or appeased within, the Communist system of rule.

The series is edited under the sponsorship of Lorton House, an independent charitable association which exists to promote the academic study of communism and related concepts.

The Bulgarian Economy in Transition

John A. Bristow
Trinity College, Dublin

STUDIES OF COMMUNISM IN TRANSITION

Edward Elgar
Cheltenham, UK • Brookfield, US

Published by
Edward Elgar Publishing Limited
8 Lansdown Place
Cheltenham
Glos GL50 2HU
UK

Edward Elgar Publishing Company
Old Post Road
Brookfield
Vermont 05036
US

British Library Cataloguing in Publication Data
Bristow, J.A.
    Bulgarian Economy in Transition. –
    (Studies of Communism in Transition)
    I. Title II. Series
    330.94977

Library of Congress Cataloguing in Publication Data
Bristow, John A., 1938–
        The Bulgarian economy in transition / John A. Bristow
        (Studies of communism in transition)
        Includes bibliographical references and index.
        1. Bulgaria—Economic policy—1989–   2. Bulgaria—Economic
    conditions—1989–   3. Post-communism—Economic aspects—
    Bulgaria.
    I. Title. II. Series.
    HC403.B75 1996   95–36671
    338.94977—dc20   CIP

ISBN 1 85278 994 8

Printed in Great Britain by Ipswich Book Co. Ltd., Ipswich, Suffolk.

Contents

Tables

Preface

For those concerned with how societies organize themselves, what has been happening in Central and Eastern Europe and the former Soviet Union in the past few years is of enormous interest, because it is unprecedented. As was discovered in the 1940s and early 1950s (and earlier in Russia), it is technically not particularly difficult to set up a one-party polity and a centrally planned economy. The reverse process has never before been attempted on both the political and economic fronts and is proving a great challenge for policy makers and for social scientists (and especially economists) who, despite their apparent confidence in offering advice to those policy makers, have little enough to guide them.

Professional attention among westerners (or, at least, among anglophone scholars) has been concentrated on Russia, Hungary, Poland and the former Czechoslovakia. Bulgaria has evoked much less interest, probably for reasons of history. Until the erection of the Iron Curtain, Hungary, Poland and Czechoslovakia were never regarded as especially remote or alien by educated westerners, notwithstanding Neville Chamberlain's crass reference to German ambitions in Czechloslovakia as 'a quarrel in a far-away country between people of whom we know nothing'. They were culturally and politically integrated with the rest of Europe. Russia was rather different, but not very: Tchaikovsky and Tolstoy were in the mainstream of European culture and the Romanovs mixed their blood with that of western dynasties. In any case, the size and geo-political significance of the Tsarist empire and the Soviet Union meant that that region occupied a large band of western observers for two centuries or more.

Bulgaria on the other hand was, during the half-millennium when Europe was taking shape politically and culturally, occupied by the Ottomans and cut off from the rest of the continent. The Ottomans were not expelled from the whole of what is now Bulgaria until 1912, and from 1944 until 1989 the country was a loyal Russian partner and one of the more closed members of the Soviet bloc — so much so that even specialists in communist affairs gave it little independent attention. The relationship with Russia is important to the history and to an understanding of Bulgaria. In 1878, the Turks were driven from most of the country by a Russian army. Although this was hardly an act of altruism, the Russians suffered massive losses and the general view since then has been to regard them as the liberators from the 500-year Ottoman occupation. In front of the parliament building in Sofia stands a fine equestrian statue of Alexander II, Tsar Liberator, and the most distinctive building in the city, the Church of Saint Alexander Nevski, was built explicitly as a memorial to the Russian soldiers who died in the war against the Turks. This particular event, when combined with the religious and linguistic affinity between the two countries, has generated ever since a generally warm attitude towards Russia on the part of most Bulgarians. At the political level, this was reinforced between the world wars when Bulgarian communist leaders such as Georgi Dimitrov took refuge in Moscow from persecution at home and then later the relationship was strengthened by the close loyalty shown to the Soviet Union on the part of successive communist heads of government.

This has produced a tendency to regard Bulgaria as the sixteenth republic of the Soviet Union[1] and not worthy of independent concern. This neglect, whatever its validity in the past, is no longer justified. To students of transition, the country offers much of interest, both because of what it has in common with other countries of the region and because of its differences.

Bulgaria's political revolution came suddenly and peaceably. The climactic event was the internal Politburo coup of November 1989 which overthrew Todor Zhivkov, effectively the boss of the country since 1954. Free elections were held within nine months.

Communism changed Bulgaria's economic structure more than that of any other country, turning the most agricultural country of the region into, with Czechoslovakia, the most industrialized. Bulgaria relied more on the Council for Mutual Economic Assistance (CMEA, otherwise known as Comecon) than did any other country and so has suffered

---

1 It appears that Zhivkov actually did offer to integrate Bulgaria into the Soviet Union — an offer which was declined (Pundeff (1992), p. 105).

more than any other from the demise of that institution. In terms of the macroeconomics of transition, Bulgaria has much in common with Poland, ending the communist period with a heavy burden of foreign debt and severe inflationary pressures. Its early transition experience also somewhat mimicked Poland's, though lagging by a year or so.

In matters of structural and institutional change, Bulgaria has made less progress than many of its neighbours, being to date rather slow in areas such as privatization and the reform of monetary and fiscal institutions. The easiest explanation for this is the apparently sclerotic condition of the legislative process, the rather unstable nature of parliamentary coalitions making radical change impossible. The more interesting question is why this should be when others in the region, also learning to use democratic institutions for the first time, seem to move more quickly.

The western economic literature on transition in Eastern Europe is, for the most part, heavily normative in tone with a prescriptive emphasis which is often misplaced. Of course, economists like to offer policy advice and they here have the opportunity of a lifetime. The policy issues are much more challenging than those in the West and, initially anyway, advisers confronted governments who were prepared to listen: they wanted to operate market economies and here were people who knew about such economies. Much has been written which takes no account of political constraints or the dynamics of institution-building; there has been much professional debate on the proper sequencing of reforms, but each contribution seemed to end up with confident policy advice; and there was even much energy dissipated in sterile controversy over 'big-bang versus gradualism'. None the less, the real world eventually takes over: governments in transition countries are now displaying much more jaundiced attitudes towards foreign advisers and, professionally more importantly, the literature has noticeably matured, especially in its recognition that privatization, monetary and fiscal reform, and generally the construction and effective operation of market-economy institutions are going to take much longer than was realised (or assumed) in the early days.[2]

This book attempts to describe and analyse the economic transition

2 A brisk and sobering review, headed with the epigramatic 'Nobody said it would be easy, and nobody was right', is provided by Portes (1994).

process in Bulgaria. The emphasis is on trying to understand what is going on rather than on devising simple solutions to complex problems. The authorities in Sofia will find some unfavourable comment but no blueprint. The longer one studies transition economies the less dogmatic one becomes, except in one's distaste for nostrums.

The first chapter sets the scene, being a superficial description of developments in communist Bulgaria prior to the watershed year of 1989. This is intended merely as an introduction and the remainder is concerned with what has been happening in the last five years or so, although further reference to the communist past continues to be made since on any topic it is impossible to understand where one is going without an understanding of where one is coming from.

A preface is the place to take out insurance against criticism and, in this respect, three points deserve mention. First, this book is not a report on research: it is synthetic and expository rather than original. It is designed to bring a little-known country to the attention of my professional colleagues and, with luck, to that of a wider audience. If it stimulates readers to conduct research on Bulgaria, then I shall be pleased. Secondly, the economics of transition cannot be understood without consideration of the politics and sociology of transition, but I am very conscious that my own professional formation makes my sensitivity to these latter aspects both superficial and naive. Thirdly, things change so quickly that, whenever one makes a generalization or a judgement, one takes one's life in one's hands. My publishers achieved the transformation of a typescript into a book with extraordinary expedition but, by the time this is published, I could be very wrong about the current state of play.

Some editorial usages are worth mentioning. Bulgarian words and names have been transliterated according to fairly standard English usage, except where a Bulgarian author writing in English has transliterated his or her name differently. The sources given for tables are the sources from which I extracted the data, not necessarily the original sources. The words 'Derived from' mean that the table contains the results of calculations I made on data obtained from the cited source. The unit of Bulgarian currency is the *lev* (with the numerical plural *leva* used in all cases) and, when attached to a number, I have used the abbreviation BGL.

I have benefitted enormously from the willingness of a large number of persons in Bulgaria to give up their time for me and to supply information. My informants extend through many ministries and other public bodies, international agencies, the private sector and academia. It would be invidious to name them and they of course bear no responsibility for what I have made of their efforts and hospitality. I could not even repay them by speaking their language with any facility but the book could not have been written without them.

My employers — Trinity College, Dublin — are thanked for financing my visits to Bulgaria and special thanks go to my friend and colleague, Ronald Hill — the series editor — and to the staff of Edward Elgar.

J.A.B.

1. The Communist Era

THE ESTABLISHMENT AND CONSOLIDATION OF A COMMUNIST SOCIETY

Political Developments

Bulgaria did all its geographical position allowed to stand aloof from the Second World War. When the war started, the country pronounced its neutrality, but German pressure became irresistible, especially after the successes against the Soviet Union in 1941, and Bulgaria declared war on the US, France and Britain at the end of that year. The German–Soviet pact and the general instability in Eastern Europe which it, and the German invasion of Poland, created had already brought territorial gains to Bulgaria. Southern Dobrudja, which had been assigned to Romania under the Treaty of Versailles, was returned to Bulgaria in late 1940 as a result of a treaty also involving Hungary and the USSR.

The main initial advantage of alignment with the Axis powers was that the Bulgarian army was allowed by the Germans to occupy Macedonia and Thrace, a move which was popular because these territories, and especially the former, had ethnic, religious and historical links with Bulgaria. Nonetheless, Bulgaria — led by a king who ironically was of a German princely family — did nothing positive to assist the pursuit of Axis aims. She never declared war on the Soviet Union, refusing to send any troops to the Eastern Front. Also, although the Bulgarian army had assisted in the deportation of Macedonian Jews, Bulgaria was the only country in Eastern Europe to use both governmental and popular power to prevent the destruction of its own Jewish population.[1]

---

1 Chary (1972).

Anti-German feeling increased from 1943 onwards: it became clear that Germany was likely to lose the war and Bulgaria was beginning to suffer (by early 1944 Sofia had been heavily bombed and both food shortages and severe inflation became manifest). Attempts to switch sides were rebuffed by the Allies who demanded the same terms as those applied to other, even only nominally, pro-Axis countries. This provided fertile ground for the development of an as yet infant organization which was to dominate Bulgarian life for the next 45 years — the Fatherland Front, a left-wing grouping of Communists, Agrarians and Social Democrats. The Front had a small membership, but focused the opposition to involvement in the war: if it had been less intransigent over its socialist policies, it might well have participated in government. Its confidence increased in 1944 as Soviet demands on Bulgaria increased and the Russians invaded Romania in August. Attempts to reach a satisfactory agreement with the western Allies failed, the Russians entered Bulgaria on 8 September and a Fatherland Front administration was installed on the following day.

All the main elements of the Front were represented in this first administration, but 9 September 1944 marked the beginning of the creation of a communist Bulgaria, assisted by the facts that the ministries of justice and the interior were given to Communists, the Red Army was in the country, and the USSR had permanent chairmanship of the allied control commission. Russian aid followed and 'Bulgaria's traditional Russophilia [was] ... assiduously nurtured [and] ... ensured that the Communists would profit from Soviet patronage and generosity'.[2] Party membership, which had been a mere 25,000 when the Russians arrived, grew ten-fold by the end of the year.[3]

The first aims were the standard ones — to eliminate opponents and consolidate the power of the party — and the means were to become familiar throughout the region — purges, sometimes but not always disguised as war-crimes trials, the growth of party committees at local level (the strength of which was to remain an important feature of Bulgarian communism), and the reconstruction of the trade unions. All members of the existing parliament were arrested and many executed, after which the focus of attention moved to left-wing, but anti-

---

2 Crampton (1987), p. 146.

3 McIntyre (1988), p. 55.

communist, elements of the Fatherland Front — notably the Agrarian Party now led by Nikola Petkov.

The end of the war saw vehemently controversial preparations for an election and the return from Moscow of the communist leaders-in-exile, most famously Georgi Dimitrov who had attracted international attention as one of the defendants in the Reichstag Fire trial of 1934. The Fatherland Front received almost nine-tenths of the votes cast in the election of November 1945, but Petkov remained adamant in his opposition. The monarchy was abolished in September 1946 and new elections for parliament announced for October. The Communists gained 277 of the 364 seats and totally dominated the Fatherland Front: it was now a straight fight between Communists and others, with Petkov leading the latter with his independent Agrarians, who had considerable support because of rural suspicions about agricultural collectivization. In November, Dimitrov became minister president and the final push to complete domination began.

February 1947 saw the peace treaty which gave Bulgaria southern Dobrudja, but not Macedonia or Thrace (thus establishing the present borders) and provided for the departure of Soviet forces. But it also abolished the allied control commission and any residual protection for anti-communists evaporated. Petkov's Agrarians were removed from the parliament (a small remnant of the original Agrarian Party had remained steadfast members of the Fatherland Front and did so until its abolition in 1990) and their leader himself was executed in September. With the destruction of the opposition, all that remained was for the Communists to consolidate their hegemony over the Fatherland Front, which was achieved during 1947 and 1948.

The last element was a new constitution, passed in December 1947. It established a typical communist polity, with a concentration of powers, lack of effective distinction between state and party organs, and sufficient generalized exceptions of the 'public interest' type to nullify any constitutional protection of citizens' rights.

The main task of the next few years was to emulate Stalin in consolidating the power of the party and the establishment of a socialist economy (see below). Dimitrov made the first steps, but he was not to last long, dying in July 1949. He may have known that his time was nigh since one of his last major political acts was to sponsor the purging and execution of Traicho Kostov, an obvious candidate for the succession. An old colleague, Vasil Kolarov, was known to be ill (he in fact succeeded Dimitrov, but died in turn in January 1950) and getting rid of Kostov gave a clear run to Dimitrov's own brother-in-law, Vulko Chervenkov — 'a replica of Stalin'.[4] He got off to a flying start by being bequeathed the overwhelming victory of the Fatherland Front in the first elections under the 1947 constitution, in which almost 99 per cent of the electorate voted and, of these, almost 98 per cent voted for the Front.[5]

Chervenkov continued Dimitrov's strategy of eliminating potential opposition both within and beyond the party. Within a year, more than 20 per cent of the party's half-million members had been purged, many being sent to labour camps. The possibility of opposition from ethnic minorities had been partially tackled by the encouragement of Jewish emigration to Israel, but the new leader turned his attention to the much more significant Turkish minority, who were notably strong opponents of agricultural collectivization and, because of their religion, of communism generally. In 1950, he announced the forced emigration of 250,000 to Turkey and, after eighteen months, when the latter closed its border, almost 160,000 had left Bulgaria. The remainder were then left in reasonable peace until a new campaign in the 1980s (see below).

The death of Stalin in March 1953 cut the ground from under the feet of Chervenkov, whose central purpose had been to mimic in Bulgaria what Stalin had done in the Soviet Union. It was made worse for him by the fact that there was uncertainty about the redirection of Soviet policy. The first step was taken at the Sixth Party Congress in March 1954 when his two jobs — head of government and head of party — were divided and the latter went to the man who came to personify communist Bulgaria for the next thirty-five years, Todor Zhivkov. Remaining as minister-president, Chervenkov put in train some elements of 'de-Stalinization', notably some redirection of economic policy away from industrial investment in favour of consumption and the release of many political prisoners, but his final downfall became inevitable after the change in Soviet policy towards Yugoslavia and Khrushchev's denunciation of Stalin. Seeing the way the wind was blowing, Zhivkov proclaimed a need to reorientate Bulgarian policies away from all

---

4 Pundeff (1992), p. 102.

5 Crampton (1987), p. 172.

Chervenkov stood for and the latter resigned in April 1956, to be replaced as head of government by Anton Yugov.

Zhivkov's avowed strategy was the close integration of Bulgaria with the Soviet Union: as he said, to make them part of a 'common circulatory system'.[6] He also needed to consolidate his domestic position by distancing himself further from the Dimitrov–Chervenkov era. To this end, Kostov was rehabilitated in 1956 and senior figures who may have remained loyal to Chervenkov purged from the party. Chervenkov was brought back into government in 1957 with the specific task of ensuring orthodoxy in the face of signs of intellectual revival — arguably as part of a perceived need to show strength in the light of what had happened in Hungary.

But Yugov and Chervenkov remained political threats, most obviously by appearing to be sympathetic to China as relations between that country and the Soviet Union deteriorated, and Zhivkov eventually moved against them. The Eighth Party Congress in 1962 was induced to expel Chervenkov (he had already lost his Politburo and government posts the previous year) and to remove Yugov from the post of minister-president and from the Politburo. Zhivkov took over as minister-president, thus reunifying the headships of party and government, and by 1964 his strength was shown by the fact that his position, unlike Chervenkov's in 1954, was not weakened by the downfall of his Moscow godfather (in this case, Khrushchev). For the next quarter-century he was essentially inviolable. The implementation of a new constitution in 1971, which vested supreme executive, and very significant legislative, power in a state council the chairman of which was Zhivkov, provided a juridical basis for his personal hegemony.

The Making of a Planned Economy

Agriculture
It has become common practice to divide agricultural reorganization in Bulgaria into phases, each successive phase being seen as a move

---

6 Pundeff (1992), p. 104. Cf. Dimitrov who is quoted as saying that 'for the Bulgarian people, friendship with the Soviet Union is just as necessary for life as the air and sun is for any living creature' (Crampton (1987), p. 174).

towards the achievement of certain long-term economic and ideological objectives. Economically, the aims were to increase agricultural productivity to such a degree that the huge transfer of labour into industry could be accommodated without resort to large-scale importation of food. This aim was to be accomplished by taking advantage of presumed economies of scale and by significant investment in the sector, though the latter was severely constrained by the overriding structural objective of transforming Bulgaria into an industrial economy. The ideological objectives were to achieve complete state control over agricultural production and marketing and to turn farm workers into members of the industrial proletariat.[7]

In the mid-1940s, Bulgaria was a land of small peasantry. In 1944 there were 1.1 million farms (fragmented into 12 million plots) with an average area of only 4.3 hectares.[8] The first moves towards collectivization came in 1945 and 1946. Rapid progress was made as regards distribution so that by the end of 1946 less than 10 per cent of agricultural exports were still organized privately and, by 1949, only 13 per cent of domestic food distribution was privately controlled.

On the production front, however, collectivization was much more difficult. Some state farms were established, but the institution upon which the collectivization programme rested was the producers' cooperative, the *TKZS*.[9] Membership of *TKZS*s was officially voluntary, but from the beginning both sticks and carrots were used to encourage peasants to join. From 1946, no person could own more than 20 hectares, the excess being distributed half-and-half between the cooperatives and, in one-hectare lots, smallholders. Among the carrots were the (uniquely Bulgarian) facts that ground rent was paid to the owners with respect to land they brought to the cooperative and that a member did not have to contribute his or her entire holding.

Initial progress was very slow (by the end of 1947 less than 4 per cent of all arable land had been collectivized), and steps were taken to

---

7 A discussion of more general political objectives of agricultural collectivisation in the region can be found in Sokolovsky (1990).

8 Commission of the European Communities (1991), Section 7.1.

9 *Trudovo kooperativno zemedelsko stopastvo.* Throughout this chapter, words like 'collective' or 'state' are used indiscriminately to identify non-private agriculture, the distinction between true state and cooperative (or collective) farming through the *TKZS*s being unimportant to the discussion.

increase the momentum. From 1948, all agricultural machinery had to be handed over to the state for the use of depots. In addition, the official 'anti-kulak' campaign was stepped up and applied to those holding more than 10 hectares (reduced to 5 hectares in 1949). This had some effect since, by the end of 1949, 11 per cent of arable land was in state hands,[10] but the authorities were increasingly dissatisfied and the elements of the drive to complete collectivization were soon put in place. First, from 1950, private farmers were obliged to deliver 75 per cent of their grain harvest for state distribution and a tough income tax was applied to the private sector. Secondly, the early 1950s saw the passage of the statutes for *TKZSs*. These were modelled on the 1935 Soviet statute, the major differences being that, for the time being, members retained the legal ownership of their land and received ground rent. Members could retain holdings of less than a half-hectare for their own use and had to contribute a defined number of days' labour to the collective. The only land transfers permitted were those to the *TKZSs*. The result was a rapid acceleration in membership, with the proportion of arable land in collective hands reaching 44 per cent by the end of 1950, 61 per cent by 1952, 77 per cent by 1956 and 92 per cent by 1958.[11]

This was not achieved without considerable opposition and disruption of production. The process was assisted by some concessions — for instance, in 1957 Bulgaria became the first East European country to extend pensions and other welfare benefits to farm workers and, in 1962, applied the industrial minimum wage to the agricultural sector — and by a surge in investment resources allocated to agriculture. Fixed investment in that sector, which in 1949 had accounted for only 12 per cent of the national total, rose to 23 per cent in 1956 and almost 30 per cent in 1960 — within five points of industry's share of investment.[12] The balance then tipped back, the percentage returning to 12 by 1970. This, combined with a dramatic fall in the agricultural labour force (a decline of 40 per cent in the period 1950–70) generated high labour-productivity growth — an annual average of 8.6 per cent in the 1960s.[13]

---

10 Crampton (1987), p. 175.

11 Lampe (1986), pp. 148–9.

12 McIntyre (1988), p. 110.

13 Lampe (1986), p. 169.

The late 1950s, aside from achieving almost total collectivization, saw the beginnings of the application to agriculture of the obsession with economies of scale which dominated communist thinking on economic structure. In 1958, the 3,450 *TKZS*s were amalgamated into 932 units with an average area of 4,200 hectares. This consolidation of collectives into gigantic units was the main feature of reforms beginning in the late 1960s, a process described shortly.

Industry
During the war, some industries were nationalized, but most of the sector was in private hands and organized in very small units. Immediately after the war, enterprises owned by those who could be tagged 'collaborators' or 'war profiteers' were confiscated but still, by late 1947, 84 per cent of industrial enterprises were private, 10 per cent cooperative and a mere 6 per cent state-owned.[14] But this structure was seen as both ideologically inappropriate and economically insufficient to provide the basis for the main thrust of Bulgaria's exercise in socialist reconstruction — the rapid industrialization of what was until then an overwhelmingly agrarian society.

The trend was set in the interim two-year plan to cover 1947–48. In one fell swoop in December 1947, all private industry was brought into state hands with no effective compensation. At the same time, the remaining 32 banks were merged into the agency which was to monopolize domestic commercial banking for four decades — the Bulgarian National Bank. With the establishment of state monopoly over international trade, all the main non-agricultural institutions of a centrally planned economy were in place.

Bulgaria chose — not surprisingly, given its close Russian affiliations — the Soviet route of economic development, based on the growth of industry (and especially heavy industry), the resources to be provided through forced saving, the central, budgetary allocation of investment and the transfer of a huge volume of labour from agriculture. This extensive approach to development through industrialization was the theme of the first three five-years plans, beginning in 1949. The first plan provided for industry to obtain 47 per cent of all investment, and for electricity supply and chemicals to get almost half of the industrial

---

14 Dobrin (1973), p. 13.

total. Over the five years, industrial output was targeted to grow by 120 per cent, with heavy industry to grow by almost twice that, and agricultural output by 59 per cent. In good Soviet tradition, the plan was declared to be achieved a year early but strains were showing, especially as a result of the extremely investment-intensive nature of the process.[15]

The second plan, for the years 1953–57, saw some reorientation away from investment, and especially that in heavy industry. The investment/NMP ratio was scheduled to halve to 14 per cent by 1956 and a 40-per cent increase in real personal incomes was planned. Furthermore, the planned increase in industrial output was only half that in the first plan, and less than the planned increase in food production. Nonetheless, the inexorable process of industrialization continued and, by the end of the plan period, industrial output outstripped that in agriculture for the first time. Furthermore, industrial concentration continued: whereas 6,000 industrial enterprises had been nationalized in 1947, by 1960 the number of enterprises had fallen to 1650, with an average labour force of 370 – over 15 times that in the former year.[16]

The drive to collectivization of agriculture in the 1950s had generated large-scale migration to urban centres and created high unemployment. The main theme of the third plan, to begin in 1958, was therefore rapid growth in production and the creation of 400,000 jobs. A new influence was that of the requirements of the intra-region trading system, the Council for Mutual Economic Assistance (CMEA, or Comecon). This organization had been founded in 1949 and developed into a kind of multinational planning system based on bilateral trading pacts. It had been unimportant in influencing the first two five-year plans, but now denominated Bulgaria as a major food supplier for the region and so forced some change in the structure of planned investment, with food processing emerging as a priority sector.

The first three plans generated the huge structural changes, indicated in Table 1.1, which were the main feature of this phase of development.

With the exception of employment creation, the ambitious targets of the third plan were not realised and this failure forced upon the

---

15 In 1951/52, the ratio of net investment to net material product was a huge 28 per cent (Lampe (1986), p. 143).

16 Lampe (1986), p. 146.

authorities a realization of the limits of extensive development. Technically, what had happened so far was the easy phase of socialist development. Capital accumulation was effected by means of forced saving through taxes, administered prices and the rationing of consumer goods; the allocation of investment towards industry was achieved by planning fiat; and labour productivity in agriculture was increased mainly through the amalgamation of holdings into cooperatives, thus making available to industry the huge additional volume of labour required for the structural transformation of the economy. In this phase, concerns for efficiency were relatively unimportant because the goal had been structural change rather than the generation of a steady increase in general living standards.

Table 1.1   Indicators of economic structure, 1948–60

	1948	1956	1960
% of NMP			
Industry	23	37	48
Agriculture	59	32	27
% of employment			
Industry	8	13	22
Agriculture	82	70	55
% of investment			
Industry	31	37	34
Agriculture	12	23	30

Source: Lampe (1986), p. 144; Dobrin (1973), p. 155; McIntyre (1988), p. 110

However, by the 1960s, the limits of this strategy had been reached. Further development required improvements in total factor productivity (or intensive development) and that decade was to see the first, albeit abortive, attempts at reforms designed to achieve this objective by relaxing some of the rigidities of central planning.

REFORM EFFORTS AND ECONOMIC PERFORMANCE

It is a conjecture beyond the ambitions of this book as to whether the desire for political freedom or the desire for higher material living standards was the more potent cause of the demise of communism in Europe. What cannot be denied is that even the totalitarian government of Bulgaria showed a continuous recognition of the fragility of power if economic performance fell too far behind the economic expectations of the population. The 1960s, 1970s and 1980s were characterized by repeated adjustments in the forms of economic organization, in an effort to raise the productivity of both labour and capital once development had gone beyond the point where growth could be achieved simply by the accumulation of capital and the transfer of labour from one sector to another. Whether these reform efforts, in the case of industry anyway, ever amounted to much more than the application of 'semantic organization theory'[17] is arguable, but they need to be reviewed since, cumulatively, they produced the situation from which transition started. Also, the last reforms — described by one observer as introducing 'profound changes in the basic principles of economic organization and management'[18] — were never put to the test. The most recent communist reform legislation of all, Decree 56 of 1989, is still partially extant and consideration of it will be left until later. Where organizational reform had very observable effects on economic performance was in agriculture, and we begin with that sector.

Agriculture

The essence of the agricultural reforms begun in the late 1960s was the desire to make farming more like industry juridically, organizationally and economically for ideological reasons (everyone would then become members of a homogeneous proletariat) but above all because of the need to raise the productivity of the labour, capital and land in the sector. The most prevalent unit, the *TKZS*, was to become organizationally similar to an industrial enterprise, shedding finally the traces of its origins as a cooperative and becoming legally similar to a

---

17 McIntyre (1988), p. 119.

18 Aroio (1989), p. 92.

state farm. Structurally, the drive was for concentration into organizations which eventually became extremely large, even by the standards of the rest of the region.

The first steps came in 1968 with new statutes for the *TKZS*s, abolishing the ground rent paid to those who had brought land to the cooperative. Minimum wages were imposed (the first place in Eastern Europe where this feature of the socialist economy was applied to agriculture) and the brigade (or work team) system introduced. The same year saw, initially on an experimental basis, the first examples of what were to become the dominant form of agricultural organization, the agro-industrial complex or *APK*[19] and its associated organization, the industrial-agricultural complex or *PAK*.

The *APK*s were at first loose federations of cooperatives but they soon became autonomous legal entities. They were designed to achieve economies of scale through horizontal integration, each complex being the amalgamation of geographically contiguous cooperatives and required to specialize in a very small range of crops and livestock. The less prevalent *PAK* was an exercise in vertical integration in the case of crops which were an input to an industrial process, the complex encompassing the *APK*s or *TKZS*s producing the crop and the industrial enterprises processing it. An early example was the production of sugar.

This amalgamation process proceeded very quickly and by the end of 1971 all of the country's 744 collectives and 56 state farms had been grouped into 161 complexes, with an average area of 24,000 hectares and an average labour force of 6,500.[20]

The intended effect on agricultural productivity failed to materialize and one reason was probably that the units became too large and serious managerial diseconomies of scale set in. As a result, some deconcentration was set in train in the late 1970s so that in 1982 the number of *APK*s was double what it had been five years previously. Furthermore, the whole *APK/PAK* concept reduced still further the motivation a farmer gains from working his own land: after all, it must have been the case that, when these organizations were established, most of their workers could remember the days when the land they worked had been owned by themselves or their relatives. Evidence for this —

---

19 *Agrarno-promishlen kompleks.* Its sister, the *PAK*, was *Promishleno-agraren kompleks.*
20 Lampe (1986), p. 207.

and, indeed, for the fact that the authorities recognized the irreplaceable incentive built into owner-worked farming — came from the experience of the continued operation of personal plots. The development of official attitudes to these plots is an interesting, and perhaps unique, example of a recognition that social and ideological incentives are insufficient for efficiency.

Personal plots were not privately owned, but their produce was: they were rather like what in parts of the English-speaking world are called 'allotments'. They originated in the late 1950s as one of the carrots in the drive to get peasants to join the cooperatives. The idea was that *TKZS* workers could have access to small amounts of land (each plot was of an area in the range 0.2–0.5 hectares) for their personal use. At the time of the establishment of the cooperatives, personal plots accounted for about 10 per cent of the cultivated land. Whilst early official attitudes were grudging and restrictive, policies changed quite dramatically in the 1970s, almost certainly in acceptance that these plots were more effective producers of food than the state organizations. Restrictions were relaxed on the number of livestock which could be raised on a plot; holders could lease further plots and were allowed access to such items as seed and equipment from the complex where they were employed; tax concessions were granted and access to credit made easier; marketing of produce in excess of the family's requirements was facilitated; urban workers could work on their relatives' plots in their spare time; and, finally, in 1977 the amount of land available for private plots was increased and plots could be leased by people who had no other contact with the complex owning the plot. The main remaining restrictions were that no-one could work a plot full-time or use hired labour.

The relative significance of personal plots can be seen from Table 1.2. Of course, these figures reveal nothing about the relative productivity of the personal and state sector: what they do show is the extent to which the authorities were willing to permit the use of personal plots in those activities where smallholdings can be efficient.[21] The continued,

---

21 Thus, personal plots were of negligible importance in the production of cereals such as wheat and barley, and the relatively high figures for meat and milk were the result of high figures for chickens, mutton and sheep or goat milk. For vegetables in general the recent figure for personal plots has been about 35 per cent and for fruits anything from 30 to 80 per cent.

and indeed growing, role of personal plots provided a good foundation for the maintenance of activity when nationalized land began to be restored to its original owners under the restitution programme of the early 1990s (see Chapter 4 below).

Table 1.2 Significance of personal plots (%), 1960–88

	1960	1980	1985	1988
Land	10	13	14	14
Milk	20	26	27	25
Meat	28	39	45	45
Eggs	50	55	52	49
Potatoes	n.a.	53	52	62
Wheat	n.a.	2	3	3

Source: Commission of the European Communities (1991), Tables 7.1–7.3; McIntyre (1988), p. 105

Industry

'What sets Bulgaria apart from the Soviet Union is the virtually unbroken process of implementing, or at least discussing, economic reform ...',[22] but it must be stressed that 'reform' in this context means organizational change designed to make the central planning mechanism easier to operate: in Bulgaria, unlike Hungary, it never meant any serious effort even partially to replace that mechanism.

In 1963 the organizational concentration of industry was increased by the grouping of all enterprises into associations, *DSOs*,[23] and these were used as the basis for short-lived reforms (probably inspired by the Liberman proposals in the USSR) instituted experimentally the following year and becoming official policy in late 1965. This was supposed to be an exercise in decentralization, or planning from below, in that enterprises could initiate their own investment programmes which were coordinated within sectors by the relevant *DSO*. Enterprises could find their own markets for production in excess of the plan target and

---

22 Lampe (1986), p. 200.

23 *Dürzhaven stopanstvo organizatsiya.*

they were now confronted with only four such targets — production, foreign-exchange earnings and maxima for inputs and investment. Wages and investment were to be more closely tied to profitability at the enterprise level.

By 1968, these reforms were largely abandoned (possibly because of the fear that they would encourage political experimentation along the lines of the 'Prague Spring', but more probably because the leadership were not truly committed to them) and the party called for a reversal of decentralization — 'the perfection of centralized planning'.[24] Throughout the 1970s, the degree of industrial concentration increased (by 1970, industry was already so concentrated that there were only 2,500 enterprises and almost half the industrial labour force was in enterprises employing over 1,000 workers[25]); the number of *DSOs* was dramatically reduced and subsequently these associations themselves became effectively redundant with the institution of a small number of yet larger organizations, one for each major branch of industry, which were to become the critical layer in the planning and coordination mechanism. But none of this did enough to remove the inefficiency and corruption endemic in the system, and the late 1970s and early 1980s saw the making of yet another U-turn — the implementation of the so-called New Economic Mechanism (NEM), which is best thought of as a continuing process of institutional change rather than the once-for-all proclamation of a blueprint.

The major objectives of the rolling reforms of the 1980s can be summarized as the improvement of productivity, the improvement of the quality of Bulgarian-made goods, an increase in competitiveness in hard-currency international trade and the stimulation of technological improvements. The first phase (roughly the first half of the 1980s) has been characterized under five headings[26]: decentralization, with much looser central supervision of enterprises and targets limited to general production guidelines, profits and foreign-exchange earnings; industrial democracy, with labour brigades exercising a leading management function; competition for investment funds based on projects to incorporate new technologies; greater responsiveness to customer

---

24 Crampton (1987), p. 193.
25 Lampe (1986), p. 213.
26 Crampton (1987), pp. 198–9.

demand; and financial self-sufficiency in the sense of less availability of subsidies and greater reliance on the internal financing of investments.

An interesting development concerned the establishment in 1982 of the Bulgarian Industrial Association, a non-governmental but nonetheless powerful Chamber of Commerce whose brief was the stimulation of new, small enterprises to exploit new opportunities. It did this by providing consultancy services and, through its close association with the Mineralbank, credit for new ventures. It was a genuine innovation in that it reflected official recognition that the standard industrial behemoth was too slow on its feet.[27]

Yet again, the reforms seemed to generate little improvement in the performance of the economy, although perhaps too much was expected of them in the short run. Decentralization requires local management to have the expertise to carry its new responsibilities but, after decades when they were merely administrators, where were managers supposed to acquire this expertise? Then, improvements in quality and productivity and the introduction of new technology could not have been achieved without a significant increase in imports from the West. Given that an overriding policy objective was the reduction of hard-currency debt, it would have been difficult to square that circle. Energy supplies, unreliable at the best of times, provided another constraint. However, despite these possible excuses, continued popular outcry against the quality and availability of consumer goods (combined with a very palpable example of economic dysfunction in the form of electricity interruptions, which reached their peak in the catastrophic drought of 1985 which made hydro-electricity unavailable and damaged food supplies) led to one more round of reform measures.

In many respects this round, initiated in 1986 and formally adopted in 1987, was more of the same.[28] For example, there was yet more shuffling of the layers of the system (with the abolition of a large number of industrial ministries and their replacement by a small number

---

27 For more detail on the early activities of the BIA (which still exists), see Lampe (1986), p. 217; McIntyre (1988), pp. 119–123; McIntyre (1992), pp. 65–9 and Jones and Meurs (1991).

28 Quite a detailed review can be found in Grosser (1989) and a thorough description of the organisational environment in which enterprises operated as a result of these reforms is provided by Aroio (1989).

of sectoral councils) and further stress on the desirability of decentralization of decision-making. Enterprises were supposed to become more responsible for their own activities and central targets for output were to be replaced by contracts with the state. The idea of industrial democracy was furthered by the institution of elections for enterprise directors.

Some changes, however, did look new in the sense that, while not in themselves tainting the ideological purity of the socialist system, they did represent some movement towards notions central to a market economy. Formal provision was made for bankruptcy, though it was never implemented. Greater flexibility was permitted in the establishment of joint ventures with foreign companies (something which had been permitted since the early part of the decade but which had produced little result on the ground) and there was some liberalization of hard-currency transactions. But the most obvious, and potentially most subversive, relaxation occurred with regard to prices and wages. The state reserved to itself the ultimate power over prices, retained complete control over the retail prices of necessities and set maxima for other retail and wholesale prices. What was interesting was the criteria which were supposed to govern these prices and those of intermediate goods: the principle was that they should be based on international prices. These were of course converted to leva by the application of a completely administered exchange rate, which could entirely nullify any influence of international over domestic prices, but the acceptance of the potential relevance of international prices in determining efficient domestic prices was a chink in the armour.

Another was a recognition that a corollary of decentralization of decision-making and the need to improve productive efficiency was the necessity of adequate personal, financial incentives. Moves were therefore to be made towards greater variation in wages (subject to a minimum) with performance-related flexibility. This apparent acceptance of the primacy of incentives over equality could have been extremely subversive.

A commentator who was usually sympathetic to the socialist system said this about thirty years of tinkering with the forms of economic organization: ' ... economic changes in Bulgaria up until 1989 can best be described as institutional innovations in the absence of reform'.[29] Whether the post-1986 changes (and especially new legislation in 1989, to be dealt with later) deserved a more optimistic interpretation is something we shall never know.

Economic performance and structure

We briefly review here what the statistics show about the main features of the Bulgarian economy under communism. All statistics have to be interpreted in the light of the circumstances of their collection and this is particularly the case in former socialist economies. Such countries had a huge statistical administration and produced, and in most cases can still produce, a veritable cornucopia of numbers: this was because such statistics were required for plan construction and monitoring. The relationship between planning and statistical provision is at the centre of the problems of interpretation. This is no place to go into detail,[30] but a few points relevant to what follows need to be made.

First, the standard western measure of an economy's output — Gross Domestic Product (GDP) — was not compatible with the Marxian distinction between productive and unproductive activity and so a more restricted concept — Net Material Product (NMP) — was employed. This included services only to the extent that they were inputs to 'productive' activity: it also excluded depreciation. The growth of GDP and NMP would therefore diverge whenever the ratio of depreciation and excluded output to NMP changed. Secondly, price statistics report the change in official prices and take no account of prices charged in unofficial markets. Furthermore, NMP was valued at these official prices, which were not market-clearing prices, the result being an aggregate which would be sensitive to changes in official pricing policies (including exchange-rate policies). So, both inflation and real growth statistics are difficult to interpret. Thirdly, and most generally, statistics in planned economies were derived from a reporting system where the reporters (enterprises) were not neutral with respect to what they were reporting: for example, failure to meet plan targets was punished whereas reported over-fulfilment could lead to more difficult targets in the future.

---

29 McIntyre (1992), p. 64.

30 A thorough treatment can be found in Marer et al. (1992).

One statistical exercise is particularly difficult and will not be attempted here. This is to attempt an answer to the question: did communist economies perform worse than capitalist economies? To obtain the flavour of the difficulties, consider the following. According to one source,[31] in 1937 the income per head of Czechoslovakia was 90 per cent of that of the adjacent Austria whereas 50 years later it was a mere 20 per cent. Such a huge decline in the relative prosperity of Czechoslovakia defies observation and common sense.[32]

With these warnings, we can proceed. Table 1.3 shows average annual rates of real NMP growth in Bulgaria for half-decades from 1950.

Table 1.3 Average annual growth rate of NMP (%), 1950–89

1950–55	12.3	*1970–75*	7.9
1955–60	9.7	*1975–80*	6.2
1960–65	6.7	*1980–85*	3.7
1965–70	8.2	*1985–89*	3.0

Source: Bleaney (1988), p. 33; Marer et al. (1992), pp. 100–1

What is significant here is the marked decline in the growth rate, except for a surge in the late 1960s, since the time when extensive growth became impracticable and increases in factor productivity became necessary. Investment continued at a high level (typically around 35 per cent of NMP at least until the mid-1980s), but there is evidence of severely inefficient investment in that the aggregate average productivity of capital fell, at least after 1970.[33] There was also a steady decline in the proportion of employment accounted for by the material or 'productive' sector — that is the part of the economy which

---

31 Solimano (1991), p. 20, where the dubious value of such comparisons is acknowledged.

32 This statistical illusion is created by the use of official exchange rates to convert the incomes of the two countries to a common currency. The use of the more appropriate purchasing-power-parity exchange rates would narrow the gap considerably, but is an issue which will not be pursued here.

33 Bleaney (1988), p. 35.

generated NMP, this proportion falling from 87 to 81 per cent in the
two decades following 1970.[34]

The change in the structure of activity already noted (Table 1.1 above)
continued though necessarily at a less dramatic pace. This is shown in
Table 1.4.

Table 1.4 Sectoral contribution to NMP (%), 1970–89

	1970	1975	1980	1985	1989
Agriculture	22	21	17	14	12
Industry	49	51	49	60	57

Source: Derived from Marer et al. (1992), pp 102–3

These changes in the structure of output are mirrored by changes in
the structure of employment, as is shown in Table 1.5.

*Table 1.5 Sectoral employment as percentage of total employment,
1970–89*

	1970	1980	1985	1989
Agriculture	35	24	20	18
Industry	30	35	37	38

Source: World Bank, 1991, Vol. I, Table 1.2.b

Finally, let us look at a measure of average labour productivity. This
is shown in Table 1.6. The most significant aspect of these figures
relates to agriculture. The establishment of the *APKs* initially had a
dramatic, positive effect on output per head in the sector. During the
1970s, it grew by an average of 8 per cent per year, in excess of
productivity growth in the material sector as a whole. The picture for
the 1980s is quite different. The 1985 figure on its own is misleading
because of the drought in that year, but the following year agricultural
productivity reached a level never attained since and over the whole
decade it rose by barely half of one per cent per year. The huge
collectives were running out of steam: in the last year of communist

---

34 World Bank (1991), Vol. I, Table 1.2.b.

rule, the real output of the farming sector was actually lower than it had been for very many years (even lower than in 1985), not something which would endear the regime to what was by now a highly urbanized population.[35]

Table 1.6 Indices of real NMP per person employed (1989=100), 1970–89

	1970	1980	1985	1989
Agriculture	40	95	89	100
Industry	34	69	89	100
Total NMP	37	72	86	100

Source: Derived from Marer et al. (1992), pp. 102–3; World Bank (1991), Vol. I, Table 1.2.a

THE END OF ZHIVKOV AND THE BEGINNING OF DEMOCRACY

Throughout the 1980s, the regime became increasingly shaky and the economic reasons for this, and the attempted responses, have already been considered. Probably the most important ultimate cause was that Bulgaria could not be isolated from what was happening in the rest of the region, and especially in the Soviet Union. Either because of loyalty to the policies adopted in the USSR or because his survival instincts told him that some relaxation was necessary, Zhivkov issued his 'July conception' in 1987. This involved, among other things, permitting the electorate a choice among candidates at elections (implemented in the 1988 elections), although the candidates had to be approved by the Fatherland Front.

Essentially, Zhivkov was unsympathetic to any notions of *glasnost* but he could not prevent the mass of Bulgarians from having access to the Soviet media which had been respectable until then. These Russian sources were now full of talk of reform and, along with the effects of

---

35 Furthermore, it is probable that the official statistics used in Table 1.6 overstate real growth in the industrial sector. For example, one estimate suggests that, for the period 1970–83, the true growth of industrial output was barely one-third of that shown by the official statistics (Minassian (1992), p. 710).

clandestine access to Western media, fuelled dissidence at home. The Bulgarian intelligentsia (with a few exceptions such as Georgi Markov, who had been assassinated in London in 1978, and the sociologist Zhelyu Zhelev who had shown dissident tendencies since the late 1970s and would soon emerge as a major figure in the move to democracy) had never provided much by way of a critique of the regime: it had been cleverly neutralized by being sucked into the communist establishment by means of privileges denied to the general population. In the late 1980s, however, it began to provide some focus to opposition. Somewhat unexpectedly, those with ecological and environmental concerns also played a growing role in the expression of opposition to the government and it was their activities, together with the treatment of the Turkish population, which brought matters to a head.

In 1988, a demonstration was held by environmental activists in Ruse, a city on the Danube notorious for its air pollution. This demonstration, and a supporting meeting in Sofia, were broken up by police, and long-standing communists who were involved in the meetings were expelled from the party. Then, as an exercise in international public relations, the government hosted a European conference on the environment in October 1989. A demonstration in Sofia in association with the conference was suppressed with considerable and very public violence. The difference this time was that the action was witnessed by delegates and journalists from the West who were attending the conference. It was a diplomatic disaster which had all the greater effect because it followed closely on another aspect of Zhivkov's policies which had attracted enormous, adverse, international attention — the renewal of action against Bulgaria's Turks.

Government suppression of the Turkish minority had never been far from the surface. Initially it took the form of the withdrawal of juridical recognition of ethnic groups: ethnicity was not mentioned in censuses since 1965 and the 1971 constitution made no reference to minorities. Positive cultural action was taken against the Pomaks (Bulgarian-speaking Muslims) in the early 1970s and the emigration of Turks was encouraged.[36]

---

36 130,000 emigrated to Turkey in the period 1968–78 (Pundeff (1992), p. 106).

The decision to attack the Turks directly came in 1984 and was implemented with brutal vigour. Overtly, it took the form of a cultural campaign — requiring Turks to adopt Slav names, banning the use of Turkish in public and forbidding certain Islamic practices — but the terms were such that the targets felt obliged to resist. The suppression of this resistance attracted considerable international attention, but this was as nothing compared to what happened when the campaign was intensified in May 1989. Resisters were now not just beaten or imprisoned; they were forced to move to Turkey with only what they could carry. By August, over 300,000 had gone to Turkey or were waiting on the border — probably Europe's largest postwar movement of population.[37] Never before had Bulgaria attracted so much attention from the Western news media.[38]

The impact of the treatment of Turks and dissidents on the international image of Bulgaria was the final nail in Zhivkov's political coffin. No-one appreciated that impact more than Petur Mladenov, foreign minister since 1971. The persistence of old-style repression by a government renowned for its loyalty to the Soviet Union was also gravely embarrassing to Gorbachev. Mladenov had unsuccessfully attempted to resign in October 1989 but, in the first week of November, paid an official visit to China. On his way home he stopped briefly in Moscow and, on arrival in Sofia, gathered together those on the Central Committee of like mind and made the final preparations to replace Zhivkov. At a meeting of the Committee on 10 November the leader of thirty-five years' standing was induced to resign and his two posts, head of state and party general secretary, were taken over by Mladenov.

At the time there was considerable speculation concerning the foreign minister's stopover in Moscow. It was obviously not a coincidence, but there is a world of difference between Moscow's engineering Zhivkov's downfall and Mladenov's prudential confirmation that, if the Bulgarian party forced out its leader, the Soviet Union would not intervene. The latter seems the more appropriate interpretation and it gives the Bulgarians credit for taking their fate into their own hands but, in the light of what has happened since in both Bulgaria and the former Soviet

---

37 East (1992), p. 24.

38 A detailed description of these episodes can be found in Poulton (1993).

Union, it is difficult to regard the issue now as more than a historical curiosum.[39]

With the obvious popular exhilaration at the fall of Zhivkov and the general mood that real reform was at last in prospect, the organization of effective political opposition became urgent and a major step was taken on 7 December with the formation of the Union of Democratic Forces (UDF),[40] an umbrella organization encompassing sixteen general and special-interest groups including parties such as the Petkov Agrarians[41] and the Social Democrats and anti-communist groups which had arisen in the previous two years such as the *Podkrepa* federation of trade unions, *Ekoglasnost* and the Club for *Glasnost* and Democracy. The chairman of the latter, Zhelyu Zhelev, became the chairman of the UDF.

The response of the Communist Party was not long in coming: it soon became apparent that its strategy (which turned out to be electorally successful) would be to give itself a reforming image. Within days of the formation of the UDF, the government proposed free elections and the abolition of the BCP's monopoly of political organization. At the end of the month, the rights of the Turkish minority were restored and on 15 January 1990 the parliament formally approved the deletion of the constitutional clause which gave a special place to the Communist Party. At a special congress at the end of January, the party changed its name to the Bulgarian Socialist Party; replaced Mladenov with Aleksandur

---

39 Tchukov (1990), admittedly writing very soon after these events, calls this a 'very important question', but this is best interpreted as a reflection of a rather typical Bulgarian sensitivity to external manipulation and penchant for conspiracy theories — a sensitivity which is perhaps understandable in the light of a history in which their country's role in international affairs had been limited to that of a pawn in disputes between greater powers.

40 In Bulgarian, *Süyuz na demokratichnite sili (SDS)*. Although practice does vary, it is more usual in English-language publications to give Bulgarian parties the initials of their English names and, henceforth, this usage will be adopted here. Thus, the Bulgarian Agrarian People's Union is BAPU (*BZNS* in Bulgarian) and the Movement for Rights and Freedoms is MRF (*DPS* in Bulgarian), the initials of the Bulgarian Socialist Party being the same in both languages.

41 A revival of that part of the old Agrarian Party which effectively disappeared after the execution of Nikola Petkov in 1947. The BAPU itself participated in the Fatherland Front throughout the communist era and re-emerged as an independent party after the abolition of the Front in January 1990.

Lilov as general secretary; appointed Andrey Lukanov as prime minister in place of Georgi Atanasov, who had held the post under Zhivkov since 1986; and adopted a programme which was explicitly Marxist but which was designed to look like that of a typical European left-wing party (although it was very vague and could be summed up as wanting some sort of market economy but with substantial social protection).

The extent of opposition was such that the government clearly did not have the legitimacy to design new democratic institutions on its own, and mid-January saw the first meeting of a round-table forum comprising representatives of the BSP, UDF and BAPU, thus giving an extra-parliamentary but legitimate role to the opposition in determining the way forward. The UDF refused an invitation to join the government (not surprisingly since its political future depended upon its being recognisable as a separate entity) and on 8 February a new, but avowedly interim, government was formally endorsed by the parliament, with Lukanov as prime minister and only the BSP represented.

The government were pushing for early elections, but the opposition was wise to this ploy and on 25 February there was a huge demonstration in Sofia demanding that elections be postponed to give the UDF time to organize. In the meantime, the round table conference was attempting to reach agreement on its own role and on the new political institutions, with most controversy being over electoral law. Agreement was eventually reached in early March on the date and form of the elections and on the veto which the forum could exercise over significant legislation. On 3 March, the National Assembly formally appointed Mladenov as president and dissolved itself in readiness for the elections.

Mladenov was not to last much longer: at a demonstration in Sofia in December 1989 he had been captured on video-tape as saying 'it's time to bring in the tanks' and, when this evidence was made public, he was forced to resign, four days before the first round of the elections. He was not replaced immediately and, with the resignation of Lukanov the following day to make room for a post-election government (which, as it turned out, was not formed until September), the country found itself with neither a president nor a prime minister for several weeks.

The rules for the elections were as follows. There were 200 single-member constituencies, to be decided on a first-past-the-post basis. The other half of the 400 seats were to be distributed proportionally among the parties according to the votes cast (that is, a list-type proportional representation). Each voter had a vote for each part of the election. Two stages were provided for the first part, there being a run-off between the best two candidates in the first stage if no candidate achieved an absolute majority. The election was held on 10 June 1990 and, in the 81 constituencies in which there was no absolute majority, the second stage was conducted a week later.

The result of the election — which had a turnout of over 90 per cent in the first round and over 80 per cent in the second — was that the BSP obtained 211 seats, the UDF 144, the MRF 23, the BAPU 16 and other parties 6, the percentages of the votes being 47, 36, 6, 8 and 3 respectively.

It had appeared that Bulgaria, by electing the BSP to the majority of seats, had gone against the trend set by Czechoslovakia, Hungary and Poland: some of the cruder Western media even interpreted this as a hankering after the old regime. In fact, the determinants of these results were quite complex. There was certainly abuse of power by the BSP, with acknowledged violations of the electoral law, but these were not on such a scale as to cause western observers to certify the election as unfair and none of the parties to the election subsequently attempted to have the results annulled on grounds of illegal practice. It is unlikely that the party manifestos had much effect because they were platitudinous and differed from each other only in emphasis.[42] Probably the most significant factor was the vast disparity in the organizational and tactical quality of the BSP compared with the UDF and BAPU. (The MRF, whose sole purpose was and is to represent the interests of the Turkish minority, obtained a proportion of the votes close to the proportion of Turks in the population.) Of course the BSP had the advantage of an organization which had been built up over 45 years and reached into every town and village, but the opposition failed, by serious tactical errors, to capitalize on the mood of the moment. The UDF was, and to a degree still is, a somewhat ramshackle grouping with little appreciation of the realities of electoral politics, but in this election its lack of tactical awareness left the door open for the BSP. Above all, it antagonised the MRF and made any kind of electoral pact impossible, especially where it would really have counted — in the

---

42 A brief summary of the manifestos of the BSP, UDF and BAPU is given in Jeffries (1993), p. 370.

constituencies where the election went to a second stage. The BAPU, who were showing about 20 per cent support in the opinion polls, made themselves vulnerable to BSP attack in the countryside by their flirtation with the UDF, whom the Socialists managed to convince the rural population were about to hand over agriculture to foreign capital. Since the cities were solidly UDF (who obtained 26 out of the 28 seats in Sofia), it was the conservative fears of the countryside (and probably those of the large number of pensioners, whose main interest lay in short-term social protection rather than longer-term economic and political prospects) which turned the election.[43]

Thus, Bulgaria now had a freely elected parliament, but it was to be some time before it obtained a government which could rule effectively, and particularly could come to grips with the serious economic difficulties facing the country.

---

43 Tchukov (1990), pp. 19–20 and Glenny (1993), pp. 174–7 have short discussions of these issues, the latter giving a lively account of the very public, very expensive, and probably counter-productive efforts of the US government to help the UDF.

2. Liberalization and Stabilization Policy: the Early Stages

As already noted, it is hard to avoid the conclusion that economic failures played a significant part in the fall of communism.[1] Zhivkov's last year in power saw supply disruptions in major industries, induced by cuts in Soviet supplies of oil and gas, difficulties in importing industrial inputs from the West because of the build-up of excessive debt, labour shortages occasioned by the large emigration of Turkish workers (which also seriously affected agriculture) and the distractions of increasing mass political activity.[2]

His successors were not reformers, but even they could not avoid an immediate confrontation with the facts of economic life — in this case the lack of foreign exchange to service the huge foreign debt which had been built up over the previous decade. This issue is dealt with in more detail later but, since it provided a major constraint on Bulgaria's transition from the beginning, a brief review would be in order here.

By the end of 1989, the country's net foreign debt in convertible currencies had reached $9.2 billion (over $1,000 per head of the population) — an increase of almost three-fold since 1985. About four-fifths of this was owed to western commercial banks and the main reason for its accumulation was that, during the 1980s, there were increasing quantitative and qualitative difficulties over inputs from CMEA suppliers, which were replaced by supplies from the West. Since these western inputs were used to produce exports to the CMEA, the economic process did not generate hard currency to repay this debt.

---

1 Minassian and Totev (1992) quote an unnamed Bulgarian economist as saying in 1988 'Our economy is in an awful state, but we know that socialism will finally win out, so the situation will no doubt improve'.

2 Economic performance in 1989 is reviewed in some detail in Grosser (1991).

Interest continued to be paid, but by 1989 the ratio of debt to annual hard-currency exports had reached 3 and the debt service ratio 74 per cent. With a hard-currency deficit on current account of $1.3 billion, this position was obviously unsustainable, but the crisis came in early 1990 because of immediate problems of liquidity. The overriding cause of the liquidity crisis was the bunching in 1990 of the debt service profile, with almost $3 billion due in that year, compared with $1.3 billion and $800 million in 1991 and 1992 respectively. Subsidiary, but nonetheless significant, problems were created by arrears in receipts from the $2.4 billion in export credits which Bulgaria had advanced to less developed countries, especially Iraq and Libya, the difficulties with the former being exacerbated by the developing crisis in the Gulf. These arrears amounted to over $700 million by early 1990.[3]

On 29 March 1990 the Bulgarian Foreign Trade Bank (the formal holder of all external liabilities) announced a moratorium on repayments of principal, which was extended to interest payments in June. At the same time, there was a four-fold devaluation of the lev for private transactions (there was a system of multiple, administered exchange rates until February 1991) and the limit on foreign currency available to travellers was halved.[4]

The unilateral declaration of a moratorium obviously deprived Bulgaria of further access to commercial credit from the West, and the restoration of normal servicing of foreign debt became a central objective of monetary policy as transition proceeded. In the meantime, the unavailability of non-official finance from abroad placed a major constraint on macroeconomic policy. Access to official credit clearly became an urgent necessity and in February 1990 Bulgaria applied to join the International Monetary Fund and the World Bank, becoming a member in September.

THE ECONOMY IN 1990

Any commentary on macroeconomic performance relies heavily on official statistics and a preliminary word on inevitable statistical problems would be in order.

---

3 The figures in this paragraph are derived from World Bank (1991), Vol. I.

4 Grosser (1991), p. 163.

The measurement of GDP in Bulgaria abounds with statistical difficulties. The concept is itself new (under communism, aggregate output meant net material product, which excluded those services which were not inputs to agricultural or industrial production) and — of increasing significance — no satisfactory apparatus has yet been installed to measure activity in the private sector. Also, there has been great difficulty in producing accurate deflators to estimate real changes. Thus, the discrepancy between GDP produced and GDP used at constant prices, after taking account of the foreign trade balance, has ranged from a negative 4 per cent to a positive 20 per cent of GDP produced.

Inflation is particularly difficult to measure and there are reasons for believing that official figures overstate the rate of aggregate price increase since liberalization. First, prior to liberalization, an unknown volume of transactions took place at black market rather than official prices, because of shortages of supply to official outlets. Black market sellers earned shortage rents. After liberalization, those rents declined and so black market prices fell relative to measured prices. Thus, to the extent that some transactions still occurred at non-measured prices, the official price index overstated the increase in the aggregate price level and, therefore, also the fall in real output and income. Then, price indices are statistical artifacts which in practice rarely measure the effects on consumer welfare of price changes. The defects of the most usual indices become very apparent when there are marked changes in the prices and quantities of goods traded. In particular, the usual price indices would tend to overstate the rate of inflation.[5]

Prices

Until mid-1990, the official index of consumer prices in Bulgaria changed very slowly, the average annual rate of increase in that index in the period 1980–89 being a mere 1.7 per cent. This was of course not a true measure of inflationary pressures. First, the index gave excessive weight to goods whose official prices were growing slowly: food prices are estimated to have risen by almost 4 per cent per year between 1970

5 These issues are discussed in detail in Osband (1992).

and 1988.[6] Secondly, prices did not clear markets and throughout the period there were significant shortages of consumer goods, and these became particularly severe by the end of the decade. Inflation was repressed.

The dam was forced to give way because strengthening political opposition was fuelled, at the popular level, by the inability of the economy to satisfy consumer desires. The only hope of generating a greater flow of consumer goods was to raise prices and, in the middle of 1990, the government (still of the Bulgarian Communist Party and before free elections) liberalized many prices and raised those prices over which it maintained control. The effect was dramatic, as is seen in Table 2.1.

Table 2.1 Monthly increase in consumer price index (%), 1990

June	4.1
July	3.6
August	10.9
September	4.5
October	4.1
November	4.9
December	10.4

Source: Bulgarian National Bank

The total increase in aggregate consumer prices in the second half of 1990 was 50.6 per cent. This process accelerated in January 1991, when the aggregate index increased by a further 13.6 per cent.

Given low short-term elasticities of supply and shortages of foreign exchange, these price increases were insufficient to remedy disequilibria in the markets for consumer goods, and rationing of basic items and petrol had to be introduced in the autumn. For short periods in October 1990 and January 1991, petrol sales for non-essential uses were suspended.

---

6 Jones (1991), p. 213. The same source suggests that the true overall index of consumer prices increased by 231 per cent during the 1980s, which is an annual increase of almost 13 per cent.

The Real Economy

GDP began to turn down in 1989, total production in that year being 1.9 per cent lower than in 1988. The decline was manifest in all sectors, with industrial output falling the least at 0.3 per cent (but perhaps most significantly since this was the first ever recorded fall in industrial output, whereas agriculture had fallen in four of the five years since 1984 and services output exhibited perennial fluctuations). As regards domestic demand, consumption was stable in real terms, but real fixed investment collapsed to 30 per cent of its 1988 level.

The main features of 1990 were an acceleration of this decline in aggregate output and, in the second half of the year, the beginnings of price liberalization and rapid inflation. Real GDP in 1990 was 9 per cent lower than in 1989 with, for the first time, the main contraction being in industry, whose output fell by 13 per cent. In addition to growing political unrest, which interrupted production, the major causes of the decline were external in origin.

First, the CMEA trading system went into progressive collapse. Exports to other members of this system declined and production difficulties in the Soviet Union reduced the supply of industrial inputs — notably crude oil and metals — from that country. This affected industrial output generally, but especially reduced Bulgaria's capacity to produce such earners of hard currency as chemicals and refined petroleum products.[7] Secondly, growing political and military tensions in the Middle East caused oil prices to increase and disrupted trade with a region which accounted for a high proportion of Bulgaria's non-CMEA trade. For example, late in the year an agreement had been reached that Iraq would repay in oil $1.2 billion of debt to Bulgaria, but this agreement could not be honoured because of the UN embargo on Iraqi oil exports. Thirdly, the debt moratorium caused non-official foreign credit to dry up and the ability to import the inputs upon which Bulgarian industry had become increasingly reliant correspondingly diminished.

This severe decline in output was reflected in a further diminution in the demand for capital — a reduction which had been apparent in several

---

7 It has been estimated that over half of the decline in output is attributable to these problems over input supply (Bulgarian National Bank, *Annual Report 1990*, p. 19).

years of the 1980s and reached catastrophic proportions in 1989, when real fixed investment was a mere 29 per cent of its level in the previous year. A further fall of 19.5 per cent occurred in 1990.

The accelerating growth of the private sector since 1989, which remains inadequately covered by official statistics, makes any precise evaluation of the situation in the labour market impossible. Employment in the official sector fell by 2.3 per cent in 1989 and the decline gathered pace in 1990, during which official employment was reduced by 12.4 per cent to just over 3.8 million, out of a working-age population of 5 million. Until the middle of 1990, however, measured unemployment was not materially affected: there had been almost perennial excess demand for labour and the decline in output was therefore not matched by an equivalent decline in employment; furthermore, a surge in emigration reduced the labour supply.

From mid-1990, the dramatic fall in output began to be reflected in the official unemployment figures, the number of registered unemployed rising from 31,000 to 65,100 between July and December of that year, whilst the number of registered vacancies fell from 58,200 to 28,400 during that period. To what extent this indicates a shift of labour supply and demand from the measured to the unmeasured sector remains a matter of conjecture.

Political Developments

The aftermath of the first free elections saw the first manifestations of a syndrome which has bedeviled Bulgarian reform efforts ever since: the extreme instability of parliamentary coalitions and the consequent difficulty of maintaining the support of the legislature for executive action.[8] After repeated efforts to find an acceptable candidate, the Assembly (which at that time still had the relevant power) eventually elected the chairman of the UDF, Zhelyu Zhelev, as national president (a post he still holds). A government, under Lukanov, was not formed until 20 September.

This government found it impossible to operate in the face of both popular and parliamentary protest. In late August there had been street

---

8 The Assembly had no difficulty with cosmetic reforms: in November 1990 it almost unanimously removed 'People's' from the state's official title.

rioting in Sofia[9] and November saw a general strike — supported by
both *Podkrepa* and the more 'official' Confederation of Independent
Trade Unions — and an opposition boycott of the Assembly. Lukanov
resigned on 29 November. Not surprisingly, the president was unable to
find a member of the Assembly who could muster majority support but,
on 7 December, parliament endorsed his nomination to the premiership
of Dimitur Popov, the chairman of the Sofia municipal court, with no
known party affiliation.[10]

This was intended to be merely a caretaker government until new
elections could be organized but, in a manner oddly reminiscent of the
election of Pope John XXIII, it found itself presiding over the first
major reform efforts.

INFLATION IN THE EARLY STAGES OF TRANSITION

Despite the fact that the lid began to be lifted from repressed inflation
seven months earlier, the starting date for the Bulgarian transition
programme is usually taken to be 1 February 1991, which was the
implementation date of Ordinance No. 8 on Price Liberalization and
Social Protection of the Population, which had been adopted by the
Council of Ministers on 29 January. It is the impact of this liberalization
which provides one of the main themes of the rest of this chapter.

With the exception of Hungary, where various components of
economic reform were introduced tentatively over two decades, most
major countries in the region initiated their economic transformation by
liberalizing international trade and domestic prices overnight, or at least
over a very short period — a process often referred to as a 'big bang'.
Except in Czechoslovakia, which had maintained monetary equilibrium
under the old regime, the immediate effect was an explosion in domestic
prices and so the most important task in this first phase was to prevent

---

9   One victim was the Stalinesque headquarters of the old Communist Party, for the past
    year occupied by the BSP. Much of its interior was gutted by fire, officially caused
    by rioters as an expression of their reformist demands but less officially attributed to
    attempts by former officials to destroy files.

10 The Bulgarian constitution does not require ministers to be members of the
    legislature, merely that they be endorsed by the Assembly. This formation of a
    Cabinet from outside parliament was repeated almost exactly two years later, when
    another government formed after an election also collapsed (see below).

this once-for-all jump from degenerating into hyperinflation. Simultaneously, aggregate demand collapsed because of the dramatic reduction in consumption occasioned by the impact of the increase in prices on real household incomes and the effects of the demise of the CMEA on the demand for exports.

Table 2.2 Monthly increase in consumer price index (%), 1991–92

	1991	1992
January	13.6	4.8
February	122.9	5.8
March	50.5	3.9
April	2.5	3.2
May	0.8	11.9
June	5.9	5.8
July	8.4	2.8
August	7.5	1.2
September	3.8	3.4
October	3.3	6.2
November	5.0	6.7
December	4.9	4.6

Source: National Statistical Institute

Bulgaria's big bang consisted essentially of four components: the liberalization of almost all domestic prices (the main exceptions being energy prices, which are still controlled); the elimination of quantitative restrictions on imports and exports; the liberalization of foreign exchange dealings, with internal convertibility of the lev and the establishment of a single, market-determined exchange rate; and a severe reduction in subsidies from the state budget. In 1991 and 1992, Bulgaria experienced the typical first phase of transition, with spectacular price increases and severe depression of output. By December 1991, the aggregate price level was 5.74 times what it had been a year earlier, and in the year to December 1992 it rose by a further 80 per cent. The month-by-month changes are shown in Table 2.2, from which it can be seen that the main explosion came immediately after the implementation of Ordinance No. 8, with further surges in June—August 1991 after Ordinance No. 106 had liberalized more prices and further increased controlled prices (especially of energy) and in May 1992.

The pattern here is, in broad terms, what might be expected: huge price increases following the initial liberalization; surges when controlled prices are administratively increased (for example, in May 1992 when energy price increases had a dramatic impact on the consumer price index); and a continuing inflationary pressure underlying the whole period. It is the last of these which is the most worrying from the point of view of stabilization policy. If the first three months of 1991 are ignored, the average monthly rate of inflation in 1992 was actually higher than in the previous year (5.0 per cent compared with 4.6 per cent).

Changes in Relative Prices

The whole point of liberalizing prices is to rectify the highly distorted nature of relative prices established under the planning regime. It is therefore to be expected that liberalization would lead to significant changes in relative prices. The distortions were known to be greatest with respect to two main sectors. First, Bulgarian development had been founded on cheap energy supplies from the Soviet Union and, as the price of those supplies was adjusted to the world price, domestic energy prices required similar adjustment. Secondly, domestic food prices were kept artificially low by a combination of unrealistic producer prices and consumer subsidies, and an important feature of the liberalization package was the phasing out of those subsidies. Thus, over the period from July 1990 to February 1991, prices of most energy items and most basic food items rose faster than the overall consumer price index. But, although the comparisons are somewhat clouded by differences in levels of taxation on the relevant items, energy prices remained considerably below those ruling in Western Europe. This was particularly the case for energy used directly by households. Immediately after the big bang of February 1991 the Bulgarian retail price of petrol was barely half that ruling in Germany and the price of electricity to households only one-eighth of the German price.[11]

Table 2.3   Changes in relative prices,[a] 1991–92

	Dec 91	Dec 92
Food	1.05	1.10
Drink	0.40	0.26
Tobacco	0.48	0.34
Clothing, footwear	0.59	0.69
Housing, heat, light	1.83	1.49
Household goods	0.90	0.89
Education, culture	0.77	0.73
Health, health products	0.97	1.14
Transport, communications	1.30	1.11
Other	0.99	0.98

[a] Index (December 1990=1) for the commodity group deflated by the total consumer prices index
Source: Derived from National Statistical Institute

The process of adjusting relative prices clearly had a long way to go, but it did continue in the expected direction, as is revealed by Table 2.3. Although there occurred in the second half of 1992 a definite slackening in the relative rate of increase in the prices of energy-intensive products (heating, light and transport), the first two years of transition saw a decided increase in the relative prices of food and energy-intensive consumption items.

The figures in Table 2.3, based as they are on broad aggregates and the consumption pattern of the average household, fail to reveal the magnitude of the increase in the cost of basic consumption items and hence the effect of that increase on the living standards of poorer households. Thus, in the first three quarters of 1991, when the official consumer price index rose by a factor of five, the price of basic foods such as bread, milk, rice and edible oil rose tenfold, that of electricity

---

11   Hughes (1991), p. 167.

went up seven times and that of central heating over eightfold.[12] An effect of this was to increase sharply the proportion of households whose income was insufficient to support the level of real consumption defined by the official poverty level. Even with a downward adjustment in that level in recognition of the impact of the price increases on the consumption capacity of all income groups, the proportion of households below the poverty level rose from 45 per cent to 66 per cent in that period, and the proportion of pensioners in that position reached 90 per cent.

Causes of Inflationary Pressure

Price determination in transition economies is not well understood. Both macroeconomic theories of inflation and microeconomic theories of individual price change were developed in demand-constrained market economies. The relevant features of such economies are that producers can be assumed to have a good feel for the demand function for their output; sellers can be assumed either to be profit-maximizers or at least to be used to operating under profitability constraints; and such price-setters rarely have to face dramatic changes in demand or cost functions, with the result that price decisions are of a fairly marginal nature so that any exogenous shock can be expected to generate a rapid convergence of prices to a new equilibrium level.

None of these conditions prevails in transition economies but, nevertheless, one may expect that familiar theories of inflation and individual price determination to be at least qualitatively applicable to such economies. Such theories stem from the proposition that prices will rise if there is excess demand at existing prices. At the microeconomic level, excess demand may arise because of a shift in either the demand or supply function. At the macroeconomic level, the analysis is essentially similar, but with concentration on the effect of monetary conditions on aggregate demand and on the effect of cost conditions on aggregate supply.

A widely observed phenomenon in transition economies is what is known as monetary overhang. This term refers to what, by the standards of market economies, was an abnormally high ratio of household

---

12 Gocheva et al. (1992).

holdings of financial assets (cash and savings accounts) to household income. Some of this high ratio (especially of savings accounts — the only non-cash financial assets permitted to households) was accounted for by the virtual absence of any system of financial intermediation providing consumer credit other than for housing. Savings accounts built up for this reason were not part of the overhang and had no particularly inflationary implications. The lack of non-monetary assets available to households also biased upwards estimates of the inflationary overhang. The high cash ratio and part of the high savings account ratio could not, however, be explained in this way.

Two major sources of overhang can be identified. First, households could not be sure that, when they wished to buy a particular quantity of a particular good, it would be available in the shops. They then held precautionary cash balances so that they could react instantly when the required goods became available. Secondly, generalized shortages gave rise to unsatisfied demand across a wide range of goods. Households could not arrive at their desired consumption ratio and there was in effect forced saving. This undesired accumulation of assets may have been held as cash or in savings accounts.

This overhang was classic repressed inflation: unsatisfied purchasing power had built up behind the dam of price controls. This kind of macroeconomic imbalance was manifest in Bulgaria. Statistical factors make it impossible to identify a pure overhang because of the difficulties of separating out the household sector: money stock data include the deposits of other agencies such as enterprises, which also held precautionary balances in liquid form in response to uncertainties in the availability of materials and other inputs. Therefore, we are forced to measure (or, more accurately, illustrate) the overhang by reference to monetary aggregates in relation to total income. Table 2.4 shows the relevant figures.

The ratio of monetary assets was considerably higher than would be normal in market economies[13] and also than was typical in Central and Eastern Europe. Thus, in the 1980s, the ratio of broad money to GDP was much higher in Bulgaria than in Czechoslovakia, Hungary, Poland

---

13 See World Bank (1991), Vol. I, p. 54 where these ratios are shown to be much higher than in an illustrative selection of Western European countries and high-income developing economies.

or Romania. By 1992, however, the Bulgarian ratio had fallen below that in Czechoslovakia and almost to that prevailing in Hungary, in both of which countries the ratio rose in the early 1990s.[14]

Table 2.4 Money supply as percentage of GDP,[a] 1988–92

	1988	1989	1990	1991	1992
Currency	12	15	16	9	9
Broad money	102	109	109	85	81

[a] Year-end broad money supply as % of year GDP
Source: Bulgarian National Bank

It is true that these figures, to a degree anyway, exaggerate the real monetary overhang. The denominator of these ratios is GDP measured at official prices, whereas it is certain that a proportion of trade in consumption goods takes place in black markets at much higher market-clearing prices. Some have even gone as far as to state that, for this reason, real monetary overhang did not exist in Eastern Europe.[15] But the extremely high monetary ratios in Bulgaria cannot be totally explained away by transactions at unofficial prices. Widespread queuing at official retail outlets was a well-observed phenomenon, which indicates that a significant proportion of consumption took place at official prices. An estimate for the Soviet Union suggested the true inflationary overhang to be of the order of 20 per cent of GDP[16] and, if a figure approximating to this also applied to Bulgaria, it would go some way at least towards accounting for the excess monetary ratios referred to above.

An overhang such as this was recognized as a grave danger to stability in Eastern Europe and various prescriptions were offered to eliminate it before the transition process was put in train. One was to sell government securities at attractive rates of interest to the public to mop up the excess liquidity in the system. Another was to engage in currency reform (such as happened in Russia) which has the effect of confiscating a proportion of the public's liquid balances. The more usual

---

14 Caprio and Levine (1994), p. 16.

15 For example, Cochrane and Ickes (1991).

16 Cottarelli and Blejer (1992).

solution, and that adopted in Bulgaria, was to allow the balances to be eroded by the process of price liberalization itself.

Two things happen. First, as long as nominal incomes do not rise proportionately, nominal balances will be run down as households seek to maintain real consumption in the face of rapid price increases. Secondly, the real value of given nominal balances declines as prices rise. The effect of these processes can be seen in Table 2.4: there has been in Bulgaria a marked reduction in monetary ratios. As can be seen from Table 2.5, most of the erosion in the real value of money balances took place immediately after liberalization began.

What this suggests is that monetary overhang contributed to the scale of the first round of price increases in the first and second quarters of 1991 (and, indeed, in the second half of 1990). The excess demand for consumer goods enshrined in those balances seems, however, to have dissipated quickly: during the second half of 1991 and in 1992, Bulgaria's monetary ratios declined towards those prevalent elsewhere in Europe. It is likely, therefore, that the remnants of the overhang contributed less to the maintenance of inflationary pressures in the later period than the initial excess liquidity did to the early response to price liberalization.

Table 2.5 Index of real value of money balances (December 1990=100), 1991–92

	Jun 91	Dec 91	Jun 92	Dec 92
Currency	27	29	22	25
Broad money	37	39	32	31

Source: Derived from Bulgarian National Bank

The massive nominal devaluation of the lev which accompanied price liberalization (see below) will also have contributed to the immediate inflationary spurt in the spring of 1991, but the exchange rate stabilized to a remarkable degree in the following two-and-a-half years (for example, from January 1992 to August 1993 the average monthly rate of nominal devaluation against the dollar was a mere two-thirds of one per cent) and so cannot be held responsible for the continuing high level of inflation.

The other most likely influence on the initial price explosion from the supply side concerns the almost complete lack of competition domestically. Indeed, a major objective of the liberalization of foreign trade is that it introduces competition into an economy whose domestic structure is overwhelmingly monopolistic in the production of goods, both industrial and agricultural (although competition did develop early, and to some extent existed under the old regime, in the distributive sector). Monopolists took advantage of the sudden expansion of monetary demand to raise prices to a greater extent than would have been profitable in a more competitive environment. In addition, price instability was created as sellers searched for market information — information which they did not need under the old planning system: they had negligible knowledge of the demand function for their products and so it is likely that there was considerable overshooting of price increases as producers searched for that function.

As already noted, one of the surprising features of Bulgarian inflation is that there has been, once the immediate impact of price liberalization was over, no systematic tendency for the monthly rate of inflation to decline. It can be seen even by casual inspection of Table 2.2 that there has been no trend in the monthly rate. The reason for this failure of inflation to abate remains somewhat of a mystery.

It is possible, of course, that the consumer prices index (CPI) overstates the true rate of inflation: the producer prices index (PPI) has risen at less than half the rate shown by the CPI since liberalization and it is of some interest as to why these two indices have diverged to such an extent.[17] The first possibility is purely statistical in that the CPI is a Laspeyres index whereas the PPI is a Paasche index, the former overstating and the latter understating the true rate of price change. Secondly, a major source of quality improvements — access to higher-quality imports — will be reflected in the CPI but not in the PPI. The third possibility is the result of informal privatization. If managers set up their own firms, sell their state enterprise output to those private firms at a low price and then sell to the consumer distribution system at a high price, then the result will be an apparent increase in distributive margins, not something which would otherwise be expected since the retail sector has become markedly more competitive in

---

17 These issues are the subject of Miller (1994).

structure since 1991. However, none of these factors explains why the 'true' inflation rate (perhaps something between the CPI and the PPI) has remained so high.

The only statistical investigation of this question known to the present author reached the conclusion that 'inflation in Bulgaria's conditions is still a phenomenon hard to explain quantitatively in a satisfactory way'.[18] It proved impossible to find a decent statistical explanation for the the variations in the monthly rate of inflation, but perhaps these variations should not be the main target for investigation. More pertinent questions are why there has been no downward trend in inflation and why the average monthly level has remained so high. This is clearly related to policy efforts to restrain the rate of inflation, and it is to this that we now turn.

INFLATION AND STABILIZATION POLICY

Most economies, to a greater or lesser degree, are subject to inertial forces which, unless resisted, tend to perpetuate inflationary pressures. Obvious examples of these forces are collective wage bargaining which links nominal wage increases to increases in the cost of living, and long-term supply contracts priced on a cost-plus basis. Both of these practices were very prevalent in formerly planned economies and so the dangers that the initial price jump would degenerate into hyperinflation were particularly acute. Somewhat different in kind but similar in effect is the role of inflationary expectations. For example, if suppliers expect prices to be higher next month, they will withhold supplies from the market this month, thus exacerbating current inflationary pressures. One aspect of this, widely observed in Eastern Europe in the early stages of transition, is the demonetization of the domestic currency whereby households held their wealth in forms less likely than money to lose their value — notably hard currency and stocks of commodities. Increased demand for foreign currency weakens the domestic currency and commodity hoarding reduces supplies to the market, both having inflationary effects.

The most important policy objective at the beginning of the transition process was therefore to ensure that the big bang did not have a

---

18   Minassian (1994).

continuing inflationary impact. This in turn required the chain along which inflationary pressures are transmitted to be broken.

The fact that there are numerous links in this chain suggests that there are options concerning the point at which the chain is to be broken. First, inflation depresses the international value of the currency and this devaluation causes further inflation. The chain may be broken by intervention in the foreign exchange market to prevent the devaluation. Second, inflation causes wages to be bid up in an effort to protect real incomes and this wage increase creates further inflation. The chain may be broken by an incomes policy which prevents this wage–price spiral from becoming established. Third, inflation increases the demand for money and, if the money supply increases to accommodate this extra demand, further inflation is generated. If monetary policy is not accommodating in this way, the chain is broken. Fourth, inflation increases nominal budget deficits which, if financed by the creation of money, generate further inflation and so the process can be interrupted by strict fiscal control.

In the literature on the stabilization of inflationary economies, the variable the control of which represents the point at which the chain is to be broken is often called a nominal anchor. We have identified four possibilities: the exchange rate, the rate of growth of real wages, the rate of growth of the money supply, and the level of the nominal budget deficit. Clearly, these options are not mutually exclusive and all transition economies have attempted to use a mixture of them.[19]

The use of the exchange rate as an anchor requires foreign exchange reserves to be available so that a central bank can intervene in a market where the inflationary forces of inflation cause downward pressure on the external value of the currency. This in turn requires a past surplus on hard-currency trade or access to a stabilization fund financed, for instance, by the IMF. For this reason, only Poland attempted to use the exchange rate as an anchor (the dollar rate of the zloty was fixed for sixteen months beginning in January 1990). Such a strategy was not feasible for Bulgaria, whose convertible currency reserves at the end of 1990 (that is, one month before the big bang of price liberalization)

---

19 For a comparative review of initial stabilization policies in several transition economies, including Bulgaria, see Bruno (1992).

provided just two weeks' cover for hard-currency imports.[20] Bulgaria's stabilization efforts were based on incomes policy and on monetary and fiscal restraint.

Incomes Policy

Because of their ability to mobilize large bodies of workers at national level, there was an early recognition that it was vital to involve the trade unions in the process of economic reform[21] and March 1990 saw the establishment of the National Commission for the Consolidation of Interests — a tripartite body representing government, employers (that is, enterprise managers) and unions — which became the forum for the establishment of the wages control which played an important stabilization role in 1991.[22]

Wage indexation was introduced by Decree No. 103 in October 1990 in an effort to maintain real wages in the face of the first surge in open inflation, Although it provided full indexation only for those with wages less than 1.7 times the minimum wage[23] (that is, about three-quarters of the average wage), this represented too much inertia in a system where the control of cumulative inflation was the most significant short-term policy objective, and the most immediate post-liberalization objective was to disconnect this indexation. In February 1991 a new formula was agreed by the tripartite commission, a formula designed to place both a floor and a ceiling on the growth of nominal wages. Each enterprise was given a ceiling for the rate of growth in its nominal wage bill for the coming quarter, the ceiling being determined by the past-quarter growth in average wages and the expected rate of inflation. It will be noted that the average wage was not a parameter of this incomes policy — it referred solely to an enterprise's total wage bill

---

20   Wyzan (1993), p. 128.

21   'The major guarantors of social peace during a period of catastrophic decline in living standards' (Vidinova (1993), p. 31).

22   This tripartite structure was replicated at sub-national levels, there being by late 1991 such organs in 11 ministries and 50 local districts (Thirkell and Tseneva (1992) p. 361). A major function at these levels was to negotiate how the national parameters were to be applied at lower levels — for instance, with regard to the trade-off between the level of employment and the average wage of those in employment.

23   Beleva et al. (1993), p. 65.

— and so an enterprise could remain within its ceiling by laying off workers. To prevent its adopting a strategy of concentrating the permitted aggregate increase on higher paid workers, the package included two other features. In February (the month of the big bang), the national minimum wage was raised from BGL165 per month to BGL435[24] and all workers received a minimum increase of BGL270. The kind of tax-based enforcement of wage-bill ceilings employed in Poland was not important in Bulgaria.[25]

The combination of a ceiling on total wages and a minimum increase for any individual worker would be expected to lead to a reduction in income differentials, and this in fact happened.[26] More important for stabilization purposes, real wages fell dramatically. In February, average wages rose only 66 per cent,[27] exactly half the increase in the consumer price index. Because inflation was higher than expected (that is, higher than the indexation factor in the determination of the ceilings), average real wages fell more than expected in the first quarter of 1991 — by 45 per cent — and the real minimum wage fell by 19 per cent. Nominal wage bills actually fell 15 per cent short of the negotiated ceiling in aggregate as wage differentials were compressed and workers

---

24 The main significance of the minimum wage is not as a minimum to what an employee can be paid but as a determinant of the level of social security payments.

25 The western literature is rather confused on this point. Bogetic and Fox (1993) state 'As in Poland, the government planned to enforce the compliance with wage bill ceilings by a tax on excess wage bill increase' (p. 43) and Grosser (1992) has 'the current wage bill increase ... is subject to steep progressive taxation' (p. 132), whereas Wyzan (1993) claims that 'a Polish style excess wage tax [was] foresworn' (p. 132). In fact, a tax on excess wage bills had been instituted in 1990 and remains in place to this day. It is, however, no more than a nuisance tax, raising negligible revenue (which could be because it is having the required effect in keeping wage bills within the ceilings but the main reason for its insignificance is that the base of the tax is a function not only of excess wages but also of profits). This tax has been of no real importance to the implementation of post-liberalization incomes policy.

26 Hughes (1991), p. 168.

27 This and other figures given here apply only to the state sector since the policy could be implemented only in that sector and, in any case, no data exist for wages in the private sector. An additional problem in attempting to generate multi-annual time series of average wages is that the sectoral coverage of official statistics appears to vary from year to year. The latter factor, however, should not materially affect estimates of growth rates of average wages.

laid off. The real average wage continued to fall during the second quarter.

This highly centralized mechanism of wage determination did not last beyond the middle of the year and what was in effect a method of enterprise-level collective bargaining took over, although such bargaining continued to be conducted within parameters laid down by the government. An important change was that, in an effort to reduce the inertia in the system, these parameters no longer included compensation for past inflation, only for expected inflation.[28] As inflation decelerated and employment declined, the average real wage increased during the remainder of the year, although by the end of 1991 it was still one-third below its level at the end of the previous year.[29]

The pattern of month-to-month changes in average nominal wages in 1992 reflected both the outcome of enterprise-level negotiations on the total wage bill and the time pattern of worker redundancies. Thus, in some months, the nominal average wage actually fell. The trend was steadily upwards but it almost reflected the trend in the general price level and so, by the end of the year, the real average wage was almost exactly the same as it had been a year earlier.[30]

Over the first two years after price liberalization, therefore, incomes policy must be judged at least a partial success despite the relatively decentralized nature of that policy. Indeed, one could properly conclude that wages were responding to the hardening of enterprise budget constraints which, if true, was a heartening indication of the success of one of the central prescriptions of transition policy. It could of course be argued that the large increases in unemployment (see below) should have forced real wages to an even lower level and the failure of average real wages to fall over 1992, when inflation ran at 80 per cent, represented an unfortunate degree of inertia in the system which helped to drive the inflationary process. However, this would have been an unrealistic expectation. Trade union acceptance of layoffs has to be bought, and the price was the maintenance of the real wages of those remaining in employment. The decline in employment fell far short of

---

28 Nenova (1993), p. 27, indicates the formula by which the ceilings were calculated.

29 Bogetic and Fox (1993), p. 45.

30 This and later quantitative statements on wages are, unless otherwise indicated, based on figures derived from various publications of the National Statistical Institute.

the decline in output over the years 1991 and 1992 and so the failure of real wages to decline after the first quarter of 1991 must have been a source of inflationary pressure. Nonetheless, things could have been much worse.

Fiscal Policy[31]

Bulgaria joined the International Monetary Fund and the World Bank in September 1990 and submitted its first request for assistance in February 1991, a standby arrangement being granted in March. Among the conditions attached to that agreement were a target for the ratio of the budget deficit to GDP and a reduction in the size of the budget relative to GDP.[32] For reasons dealt with in more detail in Chapter 7 below, one result of the abolition of the planning system and the liberalization of international trade was a dramatic decline in the base of the state revenue system: total budget revenue collapsed from 54.3 per cent of GDP in 1990 to 42.7 per cent in 1991, tax revenue falling from 43.9 per cent of GDP to 37.1 per cent. The budget deficit could be kept within bounds, therefore, only by a very significant reduction in the ratio of public expenditure to GDP.

When contemplating the budget deficit, it is important to recall that, because of the moratorium on the servicing of foreign debt, the deficit on a cash basis is very significantly smaller than that on an accruals basis. Thus, in 1991, the difference between interest accrued on foreign debt and interest actually paid was 11.2 per cent of GDP. However, for short-term stabilization purposes, it is the cash deficit which matters since it is that which has to be financed immediately.

Efforts at fiscal restraint were quite successful, considering the downward pressures on revenue and the upward pressures on expenditure endemic to transition from a planned to a market economy, the cash deficit in 1991 being 4.3 per cent of GDP compared with 4.9 per cent in 1990. Public expenditure fell from 59.3 per cent of GDP to 47 per cent. Some of this came from a reduction in public consumption

---

31 Fiscal issues are reviewed here only in the context of stabilization policy. Policy relating to fiscal structure is dealt with in Chapter 7 below. The sources of the data in this section are the Bulgarian National Bank and the Ministry of Finance.

32 Wyzan (1993), p. 129.

(that is, governmental operating expenses), which fell from 24.1 per cent of GDP to 21.9 per cent, and investment carried on the state budget almost disappeared, but the most spectacular fall was in subsidies paid to cover enterprise losses and to keep consumer prices down. This item fell by almost 11 percentage points of GDP to 4 per cent in 1991. A sharp reduction in these subsidies was an explicit component of the liberalization package introduced in February.

The significance of the budget deficit in the context of a need to control inflation lies in the way it is financed. In developed market economies, there are capital markets and large amounts of liquid wealth outside the banking system. As a result, budget deficits can be financed, at least in part, by the sale of securities to the non-bank public. In Bulgaria, on the other hand, such conditions do not exist and, furthermore, the country's inability to service its existing foreign debt made it impossible for it to finance any of its government deficit from overseas sources. The whole of the financing burden therefore fell on the domestic banking system. In 1991, about a half of the government's financing needs (the cash deficit plus financing requirements associated with inactive balances relating to past CMEA trade — a total of 5.1 per cent of GDP) came from direct credit from the Bulgarian National Bank. The remainder comprised securities issued to the commercial banks but, since there was no secondary market for such securities and the BNB had to provide the liquidity for the commercial banks to take up these issues, in effect all finance came from the BNB. This is the most inflationary method of financing budget deficits and highlights the significance of fiscal restraint.

The fiscal situation in 1992 proved even more difficult. Tax revenue continued to decline as a proportion of GDP (34.7 per cent compared with 37.1 per cent in 1991) and the fall in the ratio of expenditure to GDP, which had been dramatic in the previous year, was reversed in 1992, primarily because of increasing demands for social security benefits resulting from the continued increase in unemployment, an increasing interest bill on the domestic debt incurred in financing the deficits of the previous two years, and inertia in the public pay bill.

The outcome was a deficit which, after the comparative success of 1991, was restored to its previous level of 5 per cent of GDP. Though this may have been the best that could reasonably be expected in the face of the continued defects in the revenue system, it did nothing to mitigate the underlying inflationary pressures. Indeed, there are good reasons for claiming that the budget deficit was a major domestic source of those pressures.

Monetary Policy

In its first annual report of the transition era, the BNB defined the objectives of its policy (aside from aims relating to the restructuring of the monetary system, of which more in Chapter 6 below) as 'eliminating the monetary overhang, overcoming the inflationary pressures and stabilising the foreign exchange market in 1991'.[33]

To achieve the first of these — that is, to mop up excess liquidity — it relied on preferential schemes for the repayment of housing loans and attempted to make time deposits (i.e., relatively illiquid deposits) attractive by means of high interest rates. These interest rates may have seemed high to the BNB, but only a population subject to considerable money illusion could have been induced by them to change its behaviour. In the three months beginning in February 1991, when the increase in the consumer price index was 243 per cent, the average annual interest rate on time deposits was 42 per cent.

In April and May, the real interest rate (the nominal annual rate deflated by the annualized rate of inflation in the month in question) turned significantly positive as the monthly inflation rate dropped to very low levels, but for the remainder of the year, with the exception of October and November (when again inflation was relatively low), it was severely negative. It is therefore not credible that interest-rate policy contributed to the neutralizing of the overhang,[34] but this was not important since that overhang was almost certainly eliminated by the huge increase in prices in February and March.

More generally, although nominal interest rates were increased dramatically during 1991 (the basic, or refinancing, rate reaching 54

---

33 Bulgarian National Bank, *Annual Report 1991*, p. 39.

34 There was certainly a significant switching to less liquid assets, the ratio of lev time deposits to lev demand deposits rising from 0.3 to 1.7 to 3.0 at the end of 1990, 1991 and 1992 respectively. However, this is merely an expected response of the structure of portfolios to the dramatic increase in the return on time deposits *relative to that on demand deposits*. There is no reason to believe that interest-rate policy had any effect in increasing the ratio of total deposits to income, which would have to have taken place if such policy were to have had an effect on the overhang.

per cent and the rate on new credits 64 per cent by the end of the year), and gave rise to cries of pain from enterprise managers, the fact that they were negative in real terms indicates that they were unimportant in restraining the demand for credit.[35] More important in this respect was the imposition of credit ceilings by the BNB: that is, credit was rationed by quantity restrictions rather than by price.

Table 2.6 Net credit outstanding as percentage of GDP,[a] 1990–92

	1990	1991	1992
To government	30	40	52
To public enterprises	102	77	69
To private sector	16	10	9
Total	148	128	130

[a] Year-end as % of year GDP
Source: Derived from Bulgarian National Bank

The behaviour of the total shown in Table 2.6 of course mimics that of the broad money supply as revealed in Table 2.5 above. In 1991, nominal credit grew more slowly than nominal GDP and, to that extent, monetary policy was playing its part in the control of inflation. However, the same could not be said for 1992 where monetary policy was neutral with respect to inflation. Moreover, these figures reveal something of structural importance. The expansion in nominal credit was being driven by the budget deficit, net credit outstanding to the government increasing by over 20 percentage points of GDP during the first two years of transition. That this should have crowded out credit to the private sector, which actually fell by seven percentage points of GDP during this period, is clearly undesirable. Credit outstanding to government rose from 20 per cent of total credit at the end of 1990 to 40 per cent at the end of 1992, whereas the share of the private sector

35 Nevertheless, the high nominal rates may have had perverse effects on export competitiveness. Because of the moratorium, Bulgarian enterprises could not borrow abroad and so could obtain working capital only at rates far exceeding those paid by their foreign competitors. In the aggregate and in the long run, this effect may be expected to be offset by a devaluation of the lev, but this process provided no consolation for those caught in this trap in the short run.

fell from 11 to 8 per cent. The dramatic, relative decline in the availability of credit to public enterprises (that sector's share of total credit fell from 69 to 49 per cent in the two years to the end of 1992) is more difficult to interpret. On the one hand, bank credit under the old system was often the vehicle for enterprise subsidization and some of the decline shown in Table 2.6 is simply the counterpart of the decline in budgetary subsidies to enterprises and so is a reflection of one of the central objectives of transition policy. On the other hand, there is no way of telling from aggregate figures the extent to which acceptable credit demands from the enterprise sector remained unsatisfied because of the need to finance the growing budget deficit.

Table 2.6 of course refers solely to credit originating in the banking system, whereas one of the most prevalent features of the response to liberalization is the massive growth in inter-enterprise arrears. This phenomenon, which has made monetary control difficult in all transition economies, will be reviewed in Chapter 4 below.

To a considerable extent, the expansion of the nominal money supply was fuelled directly by exchange-rate movements. The proportion of the broad money supply accounted for by convertible-currency deposits soared from 11 per cent at the end of 1990 to 38 per cent at the end of 1991, falling back to 30 per cent by the end of 1992. This was not the result of any demonetization of the lev (that is, the switching from domestic to foreign currency as a hedge against inflation): the dollar value of convertible-currency deposits remained remarkably stable over the whole period. It was simply the result of the changing lev value of convertible-currency deposits occasioned by the changing lev/dollar exchange rate. We now turn to this issue.

Exchange Rate Policy

As already noted, Bulgaria embarked on liberalization with foreign exchange reserves quite inadequate to contemplate any kind of medium-term fixed exchange rate policy. The BNB described its approach in the following terms: 'A basic task of the exchange rate policy was to secure relative stability in the nominal exchange rate. With a floating rate and with heightened inflation, the Central Bank aimed at supporting the exchange rate of the lev on a level that would not exert inflationary pressure in the country, but would preserve the international competitiveness of Bulgarian producers in international markets'.[36] The best term for such a policy is probably 'managed float'.[37]

Table 2.7 Exchange rate (BGL/US$, end month), 1991–92

	1991	1992
January	2.88	23.82
February	20.74	24.14
March	15.17	23.28
April	18.50	23.01
May	18.25	23.21
June	17.55	23.02
July	18.69	22.76
August	17.64	22.22
September	18.95	22.64
October	20.53	23.75
November	18.73	24.70
December	21.81	24.49

Source: Bulgarian National Bank

Bulgaria introduced its liberalization package when the central, official exchange rate was BGL2.88 to the dollar and, in the initial stages, the now floating rate behaved more or less as would have been expected: the lev immediately devalued to BGL28 to the dollar but quickly began to recover, reaching under BGL21 by the end of February and remaining better than BGL20 per dollar until almost the end of the year. That is, the immediate devaluation represented serious overshooting,

---

36 Bulgarian National Bank, *Annual Report 1992*, p. 51. The Bank also says that the exchange rate performed the role of a nominal anchor, a statement which, while acceptable if taken to describe the general objective of resisting persistent nominal devaluation which would exacerbate inflation, is misleading if interpreted as implying the same role for the exchange rate as it played in, say, Poland and Czechoslovakia.

37 This is the expression used by Rosati (1994) to describe Bulgaria when categorizing the exchange-rate policies of transition economies into nominal anchor, managed float and crawling peg.

which the market (not the BNB, which had insufficient reserves for serious intervention) soon rectified.[38]

Table 2.7 indicates that the stability objective of exchange-rate policy was achieved, with almost no trend in the nominal rate between April and November, 1991, a devaluation of around 30 per cent over the following three months, and then again almost no trend up to the late autumn of 1992.

This stability in the exchange rate was attributable to two factors – a significant improvement in the balance of payments[39] and intervention in the market by the BNB, which was able to buy foreign currency as a result of assistance from the IMF and the European Union. The change in 1991 over 1990 is somewhat clouded statistically by the fact that this was the time when almost all trade payments with former CMEA members changed from transferable rubles to convertible currency. However, since all the main components moved in the same direction, the general picture is reasonably clear.

The trade balance in convertible currencies moved from a deficit of $757 million in 1990 to a deficit of only $32 million in 1991 and then to a surplus of $485 million in 1992. The current account balance was of course helped, especially in 1991, by the low level of actual (as opposed to accrued) foreign debt service, but it moved from a deficit of $77 million in 1991 to a surplus of $452 million in 1992, despite the improvement in performance in servicing the foreign debt (interest paid on foreign loans increased by $120 million between 1991 and 1992).

The main features of the improvement in the balance of payments were a creditable export performance, despite rapid domestic inflation, and the effect on imports of the depression in domestic demand. From a low base in 1990, which was Bulgaria's worst year for exports in over a decade, dollar exports rose by 43 per cent in 1991 and by a further 36 per cent in 1992. At the same time, the increases in dollar imports in the two years were only 12 per cent and 22 per cent respectively.

Support from international institutions began to flow in early 1991, starting with an IMF standby facility of SDR279 million, approved in

---

38   It appears that the government expected a rate of around BGL10 to the dollar to be established fairly quickly, although the grounds for this belief are unclear.

39   The figures used here are those of the BNB, which are derived from data on transactions through the banking system. They differ from those published by the National Statistical Institute, which derives its data from customs declarations.

March of that year, delivered in five tranches and repayable during 1994–7. This loan was explicitly designed to support the foreign exchange reserves. The first tranche ($150 million) of a World Bank structural adjustment loan (SAL) was delivered in August and this could also be regarded as support for the reserves since it was all spent on inescapable imports of oil. The second tranche (£100 million) of this SAL was withheld because of failure to meet the conditions relating to structural reform and was not delivered until April 1993. Other support from the European Bank for Reconstruction and Development and the EU was also received in 1991, 1992 and 1993, but this was of less immediate significance for the foreign exchange position since it was earmarked for import-intensive restructuring projects (such as the upgrading of electricity generation, the telecommunications system and the highway network) which, while of longer term significance, could have been delayed if the balance of payments situation demanded it. A further IMF standby of SDR155 million, to be delivered in five equal tranches, was agreed in March 1992. The first four tranches were paid during the year, but breach of the conditions of the loan caused the fifth tranche to be cancelled and the following year was a difficult one for relations between Bulgaria and the IMF, with no new assistance approved.

From this, one might judge the BNB's objectives as described above to have been achieved. Certainly, it would be difficult to lay at the door of the exchange rate the persistence of a rather high rate inflation. The performance of the balance of trade, however, seems to have been achieved despite a stability in the nominal exchange rate which might have been expected to erode competitiveness seriously.[40] It has not been possible to construct an index of the true real exchange rate because a sufficiently detailed breakdown of the origin and destination of Bulgaria's trade is not available. Trade with former CMEA members still represented over one-half of the country's trade in 1991 and over one-third in 1992. Some of these partners (those in the former Soviet Union) had inflation rates markedly in excess of Bulgaria's, and so the

---

40 There was a public difference of opinion between the minister of finance and the Governor of the BNB over the Bank's purchases of foreign currency, reflecting the conflict between the need to support competitiveness and the need to minimize the budgetary cost of foreign debt service. See Wyzan (1993), p. 137 and Izvorski (1993), p. 528.

real exchange rate with respect to those countries depreciated, whereas others had markedly lower inflation. A further complication is that OECD countries, which accounted for 30 per cent of Bulgaria's trade in 1991 and 45 per cent in 1992, did not have currencies which were fixed *vis-à-vis* the US dollar. However, concentrating on trade with non-CMEA countries, and accepting that such trading partners had inflation rates which were trivial relative to Bulgaria's, one can construct a crude estimate of movements in the real exchange rate if one simply deflates the nominal dollar rate by the domestic inflation rate. This is done in Table 2.8. So that an increase in the index indicates a real appreciation, it is based on the inverse of Table 2.7 (that is, it shows $/BGL).

Table 2.8 Index of real exchange rate (December 1990=100), 1991–92

	1991	1992
January	114	73
February	35	76
March	72	82
April	61	85
May	62	95
June	68	101
July	70	105
August	79	109
September	77	111
October	73	112
November	84	115
December	76	121

After the initial huge real devaluation in February 1991, there was a steady real appreciation until, by mid-1992, the real exchange value of the lev against the dollar had climbed back to its pre-liberalization level. By the end of that year it was 20 per cent higher. For the reasons mentioned in the previous paragraph, this is certainly an overestimate of the degree of real appreciation, but the extent of that overestimate declines over time with the decline in the relative importance of trade with the high-inflation countries of the former Soviet Union. In the light of these estimates, the export performance, with the value of exports to

OECD more than doubling and those to the EU almost tripling between 1991 and 1992, is remarkable. Whatever the explanation, exporters certainly received no help from the exchange rate. Of course, it could not last, as we shall see in the next chapter.

THE REAL ECONOMY

It has been the universal experience of Central and Eastern Europe that liberalization has been accompanied by a severe contraction of real economic activity. Although, as already noted, official figures overstate the decline in real output because they overstate the increase in the GDP deflator and fail to capture the growth of the private sector, there is no reason to doubt that the decline has been very severe.[41] Casual observation of living standards and, more objectively, what has been happening in the labour market, bear that out.

We have already seen that, in Bulgaria, the decline in real activity began well before there was any attempt to liberalize domestic prices and foreign trade — primarily as a result of constraints on the supply of imports. From 1991, this contraction was driven by demand factors.

Table 2.9   Changes in real GDP (%), 1990–92

	1990	1991	1992
Gross domestic product	−9.1	−11.7	−5.7
Industry, construction	−12.5	−18.6	−11.2
Agriculture, forestry	−3.7	7.7	−13.8
Services	−5.3	−11.3	−10.1

Source: Bulgarian National Bank

Over the three years shown in Table 2.9, GDP fell by a total of 24 per cent, with industrial production declining by 37 per cent. Since the trade balance moved favourably over this period, the implication is that domestic demand fell by an even greater extent than GDP. Real private consumption fell by 26 per cent, the decline in 1991 alone being 16 per

---

41 Winiecki (1991) suggests other reasons why the fall in output is overstated and why at least some of this decline does not represent a fall in the welfare of the population.

cent, but the collapse in investment demand was even more spectacular, the fall in fixed investment being 53 per cent and that in inventory investment over 76 per cent. Inventory investment remained positive in every year, which is perhaps surprising and may be a measurement illusion, but the collapse of the ratio between accumulation of stocks and GDP is an indication of producers' responses to the extreme market uncertainties of this period.

The different rates of output decline revealed in Table 2.9 led to a marked change in the structure of aggregate output, as is shown in Table 2.10.

Table 2.10 Composition of GDP (%), 1990–92

	1990	1991	1992
Industry, construction	51.3	48.0	43.8
Agriculture, forestry	17.7	15.4	11.2
Services	31.0	36.7	45.0

Source: Bulgarian National Bank

It has already been noted that one would expect the decline in activity to have had a number of causes — notably, constraints on the supply of inputs and the collapse of both domestic demand and export demand from the former CMEA. In addition, one might expect both structural changes and attempts to operate anti-inflationary fiscal and monetary policies to have played a part. It would be of considerable interest to understand the relative importance of these factors and some research has been done on this, although its results would have to be regarded as tentative in the extreme. One piece of work[42] attempted to measure, first, the relative importance of structural compared with macroeconomic influences and, second, the relative importance of demand-side and supply-side influences. The first conclusion was that structural factors (that is, the effect of reallocating resources to the production of output for which there is a market and away from production for which market prospects are poor) appear to have been relatively unimportant as causes of the output decline in Bulgaria: macroeconomic — or economy-wide

---

42   Borensztein, Demekas and Ostry (1993).

— factors were more significant. As regards the latter, these authors judge supply-side forces to be more important than demand-side forces. However, the procedures on which this conclusion is based can be questioned.[43]

Another piece of work[44] is interesting because it directly addresses the issue of whether the tightness of credit policy, instituted to control inflation and encourage restructuring, contributed to the decline in output. The conclusion is that it may have, though its authors are at pains to point out that this should not be taken to imply that credit policy would be able to restore output to socially optimal levels.

Employment and unemployment

Table 2.11 Employment in the public sector ('000), 1990–92

	1990	1991	1992
Total	3824	3205	2653
Industry, construction	1769	1417	1172
Agriculture, forestry	672	570	401
Services	1383	1218	1080

Source: Bulgarian National Bank

Available data on employment are defective in that they are unreliable as regards the private sector. Official estimates for private employment are published, but almost certainly understate the true situation. Statistics for the public sector (that is, state and cooperative enterprises and government) are shown in Table 2.11.

---

43 The hypothesis being tested was very simple: that sectors in which supply factors predominated should show a negative correlation between price changes and output changes, whereas a positive correlation should be expected if demand factors were dominant. The conclusion is based on the discovery of negative correlations for Bulgaria. One must have both theoretical and statistical doubts about the robustness of this conclusion. Little is known about the processes of price formation in the early post-liberalization phases of transition economies and so one must doubt the appropriateness of a model which comes straight from neo-classical comparative statics. In any case, the reported coefficients of determination (especially if adjusted for the rather small number of observations) are not impressive.

44 Calvo and Coricelli (1993).

The decline already noted in 1989 and 1990 continued at an accelerating pace, the fall in total employment in public activities being approximately 17 per cent in each of 1991 and 1992 — or 31 per cent over the two years — with particularly large reductions in industry and agriculture — 34 and 40 per cent respectively. Since the amount of industrial activity in the private sector remained very small (and will become significant in the medium term only as a result of privatization of public enterprises), the figures for public activity in that sector are a good representation of what is happening in the economy as a whole. In agriculture and services, however, the situation is quite different. By 1992, privatization of agricultural land under the restitution programme had begun (see Chapter 4 below) and private activity was moving towards domination of the services sector. The figures in Table 2.11 are therefore misleading as indicators of total employment in those sectors.

Unfortunately, no estimates exist for this period for private employment by sector, but official estimates exist for employment in the private sector as a whole. These estimates indicate private employment to have been only three thousand or so in 1991, but to have been 434,000 in 1992.[45] If these totals are included with those shown above, the fall in employment in 1992 becomes a mere 3.8 per cent, as against a fall of 17.2 per cent in the public sector. Quite clearly, this is the result of either the restitution of assets in the agricultural and service sectors or workers laid off in the public sector finding new jobs in the private sector.

Transition has seen the emergence of a phenomenon of which Bulgaria had no experience — open unemployment (see Table 2.12). All countries find unemployment difficult to measure and usually rely on a mixture of labour surveys and registrations at official agencies responsible for job-search and the payment of unemployment benefits. Only the latter can generate frequent statistics, but they are subject to serious methodological difficulties. On the one hand, persons will register as unemployed only if they have an incentive to do so — that is, if they are eligible to receive benefits or if they think registration would materially increase their prospects of finding employment. On the other hand, it is difficult to know to what extent those who register in order to receive benefits are really unemployed. It is thought that the second factor has

---

45   Bulgarian National Bank, *Annual Report 1991*, p. 17 and *Annual Report 1992*, p. 30.

been dominant in Bulgaria and so it is to be expected that the official figures derived for registered unemployment overstate true unemployment. Any observer will offer a subjective judgement of the degree of overestimation, but this is hardly reliable and so one has no option but to use official figures. Since Bulgaria provides unemployment compensation only in the short run, and since the rate of layoffs slackens over time, it is to be expected that the proportion of the registered unemployed who have jobs but who register to gain benefits will decline over time. Broadly speaking, therefore, the divergence between registered and true unemployment should decline.

Table 2.12 Rate of unemployment (%), 1991–92

	1991	1992
January	1.9	10.9
February	2.6	11.2
March	3.4	12.0
April	4.4	12.4
May	5.1	12.5
June	5.8	12.6
July	7.0	13.4
August	7.9	13.9
September	8.6	14.3
October	9.1	14.8
November	10.0	15.0
December	10.5	15.2

Source: National Statistical Institute

Again, the emergence of open unemployment had begun before the big bang but, during the two years succeeding that watershed, it grew very rapidly. From a level of 65,000 in December 1990, it reached 419,000 by the end of 1991 and 577,000 by the end of 1992. As will be noted, the increase was especially rapid during the first year, the rate of increase slowing markedly in the second year. As it turned out, it had almost reached its peak by the end of 1992, as the rate of decline in output decelerated, as those who were the first to lose their jobs ran out of eligibility for benefits (and so no longer had an incentive to register) and as job-creation in the private sector gathered pace.

3. Recent Macroeconomic Developments

The government set up under Dimitur Popov in December 1990 was intended simply to be a caretaker, pending new elections. However, there were major tasks to be confronted as regards the transition to a market economy and the design of a new national constitution and, in a rare fit of solidarity, all-party agreement was reached in January 1991 to put off elections until at least a start could be made on these tasks. Having been approved by the Assembly on the previous day, the new post-communist constitution came into force on 13 July. A major provision was for direct, presidential elections and these were scheduled for the following January.

The Popov government, as we have seen, initiated the first, major steps towards liberalization. It also oversaw the passage of legislation on such matters as land restitution. But elections could not be put off indefinitely, and Bulgaria's second free elections took place on 13 October 1991. The procedures were simpler than for the 1990 elections, involving a single-stage ballot using a list-type proportional representation. The outcome was that the UDF won 110 of the 240 seats, the BSP gaining 106 and the remainder going to the MRF. Not having an overall majority, the UDF were forced to seek coalition partners, which they found in the form of the MRF. A new government under Filip Dimitrov, the UDF leader, was formed on 8 November. This was the first government without communist or former communist participation since 1944. The success of the UDF was confirmed in the presidential elections of January 1992 when the incumbent Zhelyu Zhelev (who had been chairman of the UDF until his election by the Assembly to the presidency in August 1990) was elected president and the UDF candidate, Blaga Dimitrova, became vice-president.

The next few months were the most active so far in legislative terms, with laws on restitution, banking and, most important of all after a long drawn-out process, privatization. However, the smallness of the coalition's majority and the inherently fissile qualities of the UDF could not stand the strain of piloting the country through the difficult waters of economic reform. On 28 October 1992, the government lost a vote of confidence in the Assembly and Dimitrov resigned as prime minister. Two months of political vacuum were eventually filled when, on the penultimate day of the year, the Assembly approved the president's nomination of Lyuben Berov, a professor of economics and not affiliated to any party, as prime minister. Once again, the country had been entrusted to a government which had not been generated from within parliament. It relied for its survival on a bloc representing the bulk of the BSP and the MRF, with some breakaways from the UDF — a coalition which could not be stable in the long run since even its constituent parts were unstable. Managing to conjure up a kind of revolving majority in the Assembly, it was to have the longest life of any post-communist government so far, eventually falling in September 1994 when Berov, exhausted by fights to survive repeated confidence votes, resigned.

The Berov government, which had not only an academic prime minister but an economist turned civil servant as minister of finance, was an archetypal government of technocrats, which some see as particularly valuable in such circumstances as those prevailing in transition economies, where a technical understanding of the complex policy issues combined with an absence of personal political constituencies should facilitate the making of difficult decisions.[1] This chapter is essentially the story of a government of experts who perhaps disappointed in their expertise and who were struggling with a parliament in which even the BSP lost some of its vaunted discipline.

INFLATION AND STABILIZATION[2]

The new government came to power with every expectation that, as long as the line could be held on the monetary and fiscal policy fronts, the worst of the post-liberalization inflationary pressures were over.

---

1 Williamson (1994).

2 Unless stated otherwise, the numerical data in this chapter are derived from various publications of the Bulgarian National Bank.

They were to be seriously disappointed. At 64 per cent, inflation during 1993 was not much lower than the 79 per cent of the previous year (or an average monthly rate of 4.2 compared with 5 per cent) and 1994 was to see the nightmare scenario for stabilization policy in transition economies — a reversal in the downward trend of inflation.

Table 3.1 Monthly increase in consumer price index (%), 1993–94

	1993	1994
January	6.9	3.8
February	4.7	4.6
March	5.6	7.5
April	3.9	21.7
May	5.3	7.9
June	4.1	4.1
July	1.0	0.6
August	2.6	5.2
September	3.8	11.0
October	4.2	6.9
November	4.6	5.5
December	3.9	5.0

Source: National Statistical Institute

In addition to the continuing high monthly rates of inflation during 1993, the most obvious feature of Table 3.1 is the jumps in the price level in March–May 1994. Two things were happening here. First, the exchange value of the lev declined rapidly in the last two months of 1993 and the first two months of 1994, collapsing spectacularly during March. The effect on import prices in leva is obvious and this is clearly the main reason for the extreme instability of the domestic price level at this time. The second relevant event was the introduction of value-added tax on 1 April. This will be discussed in detail in Chapter 7 below, but it does appear that, despite the fact that the rates of VAT were set so that its replacement of the turnover tax would not have significant absolute price effects, the market power of sellers, combined with buyers' confusion over the new tax, did cause sellers' net margins, and therefore retail prices, to jump once and for all.

As in the previous chapter, we consider four possible sources of inflation: wages, monetary policy, fiscal policy and the exchange rate.

Wages

The only available data relate to the state sector and, of course, with the increasing proportion of employment represented by the private sector, these data are less and less reliable as indicators of wage movements in the economy at large. However, this need not be of great concern yet and, in any case, it is more likely that wages in the private sector will be related to productivity changes and so, if nominal wage increases were a source of inflationary pressure, the problem would be greater in the state sector.

The average real wage in the public sector declined very considerably in the early months of 1993, being in the first quarter some 17 per cent below its level in the same quarter of the previous year. It then climbed slowly until, by the end of the year, it was within 11 per cent of its level at the end of 1992. So, whereas 1992 had, taking the year as a whole, shown little change in real average wages, 1993 saw a quite significant reduction. This suggests that inflation was not driven by wages, especially since the decline in the real wage between the two years exceeded the decline in real output (see below): real unit wage costs appear to have fallen. The first quarter of 1994 saw real wages at a level only very slightly lower than in the same period of the previous year, but the remainder of 1994 was dominated by the impact of the huge price increase in April (and the larger than usual monthly inflation in March and May). In April, the real wage was only 80 per cent of its level a year previously and by June the reduction had reached 25 per cent. By the end of the year, the average real wage in the public sector was only 72 per cent of its level at the end of 1993.

The failure of nominal wages to match inflation reflects considerable success on the part of the government in preventing the pass-through of inflation. The tripartite commission had been suspended by the UDF-dominated government which had been in power throughout 1992, but the new government of Berov, in an effort to mend fences with the trade unions, re-established it in early 1993.[3] The system had been working on the basis of less than full compensation for past inflation but, in early 1994, the government insisted on returning to the original idea of relating cost-of-living-adjustments to projected rather than past inflation.[4] This had the highly desirable effect that, since the surge in prices in the spring of that year had not been foreseen, the wage-setting mechanism prevented this begetting a wage-price spiral, although not surprisingly another effect was considerable labour unrest in May.

Monetary and Fiscal Policy

The BNB continued to see its primary objectives as being to resist inflationary pressures and to maintain stability in the nominal exchange rate. Its conclusion for the year was that 'since the government's fiscal and incomes policies were not restrictive enough, BNB monetary policy failed to significantly decrease inflation'.[5] This judgement is too harsh as regards incomes policy but, as we shall see shortly, is fully justified with respect to fiscal policy. If monetary policy was ineffective, the fault lies in the Bank's inability or unwillingness to resist accommodating the inexorable rise in the state's demand for credit.

During 1993, the broad money supply increased by 53 per cent in nominal terms, which represented a real decline of 7 per cent. Some of this was accounted for by the impact on the lev value of foreign currency holdings of the one-third devaluation which occurred during the year (most of which occurred in the final quarter of the year — see below) but, as in 1992, this factor was not important in nominal money growth. This certainly represented some easing of monetary policy since the broad money supply was, at 85 per cent, four percentage points of GDP higher at the end of 1993 than it had been at the beginning of the year. Once again, the nominal money supply increased while real

---

3 Under the new title of National Tripartite Cooperation Council, with membership representing the government, the two main trade union groupings (the Confederation of Independent Trade Unions in Bulgaria and *Podkrepa*), and employers in the form of the Bulgarian Industrial Association, the Bulgarian Chamber of Commerce and Industry, and the Union for Private Economic Enterprise (*Bulgarian Economic Review*, 26 March–8 April 1993).

4 *168 Hours BBN*, 4–10 April 1994.

5 Bulgarian National Bank, *Annual Report 1993*, p. 51.

activity continued to fall, and so monetary policy was to a degree accommodating of inflation. Nonetheless, to continue to achieve a reduction in the real money supply was something of a success.

A major force behind monetary expansion continued to be the fiscal deficit. By any standards, fiscal performance in 1993 was very poor. Even the BNB was prepared to go public in its criticisms, especially of the fact that the Assembly did not approve the Budget Law until the middle of the year. 'Up to that moment it was very difficult to harmonize BNB monetary policy and fiscal policy of the government, because the latter had no clear guidelines ... The lack of efficient coordination between fiscal and monetary policies throughout most of 1993 had an unfavorable impact on macroeconomic developments ...'[6]

The budget submitted to parliament by the Council of Ministers was based on an expectation of revenue equal to 39 per cent of GDP, expenditure of 47 per cent of GDP (about one-eighth of which being for the taking-up of enterprise bad debts), and so with a deficit of 8 per cent of GDP.[7] As it turned out, revenue performed slightly better than expected (though worse than in 1992), but expenditure did the opposite, to an even greater degree. The ratio of expenditure to GDP rose from 48.7 per cent to 55 per cent and the upshot was that the consolidated cash deficit, which had been at a level of 5 per cent of GDP in 1992, grew to almost 13 per cent in 1993. As in the previous year, the main growth elements on the expenditure side of the budget were interest on domestic debt (there was also some, though small, effort to service foreign debt) and social security, with a continuing rise in unemployment. The government's inability to restrain growth in the budget deficit is perhaps the single most important policy failure on the macroeconomic front.

Once again, this had to be totally financed from domestic sources and, as in earlier years, the budget had to finance not only its own deficit but the credit balances arising from trade with the former Soviet Union. The total financing requirement was 12.7 per cent of GDP as against 6.2 per cent in the previous year. Only 22 per cent was financed directly by bank credit, the remainder coming from the issue of securities. However, almost all of the latter were taken up by the banks, the only

---

6   Ibid., p. 43.

7   *168 Hours BBN*, 12–18 April 1993.

ray of sunshine being that 1993 saw the first signs of the non-bank public taking up issues of government securities. Still, in total 89 per cent of the financing of the budget deficit came from the domestic banking system.

This burden of accommodating such a large and expanding government demand for credit was the driving force behind monetary expansion in 1993. Credit outstanding to government accounted for 49 per cent of total net credit at the end of the year, or 68 per cent of the year's GDP (up from 40 per cent and 52 per cent respectively at the end of 1992). Credit outstanding to non-financial state enterprises fell from 53 per cent of total credit to 42 per cent during the year — or from 69 per cent to 58 per cent of GDP. Some, but only a small proportion, of this was the result of the first exercises in dealing with enterprises' non-performing credits. The government initiated a policy of cleaning up enterprise balance sheets by taking over the liability for non-performing credits granted up to the end of 1990 (a policy reviewed in more detail in Chapter 6 below), and so the accounting effect is, from the viewpoint of the banking system, a matching swap of credit to government for credit to enterprises. This effect became more important as the policy got into its stride in 1994. It was of no real consequence in 1993, the main reason for the expansion of credit to government being the budget deficit. Again, the decline in relative credit to enterprises would be welcome to the extent that it represented a hardening of budget constraints which squeezed out the accommodation of credits which were really subsidies. However, one cannot tell the extent to which there was true crowding out — that is, the accommodation of government demand at the expense of justifiable enterprise demand for working capital or restructuring. One hopeful sign in 1993 was the expansion of credit to the private sector — up from 7 per cent of total credit to 9 per cent, or from 9 per cent to 13 per cent of GDP.

The monetary situation in the early months of 1994 was clouded by the direct and indirect effects of the extreme instability of the foreign exchange market (see below). In the first two months, the broad money supply and net credit remained approximately constant in real terms, but jumped (by 12 per cent in the case of broad money and 28 per cent in the case of credit) in March. This was totally the effect of a nominal devaluation exceeding 40 per cent, the lev component of both the money supply and credit outstanding remaining practically unchanged in nominal terms. This jump in real values was reversed in the following month when the domestic price level, affected by devaluation and VAT, rose by almost 22 per cent. Thereafter, the real money supply fell sharply, rose somewhat during the summer and then fell again during the final quarter until, by the end of the year, it had fallen to 80 per cent of its value at the beginning of the year.

This very considerable slackening of monetary growth compared with 1993 was to a large extent a reflection of a dramatic, and unexpected, improvement in fiscal performance. The 1994 budget was approved in March and it must have been known at the time (when the exchange rate was collapsing) that it was extremely optimistic in providing for a deficit which, in nominal terms, would be little different from the outcome for 1993. If it could be achieved, it would be a remarkable exercise in fiscal rectitude since it would have represented a fall from 13 per cent of GDP to less than 7 per cent. This budget had been framed according to assumptions which soon proved to be hopelessly unrealistic: an annual rate of inflation of 45 per cent and an average rate of exchange over the year of BGL35 per dollar. As it turned out, the price level in May already exceeded that at the beginning of the year by over 50 per cent, and at no time during 1994 was the lev as strong had been assumed. Nevertheless, the extraordinary feat of a reduction in the ratio of the budget deficit to GDP of 6 percentage points was in fact achieved, with the cash deficit for the year being exactly on target at BGL34 billion, or 6.6 per cent of GDP. Although expenditure was higher than budgeted by about 25 per cent (primarily because of under-budgeting of interest payments), the revenue system performed much better than expected. Of particular interest (because of the importance of its role in the new revenue system — see Chapter 7 below) was the achievement of the new VAT, which brought in 40 per cent more than was budgeted, contributing 38 per cent of total tax revenue or 7.4 per cent of GDP.

The main burden of monetary policy continued to be borne by credit ceilings rather than interest rates, at least into 1994. The real basic rate remained negative throughout 1993 and early 1994, becoming positive (for the first time since liberalization) in the summer, when its nominal value was increased to 78 per cent, rising to 94 per cent in September. One welcome result of the decline in the state's relative demand for credit was that the proportion of total credit taken up by the private sector rose by 5 percentage points to 14 per cent by the end of the year.

The Exchange Rate

The stability of the lev against the dollar during 1992 has already been noted, as was the concomitant steady real appreciation. Although nothing dramatic happened in the early part of 1993, there were already signs of nominal weakening: by August, the lev had already devalued by the 11 per cent by which it had depreciated over the whole of the previous year. The trickle then began to flood, the rate of depreciation over the last four months of 1993 being 16 per cent, making 25 per cent over the year as a whole. The details are shown in Table 3.2.

Table 3.2 Exchange rate (BGL/US$, end month), 1993–94

	1993	1994
January	25.59	36.32
February	26.61	37.37
March	26.52	64.94
April	26.40	56.88
May	26.41	55.59
June	26.68	53.66
July	27.21	53.31
August	27.42	57.19
September	28.03	61.20
October	29.51	64.92
November	31.17	65.04
December	32.71	65.53

Source: Bulgarian National Bank

A number of explanations can be suggested for the steady weakening of the lev in the last five months of 1993. In the first place, there was a definite deterioration in the balance of payments during the year. The trade surplus, which had been $484 million in 1992, fell to $134 million, and the total current account position moved from a surplus of

$452 million to a deficit of $339 million.[8] Most of this deterioration is the result of a decline in the dollar value of exports. The Bank[9] cites the UN embargo on trade with Serbia and Montenegro as a major cause of this, and certainly the Bulgarian air is full of estimates of the losses incurred from that embargo. It is therefore strange that figures issued by the BNB itself indicate that exports to former Yugoslavia actually rose slightly as a proportion of total exports between 1992 and 1993.[10] It is hard to resist the conclusion that the chickens were coming home to roost from the steady real appreciation of the lev already noted. By September 1993 the real value of the lev against the dollar (calculated as in Table 2.8) was 27 per cent higher than at the end of 1992.

There may have been some pressure on the lev as a result of inflationary expectations (which would cause Bulgarian residents to switch into dollars) and there may have been some outflow of money temporarily lodged in Bulgaria by foreign residents but, since the dollar value of foreign-currency accounts changed very little over the year, these factors cannot be judged significant.

This situation tested both the nerve and the judgement of the BNB since it was the first occasion when its objective of exchange-rate stability could be achieved only by selling large amounts of foreign exchange. It was not helped by the fact that the IMF had suspended its current standby agreement and so that kind of support for the reserves was not available. Gross reserves, which had reached $990 million in May 1993, fell in July, when the first pressures began to be felt, recovered slightly in August, and then went into steady and accelerating decline as the Bank struggled to sustain the lev. By February 1994 they had fallen to $593 million. The BNB very sensibly threw in the towel

---

8   The BNB (Bulgarian National Bank, *Annual Report 1993*, p. 128) very confusingly indicates a current account balance which is derived from a mixture of trade figures stated to be on a customs basis and figures for other current transactions which are presumably on a bank basis. Trade figures are also provided on a bank basis and these have been used in the text to ensure comparability between years.

9   Bulgarian National Bank, *Annual Report 1993*, p. 77.

10 Ibid., p. 127. The available breakdown of export destination is insufficient to test a conjecture that exports to the other, now independent, constituents of former Yugoslavia increased by more than the fall in trade with Serbia and Montenegro, but such a conjecture is hardly plausible. This remains a minor mystery. A fuller discussion of the impact of the embargo is provided in Chapter 5 below.

and the reserves immediately began to recover. It appears that the IMF, in negotiations for a new standby facility, had earlier advised the BNB to conserve reserves by withdrawing from the market[11] and the heeding of this advice was rewarded by the granting in April of new credits from the Fund and the World Bank, thus boosting the reserves, which rose as high as $1133 million in June. They then fell back to $581 million in July as those funds were used to buy securities to guarantee debt payments under the agreement with the London Club (see Chapter 5 below).[12] To replenish the reserves in response to these new liabilities, an additional loan of approximately $100 million was granted by the IMF in September.

It is hard not to criticise the BNB's behaviour in persisting so long in its struggle against devaluation. A managed float is always a difficult policy to operate because one can never be sure when to resist market movements and when to allow them to take their course. The Bank has ample company around the world in throwing reserves at an unsupportable currency, and hindsight always facilitates analysis. None the less, it could, and should, have been realized that the lev had become seriously overvalued since it had recovered the real exchange value it had immediately prior to liberalization in February 1991. Of course, if the Bank had given up buying leva in the autumn, there would have been a period of instability and almost certainly some overshooting in the devaluation, but this happened anyway, but six months later. In the meantime, enough foreign exchange to buy nearly a month's imports had been jettisoned to no avail. The lesson to be learned is that the market keeps its eye on the real and not the nominal exchange rate, and it behoves central banks to do the same.

Although the budget deficit is almost certainly the main cause of the high underlying rate of inflation, the surge in early 1994 is equally certainly attributable to the behaviour of the exchange rate (with, as already noted, some help from VAT in April). Further research would be needed to quantify with any precision the way lev import prices feed through to domestic prices, but a rough calculation can be made. It has been suggested that a 10 per cent nominal devaluation will create 3.3 per cent inflation in the first month afterwards and a further 1.8 per cent

11 *Bulgarian Economic Review*, 7–20 January 1994.

12 Bulgarian National Bank, *Monthly Bulletin*, various issues.

after six months, following the adjustment in nominal wages.[13] If even remotely correct, such estimates would suggest that, of the 22 per cent inflation in April, 15 percentage points resulted from the immediate impact of the March devaluation and the feed-through of the weakening of the lev in the previous autumn.

Regardless of the validity of such quantification, the qualitative conclusion is unavoidable. The dilemma for stabilization policy is then this: should all efforts be focused on the domestic sources of inflation (notably fiscal policy) and exchange-rate policy be concentrated on maintaining stability in the real rather than the nominal exchange rate? The danger when there are conflicting policy objectives is that none of them will be achieved. The underlying balance of payments situation will continue to be difficult until there is serious restructuring of domestic activity, productivity improvements and recovery in former CMEA markets. There will therefore continue to be downward pressure on the nominal value of the lev, a process which will be exacerbated as Bulgaria attempts to improve the servicing of foreign debt through its own earnings, as opposed to credit from the IMF. If domestic inflationary pressures are not contained, this in turn will lead to real appreciation, with further harmful repercussions for the balance of payments. Thus, the use of a managed float as an instrument of domestic stabilization policy is likely to be counterproductive if the real sources of inflation are not tackled.

As Table 3.2 shows, the lev strengthened again during the four months to the end of July 1994, but continued to weaken thereafter. The mid-year recovery may have been associated with improved performance on the trade front, the trade balance returning to surplus in the second quarter of the year after being in deficit for the previous two quarters. However, trade movements cannot explain the subsequent weakening of the currency since the balance remained significantly in surplus for the rest of the year. The answer may lie, at least to some extent, in an increase in non-trade, domestic demand for dollars. From the beginning of the year until the end of October, that part of broad money denominated in leva increased by 33 per cent in nominal terms, whereas that part denominated in convertible currencies increased by 55 per cent. Even more interesting is that the changes in the currency composition

---

13   Wendel and Manchev (1994), p. 20.

of the money supply match very closely the movements in the exchange rate. From the end of March to the end of July, when the lev was appreciating, the lev money supply rose by 16 per cent whereas the convertible currency money supply rose by almost exactly the same proportion. For the next three months, however, when depreciation set in again, the lev money supply increased by a mere 7 per cent but money holdings in convertible currencies rose by 25 per cent. This suggests the possibility that changes in the currency composition of the domestic demand for money, related to expectations concerning the rate of inflation and of the exchange value of the lev, provide a major part of the explanation of exchange-rate movements during 1994 after the crash in March.

Relative Prices

During the period from the beginning of 1993 to the end of 1994, food prices continued to rise faster than those of most other products, but some of the trends noted in Table 2.3 above changed direction. Significantly, one of the lowest rates of inflation was in energy for household use. Energy prices are still controlled and they tend to increase in large, infrequent jumps, as they did in May 1993 and July 1994 (a typical, politically motivated pattern of increases in administered prices at the beginning of the summer period when consumers are least likely to notice the increase), but over the long term these prices have risen less than they should have if increases in input prices were to have been passed forward to consumers.

THE REAL ECONOMY

Output

Official figures (which, we have already noted, almost certainly underestimate what is going on in the private sector) indicate that aggregate output continued to fall in 1993, though at a slackening rate. Real GDP fell by 4.2 per cent, compared with 5.8 per cent in 1992 and 11.7 per cent in 1991. Again, the decline was most marked in agriculture − 16.3 per cent, with industry showing marked signs of bottoming-out, with a decline in value added of under 4 per cent, compared with 11.2 per cent in 1992 and 18.6 per cent in 1991. As regards domestic demand, the most significant change occurred in private consumption which, in real terms, stopped falling in 1993. Investment performance continued to slump, being almost 22 per cent below its 1992 figure. So, real investment (fixed assets plus inventories) had declined by more than one-half over a period of three years.

As result of both an absolute increase in private activity and the decrease in output in the state sector, the private sector continued to account for an increasing proportion of GDP. Preliminary estimates suggest that this sector accounted for almost 20 per cent of GDP in 1993 — up from just over 15 per cent in 1992. The most significant increase was in services, which now accounted for almost one-half of private activity, compared with 37 per cent in the previous year.

The clear deceleration in the rate of decline of economic activity is confirmed by provisional estimates for the first half of 1994,[14] which indicate that GDP in the first quarter of the year was only 0.3 per cent less and that in the second quarter 1.2 per cent less than in the respective quarters of 1993.[15] Agriculture continued to perform badly, but real industrial output was actually 3 per cent higher in the first quarter than at the beginning of the previous year. The private sector continued to show above-average growth, accounting for 21.8 per cent of GDP in the second quarter, compared with under 20 per cent in 1993.

At the time of writing, only very preliminary estimates are available covering the whole of 1994.[16] Almost everyone had been predicting that the depression of output would reach its nadir during the year and this does indeed appear to have been the case. After five years of decline, the early estimates indicate that real GDP was 0.2 per cent higher in 1994 than in 1993. Industrial production increased by 4 per cent and even agriculture showed signs of recovery. The private sector is estimated to have accounted for 27 per cent of GDP during the year. It is doubtful if these numbers are sufficiently robust at this stage to

---

14 National Statistical Institute, reported in *168 Hours BBN*, 1–7 August 1994 and 10–16 October 1994.

15 The figure for the second quarter must be regarded as especially tentative because of the difficulties of deriving an adequate GDP deflator in a period of extreme instability in prices.

16 National Statistical Institute, reported in *Bulgarian Business News*, 30 January–5 February 1995.

support any detailed analysis, but they do represent a ray of sunshine in what had been a very traumatic year.

Employment and Unemployment

Employment in the state and cooperative sector continued to decline, the average figure for 1993 being 298,000 lower than in the previous year. The steady attrition continued throughout the year and into 1994. By the end of 1993, state employment was 2,148,000 compared to 2,446,000 a year earlier, and by September 1994 it had fallen yet further to 2,043,000. The largest proportional decline was in agriculture and forestry with, as a result of both the transfer of land to the private sector and the decline in output, those activities accounting for less than 11 per cent of state employment in 1993, compared with over 15 per cent in the previous year.

Employment in the private sector continued to expand rapidly, the estimate for 1993 being 742,000, compared with 434,000 in 1992. By June 1994 such employment was estimated to have exceeded 900,000.[17] If these figures are even remotely accurate, it indicates that total employment barely declined, and may actually have increased recently, which would be consistent with movements in registered unemployment.

Those movements are shown in Table 3.3. The decline in the numbers registered as unemployed has been quite significant during 1994, standing at 466,000 in October compared with 632,000 in January, only a very small proportion of this being attributable to seasonal factors. There were increases in the last two months of the year, but 1994 ended with registered unemployment − at 488,000 − 15 per cent lower than a year earlier. Further research would be needed to discover exactly what is causing the decline in registered unemployment. It is not explained by any reduction in the (officially measured) total labour force since, if anything, that appears to have been rising since the middle of 1993 (it

---

17 Bulgarian National Bank, *Report January–June 1994*, p. 10, which prefaces the estimate with the words 'although estimates may be arbitrary'. The adjective may be too strong, but it would be useful to know what these figures in fact measure. They cannot show the number of persons who work some of the time in the private sector since, by anecdotal evidence, that accounts for the majority of workers, but it is not clear that the statistics refer to full-time job equivalents.

fluctuates monthly within about 20,000 of 3.8 million). The two main possibilities are that people are leaving the register as they exhaust their eligibility for benefits and that the demand for labour is picking up somewhat. *A priori*, the most plausible hypothesis is that the rate of layoffs in the state sector is now less than the outflow from the register as a result of exhaustion of benefit eligibility. Employment in the private sector is also rising rapidly, but it is not known how many of those newly employed in that sector remain illegally on the register until they exhaust their entitlements.

Table 3.3 Rate of unemployment (%), 1993–94

	1993	1994
January	15.3	16.5
February	15.5	16.3
March	16.0	16.1
April	15.9	15.3
May	15.7	14.5
June	15.5	13.3
July	16.2	13.5
August	16.0	13.0
September	15.7	12.7
October	15.8	12.2
November	16.1	12.4
December	16.4	12.8

Source: National Statistical Institute

The difficulties of measuring unemployment have already been referred to, and these are illustrated when the figures for registered unemployed are compared with those derived from periodic surveys of the labour force. A survey conducted in June 1994[18] indicated that the total number unemployed was 721,000 — a rate of 20 per cent — compared with registered unemployed of 509,000, or the 13.3 per cent

---

18 National Statistical Institute, reported in *168 Hours BBN*, 10–16 October 1994.

shown in Table 3.3. This suggests, contrary to popular opinion which has thousands of employed persons illegally registering to obtain benefits, that the monthly registration statistics seriously understate the level of unemployment. This is exactly what international experience suggests. If large-scale benefit is very temporary, the incentive to register is equally temporary. So, the apparent conflict between the two sets of statistics is met with everywhere. This need not be a serious problem since the exact level of unemployment is rarely of great concern. More important is whether unemployment is rising or falling, and at what rate. International experience also suggests that, as long as there are no serious echo effects in the registration figures from past major fluctuations in the rate of layoffs feeding through to registrations as benefit is exhausted, the direction and rate of change as measured by the two methods is approximately the same. Thus, one continues to use registration figures because they are available more frequently than survey figures but, if the former show a significant change in unemployment, then so will the latter. There is therefore no reason to believe that the very apparent downturn in unemployment in 1994, as measured by registrations, is an illusion created by the method of measurement.[19]

The labour market is of critical importance to the transition process: it determines wage levels, which influence the rate of inflation, the exchange rate and international competitiveness, and its ability or otherwise to effect efficient transfers of resources is crucial to the whole restructuring process. It is therefore appropriate to review what is known at this juncture of the workings of this market.

Over the past decade or so there has developed a way of looking at unemployment which has a more microeconomic flavour than was traditional, and very recently efforts have been made to apply these

---

19 The Bulgarian survey is based on the methodology recommended by the International Labour Office and is subject to countervailing biases. For example, it fails to count as unemployed anyone who worked at all (even for one hour) in the previous week, but counts all such persons who claim to be looking for work (even if the respondent is, for example, a pensioner). The incentives for misreporting are evidenced by, for instance, the fact that, when grossed up, the number in the survey who stated that they were registered as unemployed fell short by about 20 percent of the number actually registered.

approaches to what is happening in transition economies.[20] Normatively, the starting point is an assertion that unemployment is essential, for three reasons. First, the collapse of planning could increase the bargaining power of workers and unemployment is needed to offset that factor. Secondly, unemployment assists in controlling the rate of growth of nominal wages. Thirdly, unemployment is necessary to effect the required reallocation of labour and, in particular, to permit the growth of the private sector and to force the acquisition of new skills. The central idea in this type of analysis is the relationship between the flow of new unemployment and the flow of new jobs (or vacancies) and, at the microeconomic level, the most important factors influencing these flows are the bargaining strength of workers, the level of unemployment benefits (paid by the state) and redundancy compensation (paid by the employer) and the scale of active labour market policies such as retraining programmes.

Attempts to apply this approach to unemployment in Bulgaria have already been made. Attention has been drawn to the fact that Bulgarian unions function within national 'social partnership' arrangements which restrict their bargaining power at the micro level, that the system of unemployment benefits is unusually restrictive, and that active employment policies have been inhibited by the fact that they are financed from the same fund as finances unemployment benefits.[21] Qualitatively, it is impossible to say whether these factors balance out in such a way as to give a higher or lower rate of unemployment than would otherwise be the case. A serious difficulty is the need to rely on official figures for unemployment and vacancies. The former has already been noted, but the latter is also difficult since it is not clear how important the official agencies are in the process of recruitment and job-search. More generally, the published data on unemployment are inadequate as regards length of unemployment and flows on to and off of the register — information which is critical to the quantitative application of the approaches summarised above. One effort to circumvent these impediments used the results of a specially conducted

---

20   See, for example, Burda (1993), from which the ensuing summary is derived.

21   Burda (1993), pp. 112–7 and Paunov (1993), pp. 222–4. Unemployment benefit depends on age and length of time in employment, but in all cases it starts with a high replacement ratio which falls rapidly month by month until, after six months it is equal to the minimum wage. No benefit at all is available after one year.

private survey of those unemployed during mid-1991 to mid-1992.[22] This suggested that more than one-third of the unemployed find jobs within a year, almost all the remainder being out of work for more than a year, with only a very small number leaving the labour force. Interestingly, this study indicates that the probability of finding a new job is not simply a reflection of the macroeconomic situation: if it were, there would be no discernible patterns in that probability. For instance, participation in a retraining programme seemed to be important for men but not for women, whereas level of education influenced women's probability of getting new employment but not men's. The use of official labour agencies seemed to have no effect on the chances of regaining employment, whereas contacts gained through political parties or trade unions were shown to be significant, which supports the point already made regarding the value of official data on vacancies.

Greater understanding of the microeconomics of flows into and out of unemployment would produce considerable dividends in terms of policy: it is just not true that the level of unemployment is determined solely (or perhaps even primarily) by the relationship between aggregate demand and aggregate capacity. Differences in unemployment benefits and active labour market policies, such as retraining, have been found to be very significant in explaining differences in unemployment rates among countries.[23] There is, therefore, every reason to expect that, in economies where structural transformation is the dominant objective, policies which influence the incentive to search for employment and policies which take account of the need to match the unemployed with potential vacancies will be critical in not only ensuring that the rate of unemployment is not higher than necessary but also in facilitating the required reallocation of labour.

THE NEW GOVERNMENT

When the Berov government resigned in September 1994, the president made efforts to construct a new administration which could attract a parliamentary majority but, not surprisingly, these efforts failed and the Assembly was dissolved with elections scheduled for 18 December. An

---

22 Jones and Kato (1993).

23 Burda (1993), p. 125.

interim government was put together from non-political figures under the leadership of Reneta Indzhova, till then the executive director of the Privatization Agency. It did little but replace a few senior officials (a depressingly typical Bulgarian practice whenever administrations change) and made noises about the fight against crime, an issue which was now looming large in the public consciousness. But it was, constitutionally and in reality, only a caretaker until the election and so nothing more could have been expected of it.

The opinion polls had been showing a strong performance by the BSP, the weakness of the UDF and some support for small, new parties. The result of the election, at which the turnout was 75 per cent, was somewhat of a surprise as regards the level of support for the BSP, now under the leadership of the 35-year old Zhan Videnov. It, along with its electoral partners the Alexander Stamboliyski Agrarian Union and *Ekoglasnost*,[24] received 43.5 per cent of the popular vote, the UDF receiving a mere 24.1 per cent and the MRF 5.4 per cent. Others reaching the critical 4 per cent mark were the Popular Union (which is a combination of the other, Petkov-inspired, agrarian party and the Democratic Party) with 6.5 per cent and a new force, thought to be 'flexible' in its attitude to the BSP, the Bulgarian Business Bloc which achieved 4.8 per cent. In the 240-seat Assembly, these votes translated into seats as follows: BSP (with partners) 125, UDF 69, Popular Union 19, MRF 15 and Business Bloc 12. Thus, compared with the 1991 elections, the BSP gained 19, the UDF lost 41, the MRF lost 9, and the new groups which had not been represented in the old parliament gained 31. This was the first time that democratic Bulgaria had a single-party government.

So, Bulgaria seems to be following the path trodden by Hungary, Poland and Lithuania in reviving the fortunes of the heirs of the communists, and for the same kinds of reason. In hard times we all seek the familiar and few in Bulgaria are convinced that radical economic reform would ease their lot. There is a deep disillusionment with party politics and the BSP were the only major grouping which offered any semblance of cohesion. Once again, they benefitted from their

---

24 The former was derived from the agrarian party which had been a member of the Fatherland Front throughout the communist era and the latter had actually been a founder-member of the UDF.

organizational strength and even from some signs of recognising how to conduct an election campaign in a democracy. The UDF, on the other hand, was its usual ineffective self, with poor organization, intolerance towards potential allies and — considering that it had been in opposition for four of the five years during which the populace had suffered so much — a remarkable inability to connect with the electorate.[25]

The new government was constructed and approved in January 1995, with Videnov as prime minister. Of the 17 cabinet positions, 14 were assigned to the BSP (though of this number only 6 of the new ministers are actually party members), the other three going to the BSP's electoral partners with, appropriately, the agricultural portfolio being given to an Agrarian Party representative and the environment ministry going to a nominee of *Ekoglasnost*. The new minister of finance is Dimitur Kostov, a senior and skilled official from that ministry.

---

25 Apparently with no sense of self-recrimination, 'Mr Dimitrov [the party's leader] believes the UDF defeat was due to the incorrect identification of the UDF with all the changes over the past five years' (*168 Hours BBN*, 19 December 1994–2 January 1995). Not surprisingly, such a leader was replaced immediately after the election.

4. Aspects of Industry and Agriculture

The macroeconomic issues dealt with so far are reflected in and are in part reflections of what is happening at the sectoral level. Any attempt at a detailed review would be out of place, but it is appropriate to consider certain major topics in the fields of industry and agriculture: services, while now accounting for about one-third of GDP, are ignored because they are increasingly dominated by the private sector and reliable data are in short supply.

INDUSTRY

Bulgaria entered transition as the second most industrialized country in the communist world, its proportion of GDP generated by industry (almost 60 per cent) being only slightly lower than that of the former Czechoslovakia. The sector was, and still is, totally dominated by state owned enterprises whose size distribution was quite different from that typical of a developed market economy with, in 1989, over one-fifth of firms having in excess of 5,000 employees, two-thirds having over 1,000 workers, and only 5 per cent employing less than 200.[1] What happens in this sector is therefore central to the success or otherwise of the whole transformation process, but it is here that the difficulties are most severe.

It is in industry that the collapse of the CMEA (see Chapter 5 below) had its most acute consequences. The country was left with a sector which had lost its dominant markets; which was inefficient in structure (because it was not related to comparative advantage); which had an obsolete capital stock producing goods which, in the main, were not of

---

1 Jones (1993), p. 8.

the quality to attract customers from the west; which was difficult to restructure because even a single liquidation could involve the loss of several thousand jobs; and whose management and workers had enormous political influence.

Privatization and related issues are postponed to Chapter 8 below. We here limit ourselves to a consideration of the performance of the industrial sector since the planning system was abolished.

Sectoral Organization

The socialist obsession with economies of scale and the consequent belief that competition was wasteful of resources produced an extraordinarily concentrated industrial structure. Not only were there few — often only one — producers of any manufactured good (that is, there was a high degree of horizontal integration), but suppliers and purchasers of intermediate products were often linked together in vertically integrated conglomerates. Efforts to break up these giants — partially to induce some competition domestically but primarily to produce units small enough to make privatization feasible — began early in a process known as demonopolization.

This process proceeded quite rapidly,[2] but there is no evidence that it has resulted in improvements in efficiency. Some of the changes were no more than cosmetic (for example, Balkan Airlines was broken up into a number of legally separate companies[3] but for all practical purposes — including privatization — is treated as a single entity), whereas in others it is just not possible, for technical or cultural reasons, to break the old links. Thus, to take another example, the railways were almost totally self-sufficient as regards equipment production and maintenance and separating these activities from the purely transportation activity could be expected to have no short-term effects at all: only the railways require locomotives and only one company maintains them. There may be minor managerial economies stemming from the reduction in the span of control, and demonopolization may

---

2 A detailed description is given in Berov (1993).

3 Demonopolization was always accompanied by 'corporatization' or 'commercialization': that is, the new units were given a legal status under the Commercial Code, which they had not previously had and which was an essential prerequisite for privatization — see Chapter 8 below.

somewhat improve the micro climate for initiative and innovation, but that is all.

Only with increased international competition and domestic competition stimulated by serious implementation of anti-trust legislation (again, see Chapter 8 below) can it be expected that demonopolization will have important economic consequences. It has made privatization a little easier since the *de jure* size of firms has been reduced,[4] but the maintenance of *de facto* integration among the former members of a conglomerate ensures that the economic, social and political implications of the liquidation or restructuring of a firm remain more or less as they were.

Inter-Enterprise Arrears

In all countries moving towards a market form of economic organization, one of the first signs that enterprises were under stress was that they failed on an increasing scale to pay their debts to each other. This was rational behaviour when the nominal cost of bank credit was extremely high and the cost of not paying one's bills was zero. The latter was the case because of the high degree of monopolization and because of the practical absence of effective bankruptcy processes. An enterprise had little incentive to take action against a defaulting customer (by, for example, withholding supplies or attempting to institute bankruptcy proceedings) since, often, it had no or few other customers. Legal action to recover the debt would have little prospect of immediate success. In any case, the mutually supportive networks of enterprise management generated a culture in which aggressive action against another enterprise was alien. So, the easy thing to do in response to such a reduction in receipts was to restore one's net cash flow by not paying one's own bills. Thus, the process grew cumulatively.

The connection to monetary control of this accumulation of debts among enterprises (as opposed to debts to the banks) is important but not straightforward. If inter-enterprise relations were on a completely closed loop, no net credit creation would take place: balance sheets would show an increase in creditors (or payables), but for the sector as

---

4 By 1991, only one-seventh of state firms had in excess of 1,000 employees (compared with two-thirds two years earlier): Jones (1993), p. 8.

a whole these would be exactly balanced by an increase in debtors (or receivables) and all that would be happening in real terms would be multilateral barter. Of course, in fact this system is not closed. As soon as an enterprise cannot cover an increase in receivables by expanding payables (if it is, for example, an importer who cannot look forward to an infinitely elastic supply of credit at zero cost from its suppliers, or it has weak domestic market power), the only way the process can continue is for that enterprise to increase its debts to the banks. This certainly has monetary implications, but is the result of the expansion in bank credit, not of the increase in inter-enterprise debts as such.

This does not, however, mean that the accumulation of inter-enterprise arrears is harmless.[5] In the first place, it is an occasion of sin for ill-disciplined banks: nothing is easier than to respond sympathetically to the demand for working capital from a client of long standing who claims that his problem is not so much selling as in getting his customers to pay. It is not known how much of the new bad-debt problem of the banks (see Chapter 6 below) is the result of accommodating this kind of demand, but it may be substantial. Even a well-intentioned bank would have difficulty in evaluating the risk of this kind of loan.

Then, in a situation where so many enterprises are fundamentally weak, a high level of current assets and liabilities makes it especially difficult to evaluate the worth of any given enterprise. In an economy where the enterprise sector at large is healthy, a high level of creditors balanced by a high level of debtors need have no consequences for the way its owners, potential investors or the market view a firm. But what if there is a low, but unknown, probability that receivables will actually be received? The situation is then quite different, and this is exactly the situation prevailing in transition economies. This uncertainty regarding the true value of debtors impedes restructuring because it reduces the quality of information regarding the net value of an enterprise — information essential if the government is contemplating support for pre-privatization restructuring, if a successful privatization is to be achieved, or even if a bank is contemplating forcing an enterprise into bankruptcy.

Furthermore, this interlinked system of mutual debts creates dangerous ripple effects if the government decides to liquidate an enterprise with

---

5 For a fuller review of these issues, see Ickes and Ryterman (1993).

poor prospects. If the residual value of its assets is insufficient to cover its arrears to other enterprises, the latter are threatened if the first enterprise is wound up. Desirable liquidation may then be postponed or avoided because of the effects on other enterprises.

Table 4.1 provides some information regarding the scale of enterprise debts in Bulgaria. Because of the rapid rate of inflation, nominal values would reveal nothing and so the issue arises of deflating such values. The aggregate consumer price index is of little relevance: of more relevance is the fact that prudent management relates the level of current assets and liabilities to the enterprise's level of activity, as measured by sales. Table 4.1 therefore shows the assets and liabilities of concern here at a number of dates as percentages of the value of sales for the quarters ending on those dates. For the earlier years of transition, available data are very patchy and so we rely on admittedly rather dubious estimates, but there is no strong reason to doubt the qualitative reliability of the changes shown. For 1992–94 the published data have been used. The figures are aggregates for state enterprises in the manufacturing sector and are not derived from consolidated accounts for that sector (which do not exist).

Table 4.1   Certain current assets and liabilities in manufacturing enterprises (% of quarterly sales), 1990–94

End of	Payable to suppliers	Receivable from customers	Short-term bank loans
Dec 1990	15	17	n.a.
Dec 1991	31	24	n.a.
Dec 1992	47	31	47
Mar 1993	67	41	60
Jun 1993	58	41	58
Sep 1993	56	43	68
Dec 1993	44	30	56
Mar 1994	46	37	54
Jun 1994	45	27	41
Sep 1994	40	26	44

Source: Derived from National Statistical Institute

The precise figures in Table 4.1 should not be taken too literally, especially for the earlier dates. Aside from data difficulties already mentioned, the deflator used (sales) may be misleading when prices are rising very quickly, unless the volume of sales is spread evenly throughout a quarter. Then, some of the increase during 1991 and 1992 may result from demonopolization: that is, what used to be intra-enterprise transactions became inter-enterprise transactions. Also, in the earlier years, enterprises were adapting to an unfamiliar, western-style accounting system and may have made errors. Finally, the figures for bank loans will be distorted if there was a conversion of short-term to long-term bank credits.

Despite these reservations, overall movements are revealing. The early transition period was accompanied by a significant expansion of inter-enterprise arrears and, what is more, an obvious widening of the gap between creditors and debtors. The latter must imply an increase in the proportion of non-bank creditors who are not other domestic manufacturing enterprises. The large jump at the beginning of 1993 is the result of a collapse of sales since the absolute value of the relevant assets and liabilities changed very little, this reduction in sales being especially notable in metallurgy, engineering, chemicals and agriculture-based manufacturing. The expansion in inter-enterprise arrears was accompanied by a more or less *pro rata* increase in short-term bank credit, suggesting that the whole process did give rise to both the macroeconomic and microeconomic dangers reviewed above. The good news is that this process has gone into reverse over the past two years. This is associated most obviously with a slight, though unmistakeable, revival of enterprise profitability since the middle of 1993, just as the pace of the earlier expansion in debts was associated with a deterioration in profitability.

Although the scale of inter-enterprise arrears, relative to sales, is declining, it is still high enough to complicate the valuation of enterprises and it is noteworthy that there has as yet been no policy response to this issue. What is important is that any policy response should involve neither the banks nor the state budget, which are sufficiently burdened as it is with the consequences of old and new bad debts, but a relatively safe procedure does seem to be feasible. This would require a scheme for the multilateral cancellation of debts within the enterprise sector. Payables to and receivables from entities outside the scheme (such as foreign suppliers or customers and suppliers or purchasers in the domestic non-industrial sector) would remain, but no-one's net worth, as measured by the accounts, would be changed since, for any given enterprise, the reduction in debtors would equal the reduction in creditors, and no-one would incur new liabilities. The result would be to remove from balance sheets net current assets or liabilities which are particularly difficult to evaluate, but which have no economic significance.

Profitability

Even in developed market economies with well-established accounting systems, profit is an elusive concept. It is measured according to conventions which may not accord with economic reasoning and, even if it did so accord, the resulting measure may say little about the underlying efficiency of the company. These difficulties are magnified in a transition economy, where enterprises are now required to report according to accounting procedures quite different from those to which they are used, where inflation is rampant and where domestic competition is significantly imperfect. All one can do is to make the best of the numbers available.

The collapse of enterprise profitability is a recurrent theme throughout this book and there is no point in repeating ourselves here. There is, however, one aspect of this which has nothing to do with the loss of CMEA export demand as such or the decline in domestic demand, and this is the impact on profitability of the move from distorted, administered prices towards market-clearing, liberalized prices. In simple terms, profitability, and more generally value added (which is the sum of factor incomes generated by the activity), will be exaggerated if output prices exceed competitive market prices or input prices fall short of those prices. This would be the result of internally administered prices, differential subsidies and taxes and administrative restrictions on international trade. In the extreme, it would be possible for an enterprise, or a sector, to have a positive value added under the distorted system of prices (as all Bulgarian sub-sectors, and probably all enterprises, did) but to have a negative value added if inputs and outputs were valued at competitive prices (as some Bulgarian activities did). The reason for this is that valuation at competitive prices dramatically reduces profitability compared with its level at distorted prices and, in some cases, this creates losses which are greater than the sum of other factor payments (mainly wages).

This phenomenon was investigated in a major research project covering several transition economies, including Bulgaria.[6] Among other things, this project studied what would have happened in the late 1980s if the inputs and outputs of Bulgarian industry had been valued at world prices (which were taken to represent competitive prices). The results were dramatic. On average for manufacturing industry, measured value added would have been more than halved,[7] but in some cases the distortion (more or less, artificial profitability) was much greater. For example, in transport equipment (which includes the famous fork-lift trucks in which Bulgaria had a CMEA monopoly), the distortions increased measured value added by almost nine-fold. In the case of basic chemicals, cement and fruit and vegetable products, value added at international prices was actually negative (which means that GDP measured at international prices would have been higher if that sub-sector had not existed). The situation became even worse after an effort to make adjustments for the alleged inferior quality of many Bulgarian products: this suggested that the industrial sector as a whole had negative value added.[8]

The exact numbers generated by this research are of no concern, especially since they have to be accompanied by many qualifications. The important point is qualitative: that the planning system generated prices which led to value added, and especially profitability, to be exaggerated. This is exactly what would be expected of a planning system which created an industrial structure which had no reference to comparative advantage, and would lead one to predict that price-liberalization itself (that is, independently of any associated or coincidental effects on demand) would lead to a decline in profitability.

Of course, it is impossible without very detailed research at the microeconomic level to disentangle all the factors which created the

---

6 Hughes and Hare (1992a, 1992b and 1994).

7 What was measured was domestic resource cost (DRC), which is the ratio of value added at actual prices to value added at international prices. Thus, with no distortion, this ratio would equal 1. For Bulgaria, the average DRC in manufacturing was found to be 2.45: that is, value added measured at distorted prices exceeded by 2.45 times value added measured at international prices.

8 Hughes and Hare (1992a), pp. 197–8.

collapse of profitability in Bulgarian industry from the late 1980s
onwards. Nor is it even possible to measure this collapse easily, since
the period of interest has seen significant changes in accounting
practices. Bearing this in mind, Table 4.2 provides some indicators of
the movement of profits over the past two years, during which
accounting procedures were standardized.

It will be noted from this table that 1993 marked a turning-point.
Since the middle of that year, losses declined until, since the spring of
1994, definite signs of renewed profitability have been apparent. How
much of this results from increased efficiency, how much from some
restoration of domestic demand, and how much is a result of the effects
on international competitiveness of the dramatic devaluation of the lev
in late 1993 and early 1994, is impossible to say at this point. What can
be shown, however, is that the improvement is not uniform across sub-
sectors of industry.

*Table 4.2   Quarterly profit in manufacturing enterprises (% of
quarterly sales), 1993–94*

Quarter	Operating profit	Gross profit
Q1 1993	−4	−14
Q2 1993	4	−9
Q3 1993	−2	−16
Q4 1993	5	−12
Q1 1994	3	−7
Q2 1994	10	1
Q3 1994	10	1

Source: Derived from National Statistical Institute

Table 4.3 shows operating profit ratios for a group of sub-sectors
which account for 80 per cent of total sales in manufacturing. Chemicals
and activities based on agriculture showed a reasonable performance
throughout the period and these, combined with metallurgy and
engineering, showed definite improvements since the middle of 1993.
This is certainly associated with the reversal of the decline in output
already noted. The exception is electricity generation which is the only

industrial activity whose output prices are still controlled. The effect of the politically motivated restriction on price increases can be seen from the persistently high level of losses in this industry (it is now the only signficant recipient of budgetary subsidies). Output prices have failed to match increases in input prices (notably of oil): at the beginning of 1993, this industry accounted for 15 per cent of total industrial sales, whereas by late 1994 that proportion had fallen to 7 percent. This bodes ill for an industry in which large-scale investment is needed for technological improvement, notably because of the great importance of obsolescent and unsafe nuclear capacity which accounts for more than one-third of total power generation.

Table 4.3   Operating profit in selected sub-sectors (% of quarterly sales), 1993–94

Quarter	Elect-ricity	Metal-lurgy	Engin-eering	Chem-icals	Food, drink
Q1 1993	–8	–23	–9	2	8
Q2 1993	–13	14	–2	4	10
Q3 1993	–12	–1	–6	6	5
Q4 1993	7	–7	–6	11	7
Q1 1994	–9	2	0	10	9
Q2 1994	–10	16	7	14	16
Q3 1994	–11	13	9	10	17

Source: Derived from National Statistical Institute

AGRICULTURE

Farming accounts for less than 10 per cent of GDP but what is happening in that sector has very important national consequences. Basic foods have a low income-elasticity of demand and so, even in a period when aggregate domestic demand is seriously depressed, failures in domestic supply harm the balance of payments. In addition, in the longer term agriculture should, because of comparative advantage, increase its share in exports and so low sectoral productivity could jeopardise the achievement of overall development objectives. It is therefore depressing that the recent past has seen such a significant decline in both production and productive capacity in this sector.

Agriculture on the Eve of Transition

By any standards, the 1980s were a poor decade for agriculture, and change would have been necessary anyway, even if the old regime had not been overthrown. This decade is difficult to characterize concisely because, primarily as a result of climatic instability, the output of almost all products fluctuated significantly from year to year. Standard statistics such as average annual growth rates are therefore misleading. Nonetheless, certain figures are revealing. The real value of gross agricultural output was lower in each of the last three years of the decade than it had been in 1982, 1984 and 1986, but even this mediocre performance was achieved only by a steady expansion in material inputs. As a result, net output (or contribution to GDP) — a much better indicator of productivity — declined consistently. In 1989 it was lower than for any other year of the decade and, in each of 1987–89, net output was lower than for any earlier year other than 1985 (when there was a serious drought). This deteriorating performance was experienced more or less equally by both crop and animal production.[9]

This failure of agricultural production had marked effects on Bulgaria's balance of agricultural trade. The need to satisfy the domestic demand for food (without increasing prices or subsidies) meant, on the one hand, a reduction in the capacity to export and, on the other, an increase in the demand for imports. From the middle of the decade, the export surplus with respect to the CMEA declined markedly, for the years 1986–89 inclusive the annual average being 15 per cent lower than in 1980–85. The balance of non-CMEA trade changed from an average annual surplus of $250 million during 1980–84 to an average annual deficit of $80 million during 1985–89. Only tobacco and wine showed any growth on the export side, almost all categories of imports (with the exception of cereals, the output of which held up reasonably well) showing significant expansion.

---

9   This and the following paragraph are based on the data shown in World Bank (1991), Vol. I, pp. 171–2 and Vol. II, p. 72; and Commission of the European Communities (1991), Tables 9.4 and 9.5. The latter provides a detailed technical review of Bulgarian agriculture in the late 1980s.

The response to this poor performance was, as in industry (see Chapter 1 above), little more than a repeated shuffling of the planning system. This need not concern us here,[10] especially since a contemporary commentator summarized what was happening in the following terms: 'Within one year and a half, people engaged in agriculture have changed the kind of organization in which they worked five times ... They felt lost in the meandering of rules and did nothing but wait for the next "fundamentally new" change'.[11]

We now review briefly the policy responses which have been made in an effort to apply general transition objectives to the agricultural sector.

Land Reform[12]

Land reform is in many ways the most radical, and the most complex, reorganization of economic activity yet attempted in Bulgaria. Although much of the poor performance of agriculture could be laid at the door of the gigantism of the *APK*s and the inadequate incentives existing within the *TKZS*s, the driving force behind land restitution was not economic necessity but political opportunism. As noted in Chapter 1, pre-communist Bulgaria was a land of owner-peasants, not one with much in the way of large estates with tenants or waged workers, and the process of collectivization had to take account of the attachment of these smallholders to their own land. Although restoration of the land to its original owners could have been expected to be resisted (as it was) by the *TKZS* bureaucracy, the number of potential beneficiaries far exceeded that of potential losers — something which made the political implications of land restitution quite different from those of industrial privatization. As a result, almost immediately after the fall of Zhivkov and before the first free elections, the BSP government, recognizing the immediate and longer-term political advantages of being associated with land restoration, set in motion the process which led eventually to the passage, under the Popov government, of the Law on the Ownership and

---

10 For a description of organisational reform in agriculture during the 1980s, see Wyzan (1990), pp. 295–8 and 300–1.

11 Quoted in Wädekin (1993), p. 252.

12 Unless otherwise stated, the source of the quantitative information in this section is the ministry of agriculture.

Use of Farm Land.[13] This law, while being subsequently amended, is still the basis for the programme of land restitution and the liquidation of the collectives.

The essence of the scheme is that previous owners or their heirs have the right to be assigned, without charge, the land they owned prior to collectivization. Where this is not possible because boundaries are ill-defined or the land has been built on, they may receive an equivalent area in the same district or may obtain financial compensation. Foreigners are not only ineligible under the scheme but may not own agricultural land at all: those who inherit it must dispose of it within three years. This is one reason for believing that the rationale of the scheme was political rather than economic.

Further indications of the same rationale are that the original legislation limited to 30 or 20 hectares (depending on the type of cultivation) the amount which could be held by any one family and proscribed the sale or leasing of restituted land for a period of three years. These provisions were subsequently repealed.

The programme is operated by liquidation councils, whose function is to wind up the collectives, and municipal land councils, to whom claimants make their applications. Claims are supposed to be submitted within 17 months of the passage of the law (one year in the original legislation) and the councils are supposed to make their ruling within one month of the receipt of a claim. The process was therefore intended to be very rapid. Land which had not been restituted under an approved claim was to be assigned to the municipal land reserve and could then be granted to landless persons who were prohibited from selling it for ten years. The law also provides that the non-land property of *TKZSs* be shared among members. Few would contest that collective agriculture had failed and that land privatization should have been a priority for policy. To that extent, therefore, the radicalism and the urgency of scheme is to be applauded. However, the political factors which generated this radicalism and urgency were allowed to overcome economic considerations.

The legal and administrative tasks involved with land restitution are daunting and, although considerable progress has been made, it has been much slower than was originally envisaged. The total land area involved

---

13 Passed 22 February 1991; published *Dŭrzhaven vestnik*, No. 17, March 1991.

is approximately 5.3 million hectares and it is thought that there are about 2 million potential applicants (thus indicating the high degree of fragmentation of pre-collectivization holdings). The average holding of 2.5 hectares is extremely small, but even this disguises the degree of fragmentation, with 91 per cent of potential owners having holdings of less than one hectare and 99.5 per cent having holdings of less than five hectares.[14] The process for establishing a claim is a nightmare. Probably 80 per cent of the original owners are dead and so the potential claimants are heirs. Bulgarian inheritance law provides for a hierarchy of inheritance and this is applied by the courts, but the process is inevitably very slow and contentious. The ministry of agriculture — which has no direct competence in these matters but which is seen as the political focus of the programme and which becomes involved by default because of the poor level of staffing of the 300 or so land commissions — receives around 300 letters per day from disgruntled claimants. An indication of the legal complexities can be seen from the fact that, where original deeds of ownership or probate documents are not available, claims may be supported by an affidavit, but the total area of land claimed under such affidavits now sums to more than the total area of the country.

In terms of the percentage of the total land area involved, the state of play by December 1994 was as follows. For 16 per cent, the final stage of restoring the land to approved claimants had been achieved and for a further 40 per cent final plans had been approved. In total, 37 per cent of the land was being farmed under the grant of interim usufruct rights, 20 points of which were yet to be included in a final plan. Thus, by the end of 1994, 56 per cent of collectivized land had either been restituted or was covered by an approved plan and another 20 per cent was subject to usufruct rights, thus leaving only 24 per cent which had yet to pass the initial stages of restitution or private use.

Regardless of the longer-term benefits of land privatization, the restitution programme has, in the meantime, been inimical to improvements in agricultural production. In the first place, it has introduced huge uncertainty. As noted in Chapter 1, about one-seventh of collectivized land was in fact being cultivated on a personal basis, and such personal cultivation accounted for a high proportion of the

---

14 National Statistical Institute, reported in *168 Hours BBN*, 7–13 March 1994.

total output of certain crops. These personal plots are of course candidates for restitution and so the existing users have no long-term assurance of continuing occupation. The same problem applies to those who have been granted usufruct rights under the programme, although in many cases these occupants may be using land for which they have made a restitution claim. More generally, the permanent ownership of much of the land has yet to be finalized. In these circumstances, investment incentives more or less disappear since current users have so little certainty that they will be able to reap the fruits of such investment. What is worse, there are signs of negative investment resulting from rational risk-aversion. Equipment and buildings are not maintained and the size of herds and flocks is being run down.

This uncertainty is the result of the complexity of the process, which in turn results from the decision to base the land reform on direct restitution to former owners. While understandable in political terms, it was not the only possible, and arguably not the best, approach to the privatization of land through the breaking up of the collectives. The problems are, first, the small size of the average holding per claimant and, secondly, the mismatch between eligible persons and those likely to wish to engage in agriculture.

Approximately 3 million hectares of land have been fully restituted or have been included in final, approved plans, but this has involved over 1.6 million claims — an average of only 1.8 hectares per claim, which is an impossibly small size of holding for modern agriculture, except in the case of certain vegetables and fruits. Then, it will be recalled that Bulgaria's development under communism was based on the transfer of large volumes of labour out of the sector — which meant a large transfer of population from the countryside to the cities. Thus, it is to be expected that a high proportion of eligible persons will have had no recent experience of agriculture. One, admittedly crude, estimate puts this proportion at 55 per cent.[15] Of these, some will not stake a claim (and so the land may eventually reach intending farmers by being assigned from the reserve in which non-restituted land is placed); others will make a successful claim and will lease or sell their land; and the remainder will claim their inheritance but will take no steps to keep it

---

15 Jackson and Kopeva (1994), p. 9.

in agricultural operation, thus reducing the total amount of land used. Few, if any, can be expected to return to the land from the cities.

The first of these difficulties (the small size of the average holding) is susceptible to two solutions. The first is the development of voluntary cooperatives among owners of contiguous holdings to take advantage of the economies of scale which continue to exist even for holdings many times the current average in size. There was a strong tradition of cooperative farming in pre-communist Bulgaria and there are already signs that this solution to fragmentation is developing. By late 1994, almost 1,900 cooperatives had been established, with 470,000 members. The other solution, which would be a response to both problems (small size and ownership mismatch), is the development of an efficient market in land. Those with holdings too small to be efficient could then sell to a neighbour as an alternative to forming a cooperative; large farms, as opposed to cooperatives, could develop; those who wish to leave agriculture could do so with a capital sum; and those who have gained holdings which they have no wish to farm can transfer them to those looking for land to farm.

However, the uncertainty already noted also acts as an impediment to the development of land markets. Because of the importance of this asset in the total wealth of a potential purchaser, freehold or leasehold title is of special significance: uncertainty of ownership or of the enforceability (by both sides) of leasing contracts would seriously inhibit both the demand for and supply of land, and would act as a disincentive to lessees to make expensive investments in land improvement. At present, the only secure legal title to over 80 per cent of the land is held by the collectives who are under an obligation to divest themselves of this land and so have no incentive even to maintain the productivity of their holdings, let alone to make improvements. They cannot legally sell to others who may have a longer-term interest and, whatever the legal position, will not be able to find tenants because the land is due for restitution. Furthermore, even when the bulk of the land has been fully restituted, the development of the markets needed to ensure effective land use will be impeded by the lack of proper legislation on leasing.

These problems are compounded by the essential role of credit in land purchase. With the current state of the agricultural and financial sectors, banks will in any case be averse to lending for land purchase and even for working capital purposes, and the lack of firm legal title exacerbates the difficulties. As one authoritative commentary says: 'Land itself is commonly advanced as collateral to secure a loan, but the slowness of restitution with property rights enshrined in law ... is a major impediment to [this] ... The circularity of the problem is obvious: as a result of a shortage of liquidity to finance land acquisition, the development of a land market is impeded. In turn, the opportunity to invest in land as a basis for securing further credit is foregone'.[16]

Many other difficulties will inhibit the growth of a land market (for example, will city-dwellers hold on to unused land simply as a hedge against inflation?), but enough has been said here to illustrate the proposition that privatization by direct restitution has almost certainly contributed to the further depression of agricultural productivity and that it then becomes urgent that policy supports the development of private cooperatives and effective land markets.

Finally, it should be mentioned that economically superior methods of land privatization are feasible. In Hungary, for example, direct restitution was ruled to be unconstitutional and so another method had to be found. Former owners or their heirs were entitled to receive not their land, but compensation certificates which were freely transferable and were the only currency accepted when collectives auctioned their land. This kind of approach builds in a land market from the beginning and, in principle anyway, overcomes the major problems associated with direct restitution. But there is no point in crying over spilt milk.

Other Agricultural Policy Issues

The agricultural sector consists essentially of four types of organization — growers (state farms, collectives and private farmers), processors (such as millers, sugar factories and industries using agricultural output to produce non-food products), suppliers of inputs to agriculture (such as chemical fertilizers) and marketing agencies. The demonopolization already noted in the industrial sector has also been proceeding here. The *APKs* were abolished in 1990, leaving the original collective, usually based on a single village, as the basic producing unit, and these collectives themselves are being broken up. The national processing monopolies have in most cases (tobacco would be an exception) been divided up on a regional basis (though they are still state-owned), as

---

16 Ibid., p. 15.

have the marketing monopolies and, to a lesser degree, the producers of industrial inputs to agriculture. However, demonopolization has proceeded fastest at the producing level and, as a result, there has been a marked change in the balance of market power between, on the one hand, the growers and, on the other, those who provide inputs to growers and those who buy growers' output, especially in the case of extensive crops (even under the old system, the marketing of fruit and vegetables, where personal plots were significant, took place in reasonably competitive markets). The share of producers' value added in the final retail price therefore declined quite rapidly, especially in the three years from 1990, with serious effects on the profitability of growers.[17]

This lack of profits at the growing stage was endemic under the old system because of the desire to keep retail food prices as low as possible, but the same problems have persisted into the transition period. The result of the poor performance in the late 1980s was an explosion in the level of agricultural subsidization. Direct subsidies to the sector — in the form of price-deficiency payments, subsidies for agricultural exports, grants to encourage expansion in the stock of animals, and special grants to mountain farmers — reached a level of BGL3.3 billion (or 7 per cent of GDP) by 1990,[18] from a negligible level three years previously.[19] The liberalization package of February 1991 put an end to that, thus leaving growers to do the best they could in the face of the uncertainties surrounding land tenure, confusion in the environment for agricultural exports,[20] unfavourable price controls (which remain for many products at the pre-retail stages), market weakness relative to input-suppliers and output-purchasers, and severe difficulties over bank credit.

Because inputs have to be purchased many months before there is output to sell, agriculture typically has an especially high demand for

---

17 See Mileva (1994).

18 Ivanova (1994), p. 17.

19 World Bank (1991), Vol. I, p. 164.

20 To protect domestic food supplies from the effects of low productivity from the late 1980s onwards, exports — notably of wheat — were subject to quotas, taxes and prohibitions in a package whose composition frequently changed, thus leaving growers in a perpetual state of uncertainty as to the conditions under which their current crop could be marketed. Wheat exports were not finally liberalized until November 1994.

working capital and so is particularly vulnerable to defects in credit supply. Furthermore, major long-term investment is required — especially to restore herd levels, to restore the productivity of perennial crops and to replace obsolete equipment. The effect of land reform on agricultural credit has already been noted, but this is only one dimension of the problem. There is a long history of low profitability and bad debts in the sector. In a precursor to the *ZUNK* scheme (see Chapter 6 below), bad debts incurred on agricultural loans up to the end of 1988 were written off by the state in 1990, but of course they continued to accumulate until, by the end of 1993, they had reached a level of around 2 per cent of GDP.[21] A banking system being urged to subject itself to hard budget constraints is going to be particularly cautious in lending to a sector which not only has such a poor profitability record but, more importantly, is probably even less profitable than before and where great uncertainties abound. In an effort to counter some of these difficulties, the abolition of direct production and price subsidies has been accompanied by the development of credit subsidy schemes, focusing almost entirely on working capital. In each year beginning in 1991, such schemes have been changed in an ad hoc way, attempting to respond to immediate crises, thus adding even more to the air of uncertainty. Nor is there any evidence that they have been effective, especially considering the high degree of moral hazard and budgetary risk which they involve.

Indicators of Post-Transition Performance

Taking account of what has been said so far, it would not be surprising if the deteriorating sectoral performance had continued into the 1990s, and this has in fact been the case, with again major year-to-year fluctuations. National accounts data show real net output in agriculture falling by 4 per cent in 1990, rising by 8 per cent in 1991, and collapsing by 14 per cent and 16 per cent in 1992 and 1993 respectively. Early estimates for GDP in 1994 suggest that the

---

21 Sturgess (1994), p. 4. This paper provides a comprehensive discussion of issues relating to agricultural credit.

agricultural decline has been arrested, with an improved performance in cereals.

Table 4.4 Index of livestock numbers (at 1 January: 1 January 1988=100), 1989–94

	1989	1990	1991	1992	1993	1994
Cattle	98	96	88	80	59	45
Pigs	102	107	104	78	66	51
Sheep	97	92	89	75	54	42
Poultry	101	86	68	52	48	44

Source: Derived from National Statistical Institute

Nothing illustrates the parlous state of Bulgarian agriculture better than the catastrophic decline in the size of the animal stock, as revealed in Table 4.4. In all major categories, the size of herds and flocks is no more than half what it was at the beginning of 1988. Furthermore, the decline continued during 1994 with the stock of cattle, pigs, sheep and poultry in October of that year being 25, 15, 13 and 11 per cent respectively lower than a year earlier. Until the late 1980s, animal products accounted for somewhat over a half of total gross agricultural output (though slightly less than a half of net output), but this serious reduction in the basic capital stock of this type of activity bodes ill for the country's capacity even to supply its own needs for milk, meat and eggs, let alone to contribute to trade in such products. This is perhaps the most palpable result of the uncertainty of the current environment for agriculture: growers who are unsure of their continued occupation of their land are acting quite rationally by failing to maintain breeding levels and engaging in premature slaughtering.

5. International Economic Relations

The performance of the overall balance of payments has been covered by our earlier discussion of macroeconomic developments. In this chapter, concern is focused on the more microeconomic issue of the structure of trade, with attention being especially concentrated on the effects of the abolition of the CMEA trading system and the reorientation, in both geographical and commodity terms, of Bulgaria's foreign trade. Also reviewed are the issues of foreign debt and the effect on Bulgaria of the United Nations sanctions against Iraq and Serbia–Montenegro.

In Bulgaria, as in most countries, there is a large volume of statistical material on the balance of payments and trade structure. Unfortunately, the quality of much of these data is questionable. First, there is a significant divergence in the statistics for the balance of payments depending on whether customs or banking data are used — a problem familiar internationally. Secondly, it is practically impossible to obtain a meaningful aggregation of trade conducted in convertible currencies and that conducted in transferable rubles, the latter being a major problem before the collapse of the CMEA in 1991, and continuing to create difficulties because a similarly artificial currency is still the basis of trade with Russia. This makes it difficult to answer with precision such a central question as: how important was the CMEA in Bulgaria's trade? Thirdly, there are often significant inconsistencies among the data from a single source.

All of these problems seriously inhibit the analysis in this chapter: it is hazardous to construct continuous statistical series spanning the pre- and post-transition periods and any judgement based on the available statistics has to be heavily qualified. However, the second issue mentioned above is so pervasive that somewhat more detailed consideration is warranted here.

The most important single question concerns the former dominance of the CMEA in Bulgaria's trade and the success or failure of the country in reorienting its trade. The starting-point therefore has to be some measure of the importance of CMEA trade. The official figures indicate that, in 1989 (the last fully effective year of the CMEA), other members accounted for over 80 per cent of Bulgaria's exports (with the USSR alone accounting for 65 per cent) and for over 70 per cent of the country's imports (USSR approximately 55 per cent),[1] but these numbers are seriously misleading. In 1989 and 1990, when CMEA trade was overwhelmingly dominant, the unit of account had no fixed, and no easily determinable, relationship with the dollar. The official aggregation from which the above percentages were derived was accomplished by measuring all trade in terms of a 'currency lev' whose exchange value was different from official exchange rates. Indeed, the relationship between the exchange value of the currency lev and official exchange rates was not constant across currencies. The overall effect was a serious overvaluation of trade denominated in transferable rubles (that is, CMEA trade) and that denominated in dollars. On top of this, the official exchange value of the lev against the dollar (which is used in the aggregation for non-CMEA trade) was itself administered and greatly exceeded the market-clearing value. This also caused non-CMEA trade to be undervalued in the aggregation.

An estimate of these biases was attempted by the World Bank,[2] which indicated that, in 1989, the CMEA accounted for 62 per cent of Bulgaria's exports (as opposed to the 84 per cent shown by the official figures) and for 52 per cent of imports (as opposed to 74 per cent). This strongly suggests that, because the official figures of trade structure prior to transition overstate the dependence on the CMEA, later indicators of changes in trade structure also overstate the degree of

---

1 These are the figures used by, for example Schrenk (1992), who provides a concise description and critique of the CMEA system, and Rosati (1992). The latter (p. 65) also provides estimates of trade-intensity coefficients which suggest that, in 1989, Bulgaria's exports to the CMEA (excluding GDR) were 5 times and those to the USSR 17 times as great as would be the case if the geographical pattern were random. The statistical problems outlined below, which cause the significance of intra-CMEA trade to be overestimated, also apply here but do not nullify the qualitative point that the country's trade was massively concentrated.

2 World Bank (1991), Vol. I, pp. 152–3.

trade-reorientation and, more generally, of the impact on Bulgaria of the changing trade regime. This theme runs throughout much of this chapter.

Of course, notwithstanding these statistical problems, the dominance of CMEA trade for Bulgaria cannot be doubted and so the country had more than any other member to lose when the system collapsed.

THE CMEA AND ITS DEMISE

The Council for Mutual Economic Assistance was established in 1949, its membership consisting of the USSR, all European communist countries other than Albania and Yugoslavia, and certain non-European communist states. Although it had an investment bank which organized finance for multi-member capital projects, primarily in the energy sector, its most important institution was the International Bank for Economic Cooperation which managed the clearing accounts for inter-member trade.

Intra-CMEA trade was organizationally noteworthy for four main reasons. First, that trade was conducted on the basis of bilateral agreements of an essentially barter nature, extending the physical 'material balance' planning concept to international trade. Secondly, the system was explicitly designed to promote national specialization based on the assumed existence of economies of scale but having little to do with comparative advantage. This is why, for example, Bulgaria became the world's largest producer of fork-lift trucks whereas its natural endowments would have indicated specialization in agriculture. More generally, this inefficient international allocation of resources reflected the old Stalinist notions of socialist development, which equated socialism with heavy industry. Thirdly, the implicit exchange rates and relative prices for this trade were not equal to world prices and were not even equal to domestic relative prices. Fourthly, for the purposes of clearing, planning and statistics there was developed an artificial currency, the transferable ruble, which was no more than a unit of account and had none of the other features of money. In general, the system could be considered as the international equivalent of the physical, non-market, planning processes used to allocate resources domestically.

Although, as noted in Chapter 1 above, the CMEA was not initially of much significance for Bulgaria, from the 1960s onwards it became the most important external influence on the country's economic development. Primary energy and industrial materials were imported from other members (notably the USSR) and transformed into generally 'soft goods'[3] exported also to other members (again, mainly to the USSR).

Difficulties over the supply of imports from the USSR became apparent during the 1980s and resort was increasingly made to western sources of supply. This was the origin of the debt problem reviewed below. Furthermore, as Russian oil prices moved towards world prices in the later part of that decade, Bulgaria not only experienced a deterioration in the terms of trade but had decreasing opportunities to earn the large profits it had been reaping by selling onward to non-members. Thus, the shock of the collapse of the system was to an extent expected, but was nonetheless overwhelming when it arrived.

The *coup de grâce* was administered in January 1990 (ironically at a meeting of the CMEA Council held in Sofia and chaired by a Bulgarian) when the USSR, upon whom the whole system depended, announced that, with effect from a year later, it would implement trading arrangements based on convertible currencies. The institution became formally defunct on 1 January 1991.

The qualitative effects on the Bulgarian economy of the termination of the CMEA have already been noted, but quantitative estimates are extremely difficult, especially because of the statistical difficulties of measuring the importance of the CMEA in the country's trade. One set of estimates, referring to the change between 1989 and 1991, suggests the following.[4] The first effect results from the collapse of export markets in the former Soviet Union, which is estimated to have generated a decline of around 40 per cent in total export volume over the period in question. Some of this could have been expected to have been compensated for by a reorientation of exports to other markets, but a figure of 33 per cent is suggested for the proportion by which import volumes would have had to diminish to preserve external balance. Then,

---

3 This expression refers to products which were uncompetitive on world markets (usually for reasons of quality) and which, because the CMEA as a whole employed physical restrictions on imports, could only be disposed of through the bilateral agreements with other members. By contrast, 'hard goods' were those tradeable in world markets.

4 Organisation for Economic Co-operation and Development (1992), pp. 52–55 and 99–101.

the move to world prices for intra-CMEA trade produced a serious deterioration in the terms of trade on both sides of the account. Dominating Bulgarian imports were fuels from the former Soviet Union (FSU) and, over the two-year period, prices of these products more than doubled. On the other hand, the country's major CMEA exports were machinery and equipment, of which prices fell somewhat.[5] The overall terms-of-trade effect (that is, the decline in import volumes required to preserve external balance with no change in export volumes) was estimated to be 27 per cent. In other words, the two effects together required a 60 per cent reduction in the volume of imports if the balance of payments were to be unaffected. Such a reduction would have represented something between 12 and 25 per cent of 1989 GDP.[6]

These estimates should not be taken too literally (and even their authors warn that they involve a series of unverifiable assumptions necessitated by data deficiencies and so are only very approximate orders of magnitude), but no reasonable estimation procedure could refute the hypothesis that the fall in exports to the FSU and the deterioration in the terms of trade administered a catastrophic shock to the Bulgarian economy — a shock which is more than enough to explain why the output decline since 1989 has been deeper than in any other country of the region. Figures for the same trade, but viewed from the Soviet side, also support this conclusion. In 1991, total Soviet imports were 44 per cent lower than in the previous year, imports from all CMEA partners were 56 per cent lower, but those from Bulgaria had declined by 63 per cent.[7]

In addition to these real effects, mention should be made of the adverse effects of the inadequacies of the financial regime under which

5 This deterioration in the terms of trade, especially with respect to the FSU, would seem to support a long-standing claim that the CMEA system involved large implicit subsidies from the Soviet Union to other members: that is, the USSR underpriced its exports and purchased overpriced imports. This claim has, however, recently been challenged — Poznanski (1993).

6 The size of this range is a reflection of the fundamental statistical problem that there was no reliable method of aggregating trade flows, part of which were denominated in convertible currencies and part in transferable rubles. Official figures suggested the import/GDP ratio to be only about 20 per cent, whereas other estimates put that ratio in excess of 45 per cent.

7 Koves (1992), p. 61.

Bulgarian–FSU trade has been conducted since the collapse of the CMEA. Under the old system, if a bilateral clearing account failed to balance in transferable rubles, no debt in the financial sense was established: the debit or credit was simply used as the starting-point in future physical barter agreements between the two countries. Unfortunately for Bulgaria, this system came to an end at a time when the country was in credit in its balance with the Soviet Union (by one estimate, to the tune of $300 million[8]). Since the Bulgarian exporters had already been paid in leva by the Foreign Trade Bank, the Russians were in effect debtors of the Bulgarian government and the latter had to carry the financial costs. This is one reason why the state's financing requirement has exceeded its budget deficit. Since the credit was interest-free but its financing was not, the existence of this unredeemed debt added a burden to the Bulgarian budget.

Trade between the two countries has, from 1991, been conducted in so-called 'clearing dollars'. These are still really only units of account but balances are domestically transferable at a publicly quoted exchange rate — but a rate which bears no real relationship to the lev/US$ rate. Trade continues to be on a negotiated bilateral basis, but the newer system may be slightly less distorted than the old transferable ruble in that price-ratios for traded goods may bear a closer relation to international price ratios than they did.

THE ORIGIN AND DESTINATION OF TRADE

In many respects, the issues here are at the very centre of the transition process. The ability to reorientate trading relationships in the face of the collapse of traditional markets in the former CMEA is the key to Bulgaria's future economic success. It is therefore particularly unfortunate that the statistical difficulties mentioned above are most severe when it comes to tracking changes in the geographical structure of the country's trade.

Table 5.1 gives the story as related by official Bulgarian statistics.

---

8 Lazarova and Harsev (1994), p. 16. These authors review a range of more technical issues relating to the post-CMEA system of clearing between Bulgaria and the FSU.

Table 5.1 Geographical structure of trade (%), 1989–93

	1989	1990	1991	1992	1993
Exports					
Former CMEA[a]	78.5	77.6	55.1	29.0	25.8
(Of which FSU)	65.2	64.0	49.8	22.4	19.4
OECD[a]	13.6	11.9	26.3	42.2	43.1
(Of which EU[a])	11.0	7.9	15.7	29.4	28.1
Other	8.0	10.6	18.6	28.9	31.1
Imports					
Former CMEA[a]	67.9	69.7	46.8	36.8	43.1
(Of which FSU)	52.9	56.5	43.2	28.6	36.2
OECD[a]	23.0	21.6	32.8	43.8	42.6
(Of which EU[a])	16.1	16.3	20.7	31.1	30.2
Other	9.1	8.8	20.4	19.4	14.1

[a] For continuity in the series, the former German Democratic Republic is throughout counted as OECD and EU rather than as former CMEA. That country accounted for 5.5 per cent and 2.9 per cent of exports in 1989 and 1990 respectively, and for 5.8 per cent and 6.7 per cent of imports in 1989 and 1990 respectively.
Source: Bulgarian National Bank

The table appears to indicate a very dramatic change in the geographical pattern of Bulgaria's trade, with the proportion of exports accounted for by the former CMEA (excluding GDR) declining by over 50 percentage points and the proportion accounted for by OECD increasing by 30 percentage points. Qualitatively similar though quantitatively less dramatic changes are shown for imports. The problem is to know how much of this is real reorientation and how much is statistical illusion.

The potential illusion has two, related sources. First, there is the general problem of aggregating trade in transferable rubles with trade in convertible currency, a problem which causes the official figures to overstate the relative importance of trade conducted in non-convertible currency. Since, from 1991 onwards, trade with the former CMEA other than Russia has been conducted in convertible currency, this statistical bias correspondingly diminishes and so changes between the pre- and post-transition years are exaggerated. The other factor confusing the picture is the devaluation of 1991 when the lev/dollar rate was unified and became market-determined. Since the method of valuing trade with Russia did not adjust proportionately, the effect of the devaluation was to increase the significance of dollar-denominated trade relative to trade denominated in transferable rubles.

Thus, Table 5.1 is misleading as a statistical picture of the change in the geographical structure of Bulgarian foreign trade. However, there is no reason to believe that it is misleading qualitatively. No data exist for trade volumes (and, even if they did, some of the same issues would arise since such data consist of value figures deflated by price indices, the latter being notoriously difficult to construct reliably) but there can be no doubt that there has been a reorientation away from the FSU, especially on the export side.

THE COMMODITY STRUCTURE OF TRADE

Table 5.2 reveals very clearly the nature of Bulgaria's international trade in the last full year under the old system. In relation to the CMEA, the country was predominantly one which imported equipment, fuels and minerals and used them to produce capital goods for export. In addition, it had net exports of food products and of manufactured consumer goods.

As regards non-CMEA, the picture is different with, at the level of product differentiation shown in the table, quite a close match between the commodity structure of imports and exports (one exception being agricultural produce, which includes wine and tobacco). However, the table disguises important differences between trade patterns with, on the one hand, OECD members and, on the other, developing countries. For most of the 1980s, Bulgaria's exports to developing countries considerably exceeded those to the developed world, whereas the situation as regards imports was the reverse. In 1989, 64 per cent of imports from developing countries consisted of fuel and minerals — a reflection notably of growing oil imports from the Middle East and North Africa — and machinery accounted for 38 per cent of exports to developing countries. Bulgarian capital goods were, however, less successful in penetrating western markets (machinery representing only 10 per cent of exports to developed countries) and exports to those countries consisted particularly of food and materials (27 per cent) and fuels and minerals (44 per cent). Imports from OECD members consisted especially of machinery (36 per cent) and food and materials (25 per cent).[9]

Table 5.2   Commodity structure of trade (%), 1989

	CMEA	Other	Total
Exports			
Machinery, equipment	65.4	24.2	49.8
Fuels, minerals,	3.4	33.0	14.6
Chemicals, rubber	2.8	7.3	4.5
Non-food materials	3.0	8.5	5.1
Food, related products	13.3	17.8	15.0
Consumer goods	11.7	7.6	10.1
Other	0.4	1.7	0.9
Imports			
Machinery, equipment	48.5	25.2	37.2
Fuels, minerals,	36.1	32.2	34.2
Chemicals, rubber	3.4	9.8	6.5
Non-food materials	3.4	13.5	8.3
Food, related products	3.0	12.5	7.6
Consumer goods	4.8	6.4	5.6
Other	0.7	0.5	0.6

Source: Derived from World Bank (1991), Vol. I, pp. 152–3

Transition has brought very significant changes in the commodity structure of Bulgaria's trade, as is shown if Table 5.3 is compared with the final column of Table 5.2.

---

9 The source of the figures in this paragraph is the Bulgarian National Bank.

Table 5.3 Commodity structure of trade (%), 1991–93

	1991	1992	1993
Exports			
Food, drink, tobacco	25.4	26.7	21.0
Minerals, fuel	4.5	7.5	10.1
Chemicals, plastics	27.1	14.5	16.9
Metals	6.6	15.0	18.5
Machinery	29.3	18.7	15.2
Other	7.0	17.6	18.3
Imports			
Food, drink, tobacco	10.4	8.0	9.4
Minerals, fuel	55.5	38.0	37.6
Chemicals, plastics	7.8	11.7	12.3
Metals	2.8	5.7	6.0
Machinery	15.5	24.0	22.0
Other	8.0	12.5	12.7

Source: Bulgarian National Bank

From 1991 onwards, statistical reporting is on the basis of international customs classifications, and so it is not possible to show a continuous series. There are, however, definite statistical weaknesses which cast doubt on some of these numbers. Just one example of inconsistency is that the Bulgarian National Bank, *Annual Report 1992*, p. 130 shows chemicals and rubber accounting for 22.2 per cent of exports in 1992 whereas the *Annual Report 1993*, p. 126 gives a figure for 1992 of 14.5 per cent (which is used in Table 5.3). Nonetheless, the broad pattern is clear, and it shows just how much the structure of trade was distorted under the dominance of the CMEA, especially on the export side. Machinery and equipment had accounted for almost half of total exports in 1989, and two-thirds of exports to the CMEA, whereas the contribution of those products to exports fell to 15 per cent by 1993. This is not surprising, given the collapse of major markets and the time needed to penetrate new markets. The longer-term prospects are, however, not encouraging since (apart from computers and related products) the structure of Bulgaria's engineering exports bears little resemblance to the structure of OECD imports of such goods.[10] On the other hand, food, drink and tobacco — where some comparative advantage exists — have increased their contribution noticeably. In general, total export structure in 1993 was quite similar to the structure of non-CMEA exports in 1989, as would be expected with the dramatic reduction in the effect of distorted CMEA trade patterns. The change on the import side is less marked, primarily because of the low price-elasticity of demand for energy from the FSU: the contraction in the volume of fuel imports has been small relative to the huge increase in prices. Nevertheless, again the total commodity structure is moving towards the earlier non-CMEA structure.

Preliminary data for the first nine months of 1994 suggest that these trends are being maintained, especially as regards exports, the share of machinery and equipment falling yet further, that of fuels, minerals, metals and chemicals continuing to rise, and that of food, drink and tobacco restoring the rising trend which had been interrupted in 1993.

THE FOREIGN DEBT PROBLEM

After the collapse of the CMEA, the legacy of hard-currency debt has been the most severe constraint on Bulgaria. Table 5.4 shows how this debt developed during the 1980s. One measure of the burden of that debt, the debt/export ratio, is shown in Table 5.5. The situation since transition began is not shown because there has been no access to commercial or inter-governmental foreign borrowing since the announcement of the moratorium in 1990 and movements in foreign debt since then reflect solely the granting of loans by multilateral agencies such as the International Monetary Fund and the World Bank.

At the end of 1989, 49 per cent of this debt was denominated in US dollars and 30 per cent in Deutschmarks, the remainder being divided approximately equally among Japanese yen, Swiss francs and Austrian schillings. The main creditor countries were West Germany (21 per cent of the total), Japan (20 per cent), the United Kingdom and Austria (13 per cent each).[11]

---

10 Kostov (1992).

11 World Bank (1991), Vol. I, pp. 157–8.

Table 5.4   Gross foreign debt outstanding ($bn: end year), 1980–90

Year	Debt	Year	Debt
1980	4.7	1986	5.5
1981	4.1	1987	7.4
1982	3.5	1988	9.1
1983	3.1	1989	9.2
1984	2.9	1990	10.0
1985	4.1		

Source: Bulgarian National Bank

Table 5.5   Debt/export ratio (%),[a] 1980–90

Year	Ratio	Year	Ratio
1980	129	1986	194
1981	108	1987	204
1982	99	1988	231
1983	105	1989	261
1984	79	1990	357
1985	115		

[a] Debt outstanding at end of year as percentage of sum of merchandise exports and net earnings from services (excluding interest) in convertible currencies during the year
Source: Derived from Bulgarian National Bank

Although external debt had increased in the 1970s, primarily to finance the importation of capital goods and other industrial inputs from the west,[12] the first half of the 1980s saw significant retrenchment as capital imports declined and the current balance of payments was helped by the re-export of Russian oil products. By 1985, 'Bulgaria was widely regarded as a good borrower'.[13] Serious deterioration then set in, with

---

12 Ganchev (1992) presents an econometric analysis of the origins of changes in external debt from the mid-1970s to the mid-1980s.

13 Organisation for Economic Co-operation and Development (1992), p. 96.

the outcome as shown in the tables. Supply difficulties regarding imports from the Soviet Union, combined with some politically motivated relaxation of physical restraints on imports of western consumer goods in response to manifest discontent among the population, created a marked change in the balance of payments in convertible currencies. By 1989, hard-currency imports were 44 per cent greater than in 1984 but exports were 5 per cent lower.[14] Further difficulties were created towards the end of the decade by the failure of certain developing countries — notably Iraq and Libya — to service the large credits which Bulgaria had extended to them to finance imports of machinery and construction projects. By early 1990, outstanding credits of this type amounted to $2.4 billion and arrears amounted to $0.75 billion.[15] Negotiations were concluded to deal with the most significant arrears by means of oil shipments but, in the case of the most important debtor (Iraq), such agreement was frustrated by the Gulf Crisis (see below).

This huge volume of debt appears time and again in our story: inability to borrow abroad has inhibited exchange-rate policy, has forced the government to use the most inflationary method of financing budget deficits, has inhibited hard-currency exports because of lack of access to trade credit, and has severely limited restructuring strategies since direct investment has been the only means of access to foreign capital. It is no wonder that so much effort has had to be extended in efforts to reschedule the debt. Success was finally achieved in 1994 and, since no purpose would be served by a history of these negotiations, we here simply describe the agreement which was reached with the commercial creditors of the London Club. Having been the subject of intermittent and frustrating negotiations for four years, an agreement with the commercial creditors for debt forgiveness and rescheduling finally came into effect on 28 July 1994. Since most of the debt was short-term and had been incurred in the 1980s, it was all past maturity by the time of the agreement.

The basis of the agreement was the substitution of new instruments for existing debt and, for this purpose, the latter was divided into two parts — principal and accrued interest. The first action, performed

---

14 Bulgarian National Bank, *Annual Report 1990*, p. 76.

15 World Bank (1991), Vol. I, p. 24.

instantaneously, was a buy-back at a 75 per cent discount of 12 per cent of the principal and a portion of the accrued interest. The remainder of the principal was dealt with by two instruments.[16] The first, covering 62 per cent of the principal, replaces debt with government bonds at a 50 per cent discount and with a 30 year maturity. These bonds pay interest at LIBOR (the London Inter-Bank Offer Rate) every six months and redemption will occur in a single tranche on maturity. The second, which covers the remaining 26 per cent of the principal, is a front-loaded interest-reduction bond. It pays an increasing rate of interest, beginning at 2 per cent for the first two years and rising in periodic steps to slightly above LIBOR after seven years. This bond has a full maturity of 18 years, with redemption taking place in tranches beginning in the eighth year.

These two bonds are fully collateralized by US Treasury Bonds and other foreign government securities. The acquisition of this collateral occasioned a fall of over $700 million in foreign-exchange reserves in July.

The remaining instrument, which covers most of the accrued interest, is a non-collateralized interest arrears bond. With a full maturity of 17 years, it is to be redeemed in stages beginning in the eighth year and pays slightly above LIBOR from the outset.

By any standards, this is a satisfactory deal for Bulgaria, although no-one gets all he would like from any negotiation. Of the principal, 40 per cent has been written off, 31 per cent involves only interest payments for 30 years, 26 per cent requires only interest for 7 years, and only the remaining 3 per cent had to be repaid immediately.

This agreement signalled the end of the moratorium which had been in operation since early 1990 and which, although very slightly relaxed with some debt-service in 1992 and 1993, had effectively isolated the country from any credit from non-official sources, be it import/export credits for Bulgarian hard-currency trade or foreign participation in the financing of the budget deficit. With the current state of their balance sheets, even after the bad-debt scheme (see Chapter 6 below), most commercial banks (certainly the state-owned ones and possibly the private ones too) would be a very poor credit risk, especially if the

---

16 Known popularly as 'Brady bonds' after a former US Secretary of the Treasury who gave his name to a similar scheme for the foreign debt of developing countries.

Bulgarian National Bank desists from its practice of generous support and is prepared to harden significantly the budget constraints under which the banks operate. Certainly, any foreign bank will for some time be very careful about the collateral on offer before lending to most commercial banks in Bulgaria, although a window may be provided by the expected expansion of local branches of foreign banks.

Table 5.6   Foreign creditors and debtors ($bn), end October 1994

Creditors	
London Club[a]	5.1
Paris Club[b]	1.2
IMF	1.0
World Bank and others[c]	0.6
European Union	0.4
IBEC and IIB[d]	1.0
Other	0.7
TOTAL	10.0
Debtors[e]	2.2
Foreign reserves	0.9

[a] Bonds issued under rescheduling agreement
[b] Official creditors for which no rescheduling agreement yet reached
[c] World Bank, European Bank for Reconstruction and Development and European Investment Bank
[d] The institutions of the former CMEA. Conjectural and subject to negotiation
[e] Loans to developing countries and credit balance on CMEA trade with Russia
Source: Bulgarian National Bank and *Bulgarian Business News*, 2–8 January 1995

Direct financing between foreign and Bulgarian traders, ultimately based on foreign bank credit, is already showing some small signs of having been influenced by the London Club agreement. There are reports that the terms, hitherto completely unrealistic, offered by foreign banks for such deals are relaxing somewhat.

Table 5.6 shows the relevant parts of the most recent government balance sheet with respect to foreign transactions. (There are in addition some outstanding credits and debits denominated in transferable rubles, arising as they do from loans to and from, and uncleared trade balances with respect to, former CMEA members other than Russia. These are, however, small in net terms and controversial.) Even after the London Club agreement, and even if foreign debtors were servicing their debts to Bulgaria (which they are not), the net servicing requirement is still very significant. If the average interest rate on this debt were 6 per cent, interest liabilities alone would amount to over $400 million per year, or more than 10 per cent of merchandise exports in 1994. Although in principle these apparent net liabilities are balanced by the assets (at least some of which are fixed assets owned by state enterprises), these assets are probably predominantly non-performing — they are loans to enterprises — and more certainly non-performing in terms of hard currency. This being so, Bulgaria has significant negative net worth in foreign transactions and this will give rise to a continuing fiscal burden for many years to come.

UNITED NATIONS EMBARGOES

Regardless of the general merits or otherwise of UN-imposed trade embargoes as an alternative to warfare, little consideration has been given to the effects on innocent parties, and Bulgaria has suffered spectacularly in this respect. Immediately before the invasion of Kuwait by Iraq, an agreement was concluded under which the latter contracted to deliver oil to the value of $1.2 billion as payment of debts to Bulgaria. This agreement could then not be fulfilled because of the United Nations prohibition on Iraqi oil exports. But that was not all. The Gulf War came at a time when Bulgarian firms were carrying out major construction projects in Iraq. These projects were halted, no payments were received and large amounts of equipment were destroyed by American bombing, were confiscated or simply had to be left in place. Semi-official estimates (which are very probably over-estimates) put the losses on contracts and from the loss of equipment at $3 billion. Even the Iraqis admit to a debt of $2 billion.[17] More generally, Iraq had been an important trading partner (in the late 1980s that country had accounted for about one-sixth of Bulgaria's exports outside the CMEA)

---

17 Iraq's ambassador to Bulgaria, reported in *168 Hours BBN*, 12–18 September 1994.

and the enforced cessation of trade involves substantial losses at a time when every export opportunity is needed.

Even more damaging have been the effects of United Nations Resolutions 757, 787 and 820 imposing sanctions on Serbia and Montenegro. The problem here is not only, or even primarily, the loss of markets in Serbia itself, but the isolation inflicted on Bulgaria by the embargo on transit traffic. Bulgaria's geographical position had brought with it major earnings from the transportation of goods between Europe and the Middle East and a central transition strategy involves the reorientation of her own trade in the direction of Central and Western Europe. The only realistic routes lie through Serbia, the alternatives through Romania being totally inadequate. There is no bridge across the Danube between Ruse and the Bulgarian–Serbian border and Romanian roads from the south to the west are incapable of carrying serious traffic. It is this physical isolation which has created the damage.

A study carried out by the ministry of trade in association with the United Nations Development Programme has produced some estimates of the scale of this damage. For the period from the establishment of the sanctions in mid-1992 up to August 1994, total losses are estimated to be $6.2 billion, trading margins on Bulgarian trade with Europe accounting for $2.2 billion of this and the value of exports lost accounting for $3 billion. The basis of the latter is unclear, however. The effect on the balance of payments depends upon the import content of the lost exports[18] and the effect on GDP depends also upon the domestic opportunity cost of the resources not employed as a result of the loss of markets.

Nonetheless, whichever way one looks at the figures, they add up, not only to a significant depressive effect on domestic activity, but to a high proportion of Bulgaria's external debt. Though the charter of the United Nations makes no provision for direct compensation in cases such as this, some hope exists that it will be taken into account by the UN-associated multilateral lending agencies when considering infrastructural assistance.

---

18 An unattributable estimate by an international organization suggested that, for the 18 months up to the end of 1993, the balance of payments loss was of the order of $1.1 billion.

RELATIONS WITH THE EUROPEAN UNION

In March 1993, Bulgaria became the fifth transition economy to conclude an association agreement with the European Community (now the European Union), the others being the former Czechoslovakia, Hungary, Poland and Romania. Trade aspects were dealt with under a so-called interim agreement which was intended to become operable in July, but was postponed for six months. The agreement provides for the establishment of a mutual free trade area over a period of ten years, the rate of elimination of tariffs and non-tariff barriers varying very significantly among products. In the generality, EU tariffs will be removed immediately and the overall complexion is asymmetrical in Bulgaria's favour — that is, trade barriers will be eliminated more quickly by the EU than is required of Bulgaria. However, this apparent favour is offset by the choice of goods for which free trade is to be delayed.

The goods in question are 'sensitive' products — notably iron and steel, chemicals, clothing and textiles and, above all, agriculture. As regards the industrial products in this list, EU trade barriers will be dismantled on a phased basis, the period in question varying among sectors. Of course, the EU's common agricultural policy is the very antithesis of free trade and this is reflected in the agreement, under which the mixture of quotas and tariffs will, for most products, continue to operate.

While the agreement is clearly welcome in providing opportunities for trade reorientation, its value to Bulgaria is restricted as a result of the special provisions for trade in sensitive goods.

In fact, imports of sensitive products from the five associate members have historically been of no significance to the EU, in the mid-1980s equalling much less than one per cent of EU output and only about 4 per cent of total EU imports of those products. However, such products are of much greater consequence to the associate members, and especially to Bulgaria. In 1989, sensitive products accounted for 50 per cent of Bulgaria's exports to the EU — higher than for any other transition economy except Hungary. Furthermore, exports of those products from Bulgaria to the EU increased by 45 per cent in the next two years — the highest figure for any of the five associate members.[19]

The restrictions on access therefore have the capacity to deny to Bulgaria considerable opportunities to expand trade, but that is not all. Trade restrictions reduce the incentives for EU firms to invest in transition economies and, more generally, inhibit the efficient restructuring of economic activity which the movement to a market economy is designed to achieve. In a package of policies which defies economic logic, the EU harms itself through these restrictions and at the same time devotes resources to direct financial assistance through, for instance, the PHARE programme. This is an excellent example of the domination of economics by the imperatives of inter-member federal politics and is summed up by one commentator (writing about the agreements with Czechoslovakia, Hungary and Poland, but equally relevant to the Bulgarian agreement) as follows: 'Throughout the Europe Agreements one finds the stamp of the EC's powerful internal enemies of change ... The EAs are indeed a missed opportunity for doing well out of doing good'.[20]

---

19 The figures in this paragraph are taken from Rollo and Smith (1993), pp. 146 and 149–50.

20 Winters (1992), p. 28.

6. Reform of Financial Institutions

This chapter considers two areas of activity the reform and development of which are crucial to the success of both stabilization policy and the creation of a dynamic economy: banking and capital markets. Much greater attention will be given to the former since, of course, a banking system existed before transition and the task is to transform it into an activity suitable for a market economy, and it is always more difficult to effect radical reform of existing institutions than to set up with a clean sheet an institution such as a stock market which did not exist.

The scale of the differences between banking under central planning and banking in a market economy is so great that, in order to provide a context for a discussion of Bulgarian reform needs and policies, we initially offer a brief review of general issues.

GENERAL ISSUES OF FINANCIAL SECTOR REFORM

Banking in Planned and Market Economies

In a market economy, investment capital is provided through the issue of equity or debenture stock to the public through the stock market, through reserves accumulated from past profit not distributed to shareholders, or through long-term bank loans. Working capital is typically financed from short-term bank or trade credit. In all these cases, the market or the banks in effect evaluate the purposes for which the capital is required and reject projects which are judged an unacceptable commercial risk. (The same mechanism in principle exists indirectly even for internally financed investments, but in practice tends to be weak in such cases.) In a planned economy, on the other hand, investment was determined by the strategic priorities and immediate production targets enshrined in the plan and was financed by allocations from the budget and bank credit, the latter being automatically provided to enterprises if needed to meet the requirements of the plan. Not only did this mean that the supply of credit was in effect infinitely elastic at the officially determined interest rate, this being administered like any other price, but that the banking system was little more than that part of the bureaucracy which organized the financial flows required by the plan. Although commercial banks existed, they were essentially specialized branches of the central bank, which was in turn just as much a part of the planning mechanism as any ministry. Any transaction approved by the plan was automatically financed by the banks: capital was no more subject to market judgements than any other good, service or factor of production.

The macroeconomic implication of this was that monetary policy was entirely passive: the supply of money merely responded to demands sanctioned by the plan. The microeconomic implication was that capital was allocated like any other resource, by fiat at an administered price, and not by a market mechanism. To be effective contributors to stabilization and economic dynamism in a liberalized context, monetary institutions need to be changed and, within them, perceptions of their economic and social function have to be revised.

The main institutional requirements are a separation between the central and commercial banks, the development of a competitive structure and spirit among the commercial banks, and a degree of independence for the central bank. Among the market economies of the developed world, there is considerable variability in the extent to which the central bank is independent of government and it would be inappropriate to be dogmatic as to the needs of transition economies in this respect. Thus, in the US and Germany, the Federal Reserve Board and the Bundesbank respectively are entirely independent and frequently find themselves in conflict with government over such matters as the proper level of interest rates. This is a reflection of an overriding belief that governments, because of the imperatives of popularity in a democracy, have inherently inflationary instincts and there is a need for an independent agency to take responsibility for the value of the currency. The Bank of France and the Bank of England, on the other hand, are located in countries where, historically, such attitudes were weaker, but it is noteworthy that recent years have seen a marked increase in the degree of independence claimed by the central banks. The most that can be said at this stage is that central banks need more independence than they had under the planning system, if only to provide some public restraint on governments. Especially, the automatic monetary financing of budget deficits has to be avoided. On the other hand, there is always the danger of the Russian experience whereby the central bank turned out to be more attached to the old way of working and therefore more inflationary in its actions than the government itself.

As regards the commercial banks, the need is for them to be driven by the profit motive to act as filters with respect to the demand for credit. This is a complete change of culture. The only requirement for credit to be granted under the old system was that the purposes for which the credit was wanted were approved by the plan. It was quite unnecessary for the bank to evaluate the project or concern itself with the risk of default by the client since future plans provided for the repayment of credits to banks. Life will now be more complex: banks will have to evaluate the risk attached to any credit since they have no protection against defaulting debtors, other than what may be provided under new commercial and bankruptcy laws.

Furthermore, banking will cease to become a branch of state budgetary activity: it will become a commercial activity like any other and, as in other industries, the best spur to efficiency will be competition. There may be some specialization among banks, as there is in market economies, but in general customers will be able to shop around for credit. The ability to provide credit will depend on the ability to attract deposits and survival will depend on a bank's ability to evaluate risk and to set the correct conditions for deposits and advances.

This is of course a somewhat stylized — indeed, idealized — picture in two respects. First, even in the most liberal market economies, banks are not exactly like other businesses. From country to country there are variations in the freedom given to retail banks and in the degree to which they operate collusively. Also, the history of all market economies is that governments will not allow major retail banks to fail. The recent savings and loan episode in the US is just one illustration of the extent to which even the most laissez-faire governments are willing to commit large sums of public money to protect depositors.

Secondly, the structural change required in the banking sector exceeds that needed in any other sector during transition. Factories may have to change from making trucks to making toasters and may have to find new markets domestically and abroad, but they are unlikely to be required to do something totally remote from their experience. This is exactly what the banks will have to do. They are fortunate in that the change will not require the kind of massive investment in new fixed assets essential in the manufacturing sector, but they will have to invest heavily in personnel development. This kind of process will take time and it is to be expected that transition will be especially tentative in this sector.

In principle anyway, banking reform is comparatively simple: the banks will never want for customers and so do not face the problems of an industrial sector a large proportion of whose market has simply disappeared with the collapse of the planning system and the CMEA. Furthermore, with one exception, banking organization in developed market economies is fairly uniform and so there is a reasonably standard model on which to base reform. The exception relates to the role of banks in the ownership of non-financial enterprises, and this will be referred to later. However, in one respect the old system has left a cancer at the very heart of the financial system, a tumour which must be excised if a healthy banking structure is to develop — the high proportion of banks' assets accounted for by non-performing loans to enterprises: indeed, by most estimates, the commercial banks in most transition economies are insolvent.

Bad Debts

This problem arises directly from the role of banks under the planning system. It was not that bank managers were stupid, inefficient or venal (though they, like any other arbitrarily chosen group of people, may have been), but that the planning system did not require loans to perform, provided no incentives for enterprises to service their debt and provided no incentives for the banks to enforce debt-service by their customers. When the planning system is removed, the banks find themselves standing naked in a gale. Their balance sheets contain a high volume of loans which are not being serviced and which have even less likelihood of being serviced than in the past since one of the first effects of liberalization is a dramatic decline in the profitability of the enterprise sector.

The magnitude of the problem is difficult to measure and estimates vary quite widely. An authoritative source suggests that, at the end of 1991, non-performing loans represented 44 per cent of total loans in

Bulgaria, 55 per cent in Czechoslovakia, 50 per cent in Hungary, 40 per cent in Poland and 37 per cent in Romania.[1]

Since the banks made no provision for bad debts (they had no incentive to do so), the writing down of assets to reflect the true market quality of the portfolio would reveal most banks to have negative net worth. They are therefore in no condition to play their role in transition. That restructuring role requires a tightening of banks' attitudes to giving enterprises credits — that is, it requires the use of the banks to enforce a hard budget constraint on enterprises and so to use market disciplines to force the real weaklings out of business. One approach would be to start by imposing hard budget constraints on the banks themselves and so forcing them to file for the bankruptcy of enterprises who fail to service their credits.

However, such a simplistic approach contains several kinds of perverse incentive. First, most enterprises are experiencing trading losses and need credit to stay in business. If a bank refuses the credit, the firm will cease operations, whereas this may be a firm which has good long-term prospects and so all the bank has done is to remove for ever the prospect of recovering the existing debts from that firm. So, there is little incentive to tighten up on new credit if that carries a risk of reducing the capability to service existing debts to the banks.

Secondly, if the government imposes a hard budget constraint on the banks, and tells them to work out their own salvation, it is likely that banks will increase the spread of rates between deposits and credits, which is harmful to economic efficiency and, less abstractly, means increasing the cost of credit to those who are expected to be good payers — that is, those with good trading prospects — so as to maximize short-term income. This is the opposite of what is required in the interests of enterprise restructuring.

Thirdly, and the most important form of perverse incentive, no banking system in the region (or anywhere else, for that matter) believes that the government will leave it to sink or swim. This is a reasonable

1 Thorne (1993), p. 977. The measurement difficulty is illustrated by the fact that another source, which provides an extremely thorough review of the whole range of financial reform issues, comes up with quite different estimates: Czechoslovakia 21 per cent of total loans, Hungary 11 per cent and Poland 26 per cent (Blommestein and Spencer (1994), p. 145). The latter refer to 1992 rather than 1991, but improvements in the meantime cannot explain the large discrepancy between the two sets of estimates.

expectation because there is no social value in pushing state-owned banks into bankruptcy, given their crucial role in the transition process. So, the banks know that, at some stage, public money will be available for recapitalization — that is, some sort of state acceptance of the banks' bad debts. In these circumstances there is moral hazard and the banks have no incentive to improve their own bad debt situation.

Nowhere, except perhaps in regard to privatization, have the imaginations of observers been more fertile in devising prescriptions than in relation to the problem of banks' bad debts.[2] This is no place to attempt a review of this large and complex literature, especially since, whatever the details of the various proposals, they all have one thing in common. No-one has yet devised a scheme which is speedy, feasible and addresses the magnitude of the problem but which does not involve, sooner or later, a serious burden on the state budget. The banks need to be recapitalized and the only source of this is the state. Ultimately, what is involved is some kind of swap, with the government giving bonds to the banks in exchange for their bad debts. It is the servicing of these bonds which creates the burden. Of course, if government accounts were like commercial accounts, no new burden would exist. If the state owned the banks and the defaulting enterprises and so was the ultimate source (directly or indirectly) of the original credit, the burden of non-performing credits was there anyway. It was not revealed because few governments construct a balance sheet or a profit and loss account on an accruals basis. The debt–debt swap simply makes the whole process explicit: it substitutes additional expenditure, which is shown in the budget accounts, for revenue foregone, which is not. But this cuts no ice with all those whose market responses are influenced by the explicit budget deficit and by the extra taxes needed to reduce it.

Domestically, one obvious possibility is to use privatization proceeds to finance at least part of such an operation, but it is contentious as to whether the generation of fiscal revenue should be an objective of any privatization scheme (see Chapter 8 below) and, in any case, bank recapitalization is so urgent that it cannot wait for significant sales of enterprise assets. This, combined with the fact that transition brings with it other major pressures expanding the budget deficit (see Chapter 7

---

2 See, for but one example, Hexter et al. (1993).

below), is why the financing of bank recapitalization programmes is a priority target for assistance to governments from multilateral agencies.

Again, however, such programmes run the risk of moral hazard. The government can engage in bank recapitalization only on a once-for-all basis (otherwise incentives will be totally perverse) but this is difficult to effect. The state of banks' debt is such that it cannot be ignored and governments have been making budgetary provision for assistance. The ideal would be to state that only credits granted up to a particular date will be subject to assistance. The problem is to pick the date. If it is in the past, some banks may still be left in a bad state. If it is in the future, the banks will have an incentive to be very soft in the meantime, thus making the problem even greater when the relevant date arrives.

The only chance of the banks' dealing with any of this problem themselves is for them to engage in debt–equity swaps with their debtor enterprises. This is not much help to a bank's solvency in the short run, but it does introduce some flexibility into the system, especially if associated with an enterprise privatization programme. It does, however, raise a rather contentious issue: what is the appropriate role of the banks in providing long-term capital for non-financial activities?

The two generic models are the 'insider', associated with much of continental Western Europe and with Japan, and the 'outsider', associated with anglophone countries. In the former, banks are significant equity-holders in non-financial enterprises and often play an important role in corporate governance, having representatives on enterprise boards. In the latter, the banks do not invest in equity, their provision of long-term capital being solely in the form of loans: they are creditors but not owners. The main argument for the former is that it relieves some of the market failures created by excessive risk-aversion on the part of banks and stimulates a valuable synergy between real enterprise development and its financing. The main argument for the latter is that prudential banking requires banks to avoid risky assets. This latter point is clearly important for transition economies who are trying to base their development on very sick banking systems and where prudential banking regulation is in its infancy. On the other hand, the absence of developed stock markets and of non-bank financial institutions gives, by default, a potential role for the banks which they do not need to play in developed market economies. No firm conclusion is warranted here:[3] a pragmatic mixture of the two models is what is actually happening in the region (including Bulgaria — see below).

Securities Markets

Finally, some reference must be made to non-bank capital markets. In a market economy, significant parts of the supply of capital are securitized: fiscal deficits are typically financed by the issue of fixed-interest securities, and major expansions or other restructuring by enterprises are frequently financed by the issue of debentures or equity. The problem is not a primary market (the mechanism through which the securitized transaction is initially effected), but the existence or otherwise of secondary markets — that is markets through which the initial holders of securities may dispose of them when they wish to change their portfolios.

The development of such secondary markets is critical to transition programmes for three major reasons. First, the least inflationary way to finance a budget deficit is to sell securities to the non-bank public, but the attractiveness of such securities is severely reduced by the absence of a secondary market. It has already been noted that Bulgaria has run up against this problem. Throughout the region, stock markets are developing, but nowhere have they yet become important in the trading of government securities. Secondly, a huge volume of capital has to be mobilized to finance enterprise restructuring and, although the absence of significant holdings of liquid wealth means that public share issues are unlikely to be a major force in this process in the medium term, the longer-term relevance of secondary markets in enterprise debt or equity is obvious. Thirdly, and of more immediate relevance, the absence of secondary markets could seriously inhibit privatization programmes, whether they involve the selling of shares or are mass privatization schemes (see Chapter 8 below).

---

3 Though some commentators offer one: see, for example, Corbett and Mayer (1991), where the case for bank involvement in corporate ownership is urged. Similarly, Phelps et al. (1993) argue the desirability of the involvement of financial intermediaries, although doubts are expressed about the ability of banks in their present condition to take on such responsibilities.

THE BANKING SYSTEM ON THE EVE OF TRANSITION[4]

Banking Organization

The banking system was nationalized in 1947 and, until 1987, was essentially of the mono-bank type typical of the region. On nationalization, there were three banks: the Bulgarian National Bank (BNB), which issued currency and provided short-term credit to enterprises; the Bulgarian Investment Bank, which provided long-term finance; and the Post Credit Bank, which dealt with the general population. In 1951, the latter was replaced by the State Savings Bank (SSB); in 1964 the Bulgarian Foreign Trade Bank (BFTB) was established to deal with all transactions involving foreign currency; and in 1967 the Investment Bank was abolished and its functions transferred to the BNB. Thus, by 1981, the system consisted solely of three institutions: the BFTB dealing with foreign exchange, the SSB — the only institution which took deposits from the general public or provided for the credit needs of households (especially for the construction, purchase or refurbishment of housing) — and the BNB which performed all other banking functions — that is, it was the central bank and its branches constituted a commercial banking network for enterprises. In an effort to provide some flexibility and dynamic to the financial aspects of central planning, there was set up in 1981 a bank (Mineralbank/Bank for Economic Initiatives) designed to finance productive activities which were outside the plan, or production in excess of plan targets, and whose main importance was as a source of finance for small and medium-sized enterprises. Its own finance came from the BNB.

The beginnings of at least the organizational loosening of the mono-bank system came in 1987 when the BNB decentralized its functions of supplying credit to enterprises by setting up seven new commercial banks, each with responsibility for a particular economic sector. These were Electronic Bank, Biochemical Bank, Autotechnical Bank, Agricultural and Cooperative Bank, Construction Bank, Transport Bank,

---

4 The information in this descriptive review is derived primarily from the following sources: Bulgarian National Bank, *Annual Report 1990*; Daviddi (1989); Hunter (1993); Mladenov (1992); Thorne (1992); and World Bank (1991), Vol. II, Chapter 5.

Bank for Economic Projects, and Economic Bank (which served sectors not covered by the other banks). Capital was provided by loans from the BNB, balanced by a transfer of assets in the form of outstanding credits to enterprises in the relevant sector. The banks were established as joint-stock companies, with ownership divided among the BNB and sectoral enterprises, thus giving rise to a potential conflict of interest in that an enterprise could be both an owner and a major debtor of its sectoral bank.

Further structural changes came in 1989 when 59 new commercial banks were created from branches of the BNB, financed by the transfer of deposits, balanced by further transfer of loans to enterprises. Ownership was again divided among the BNB, the BFTB, the sectoral banks and enterprises, and these new banks, based as they were on the old network of BNB branches, had a strong regional specialization. In terms of banking functions, the 1989 reforms, which became effective in 1990, represented an important step along the road to the creation of the type of banking familiar in market economies. Until then, banks were almost totally specialized in their functions: enterprises lodged their deposits in and received their credit from the appropriate sectoral bank and households dealt solely with the SSB, but now as regards domestic transactions the commercial banks could become universal banks. A small degree of competition had been introduced, but the interlocking ownership patterns were inherently inimical to true competition. One sign of the future was the establishment in 1990 of the first private bank (helpfully named the First Private Bank).

System Weaknesses

Although, by the end of the communist era, some of the features of a banking system appropriate for a market economy had been put in place, in many important respects Bulgarian banking was ill-suited to provide the kind of financial infrastructure essential for successful transformation.

In the first place, although universal banking had been provided for in the 1989–1990 reforms, methods of financing were still dominated by the means of financing their establishment — that is, in the case of the sectoral banks, which were dominant in size, by credits from the BNB. On average, the ratio of such credits to total liabilities in the sectoral banks was 57 per cent in 1990 and in the new banks, which had been financed partially by the transfer of deposits, 22 percent.[5] The BNB had a central role in the underlying financing of the other banks with, at the end of 1990, 63 per cent of its assets consisting of outstanding credit to banks. What is more, the BNB was the vital link between household savings and enterprise borrowing: 42 per cent of its liabilities consisted of the excess deposits of the SSB, which were held in the BNB.[6]

Allied to this is the question of capital-adequacy — that is the ratio of equity to assets. In 1991, the thirteen largest commercial banks (including the sectoral banks and the First Private Bank) had an average ratio of only 5.3 percent. Of these banks, only the Mineralbank (at 16.8 per cent) and the new Post Bank (11.3 per cent) had ratios in excess of 5.5 per cent. The Economic Bank, whose assets accounted for 42 per cent of the total in this group of banks, had a ratio on merely 1.4 percent.[7] Nor has the situation improved in the meantime. At the end of 1993, the total capital/assets ratio of all commercial banks had fallen to 3.4 per cent and, if claims on non-financial clients are taken as an indicator of risk assets, the ratio of capital to risk assets was 8.6 percent.[8] The latter may seem satisfactory in relation to the international recommended norm of 8 percent, but this ignores the fact that a significant proportion of the assets in question take the form of non-performing credits to enterprises. Given this, and the inexperience of the banks in credit management in a liberalized setting, prudence would indicate that capital/asset ratios should be considerably in excess of those prevailing in developed market economies.[9]

Then, the ownership structure of the commercial banks was unsatisfactory. This is not simply because most of them were, and still are, indirectly owned by the state. The problem was that ownership was entirely held by a mixture of the banks' debtors (in the case of the sectoral banks created in 1987) and other banks (especially in the case of the common commercial banks created in 1989, whose shares were concentrated in the hands of the BNB and other commercial banks).

---

5 Thorne (1993), p. 81.

6 Bulgarian National Bank, *Annual Report 1990*, balance sheet, p. 63.

7 Minkov (1993), pp 38–39.

8 Calculations based on Bulgarian National Bank, *Annual Report 1993*, p. 137.

9 For example, Rostowski (1993), p. 448, suggests capital/asset ratios in the range 25–30 per cent and Caprio and Levine (1994), p. 12, recommend 15–20 per cent.

Perhaps the single most important requirement of successful transition is the imposition of hard budget constraints on enterprises and, since bank credit unrelated to commercial risk was a major example of a soft budget constraint, tougher attitudes by the banks towards their debtors must be a vital element in transition strategy. This is difficult to effect when enterprises with debts to the banks, and those seeking credit from the banks, are themselves major bank owners. Ironically, one of the suggested solutions for the bad-debt problem is to reverse this relationship — that is to make banks the owners of enterprises. Furthermore, the significant participation of the BNB in bank ownership, and the network of cross-ownership between commercial banks, were not conducive to the kind of competition required by efficiency and give rise to a potential conflict of interest when the BNB is both the owner and regulator of commercial banks.

The number of commercial banks also gave a misleading impression of the potential for competition since not only were they highly specialized on a sectoral and regional basis, but there was great concentration in terms of size. Of the 59 common commercial banks, the largest five held 44 per cent and the smallest five held one per cent of the total deposits of these banks at the end of 1990.[10] Of the total assets held by the 13 largest sectoral and common commercial banks at the end of 1991, 42 per cent were held by one bank (the Economic Bank), the next largest (Mineralbank) held 19 per cent and the smallest eight held only 18 per cent.[11] The large number of very small banks, whose survival was doubtful in an environment where economies of scale exist and where large-scale investment in staff development would be vital, presented a serious policy issue.

Aside from these structural defects, the system was, by western standards, extremely ill-equipped at the retail level. In 1990, 39 of the commercial banks had no branches at all other than their head offices and the remainder had on average less than four branches each. This compared with the 3,500 outlets of the SSB (including branches and offices in enterprises and post offices). Including these SSB branches, Bulgaria had approximately one bank retail outlet per 20,000 of the population, whereas the typical ratio in Western Europe would be of the

---

10   Thorne (1993), p. 80.

11   Minkov (1993), p. 38.

order of 1,500–3,000.[12] In addition, payments systems were positively antediluvian, with ill-developed chequing and nothing in the way of giro transfers, credit cards or automatic cash machines. Furthermore, inter-bank clearing was extremely slow, anecdotal evidence suggesting that delays of several months were not uncommon.

Finally, there is the fundamental problem of bank insolvency because of bad debts, which has already been reviewed in general terms and Bulgaria's response to it will be discussed below.

REFORM OF THE BANKING SYSTEM

Legal Foundations

The new system is governed by two pieces of legislation, one concerning the BNB and the other the commercial banks, passed in 1991 and 1992 respectively.

The BNB was re-established by the Law on the Bulgarian National Bank[13] and the main points of interest concern its functions and its relations with government. The latter is important because the Law (Article 2) describes the Bank's main task as maintaining the internal and external value of the currency and, to this end, *formulating* and implementing monetary policy. It also is required to regulate and supervise the banking system and is the sole note-issuing authority.

The BNB's managing board consists of the governor and three deputy governors — all appointed by the Assembly — and five other members appointed by the president of the state on the nomination of the governor. Members may be removed during their term only if convicted of a criminal offence or if they are unable to perform their functions for more than a year. It will be noted that there is no provision for their removal on grounds of incompetence or (for which incompetence would be the stated reason) for disagreement with the government. Overall policy is decided by a Plenary Council consisting of the managing board along with six others, appointed by the governor for three years and described by the Law (Article 19) as 'leading specialists in the

---

12 World Bank (1991), Vol. II, p. 101.

13 Passed on 6 June 1991; published in *Dürzhaven vestnik*, No. 50, June 1991.

monetary, financial, business and scientific fields'. No provision is made for the early removal of such members.

The BNB's role as a *central* bank is firmly established by denying it any residue of the commercial banking functions it had previously exercised. Thus, it may discount paper presented by or extend collateralized credit to financial institutions or extend non-collateralized credit to banks if these are 'extremely necessary' (a hazardously vague term, but probably unavoidable in present circumstances) to preserve the debtor's liquidity (Article 30); it may lend short-term to the state (Article 46) — subject to such loans not exceeding 5 per cent of the state budget — and may purchase government securities (Article 48); it is the government's banker and broker (Article 45); and may accept deposits from financial institutions, the government and municipalities (Article 38), but from no-one else. That is, its old role as banker to enterprises is excluded. This legislation also makes the BFTB redundant in that Article 34 gives the BNB the duty of managing the country's foreign exchange reserves and of reporting, and recommending remedial action, to the Council of Ministers when, in the Bank's judgement, reserves are dangerously low. As a result, the BFTB, once the foreign-debt agreement had been reached with the London Club (see Chapter 5 above), became in effect just another commercial bank.

It is clear that the legislators intended that the BNB be independent of government. It is accountable to parliament (Article 2) — although the law is silent as to what the Assembly can do if it disapproves of the BNB's actions (as already noted, it can dismiss its appointees only in well-defined circumstances which do not refer to disagreement over policy) — and Article 47 is worth quoting in full: 'In performing its functions the Bank shall be independent from instructions from the Council of Ministers and other state bodies'. Especially when combined with the restrictions already noted on the furnishing of credit to the state, this is a very important provision in that it gives the Bank legal authority to resist exactly the kind of monetary actions, originating from the budget deficit, which could jeopardise the internal and external value of the currency. No law can protect totally from the informal pressures generated within the very small group responsible for the banking and governmental aspects of monetary policy, and there have been public manifestations of these pressures in Sofia, but the BNB has done rather well in this regard so far.

Finally, the BNB, under Section VI of the Law, regulates the commercial banks, but this function is best considered in the context of the more general legislation on banking, to which we now turn.

The Law on Banks and Credit Activity[14] is a fairly standard piece of banking legislation concerning licencing, capital adequacy and other prudential requirements. Banking[15] may be conducted only on receipt of a licence from the BNB and the Law lays down the necessary conditions for the granting of such a licence and the reasons for which a licence may be refused. Some of the latter reflect what one hopes will be temporary fears that the establishment of one's own bank is a convenient way of laundering money acquired through crime or as a result of holding positions of power under the old regime.[16] From the economic viewpoint, an issue of concern would be the interpretation of Article 14(1)(2), which states that a licence may be refused if the proposed activity 'does not correspond to the local needs or to the interests of the Bulgarian economy'. If this is meant simply as a portmanteau clause to capture things which were not thought of when the Law was framed, then such completely undefined discretion for the BNB is acceptable. However, this provision looks suspiciously like a reflection of old attitudes, which regarded competition as wasteful, and it could be used to inhibit competition. Time will tell.

As regards capital adequacy and reserve requirements, the Law (Article 21) leaves it to the BNB to determine from time to time such matters as the minimum shareholders' equity and reserve ratios. Discretion in relation to the former is inescapable in these times of high inflation and discretion as regards the latter is actually a normal instrument of monetary policy. The Law does, however, contain the prudential requirement that equity shall not be less than 8 per cent of

---

14 Passed on 18 March 1992; published in *Dŭrzhaven vestnik*, No. 25, March 1992.

15 Banking activities are defined by the Law (Article 1) and, for these purposes, exclude such organizations as the Post Office, insurance institutions, and housing savings and loan institutions (Article 2).

16 Thus, Article 14(6) provides that a licence may be refused if persons holding over 10 per cent of the voting shares 'may harm the reliability or security of the bank' and para. 9 of the transitional provisions exclude, for five years, from the managing board of a bank those who held high office in the Communist Party and its affiliated organisations, and officers of the State Security. Only university graduates may be on managing boards (Article 8(1)(2)), the reason for this being a mystery.

what are called 'risk assets'. It is not stated how the denominator of this ratio shall be defined or calculated.[17]

The prudential requirements (which are essentially aimed at protecting depositors from obviously unwise investments by their bank) are of interest because of a point raised earlier: what is the proper role of the banks as owners of non-financial activities? On balance, it can be judged that Bulgaria has leaned more towards the outsider than the insider model, which is perhaps understandable in an unstable period when depositor-protection is regarded as outweighing any consideration of the potential of the banks to mobilize capital for restructuring the enterprise sector. Thus, a bank must receive the permission of the BNB before it may acquire more than a 10 per cent stake in a non-financial enterprise (Article 17(2)(1))[18] and 'the total amount of the bank's investments in real estate, equipment, shares and interest in non-financial institutions shall not exceed its shareholders' equity' (Article 29(1)). This is very restrictive. First, shareholders' equity need represent only 8 per cent of risk assets. Secondly, this provision refers to all investments of the type stated, not such investments in an individual enterprise. Thirdly, it includes real estate, which (aside from industrial buildings) would not usually be regarded as a risky asset. It would appear that this provision will restrict the participation of the banks in what one would expect to be very profitable urban developments. The restrictions referred to in this paragraph clearly rule out any extensive participation of the banks in privatization programmes.

Restructuring the Banking Sector

Two major, structural issues identified earlier are the large number of very small banks and bank privatization. To deal with these issues, the Bank Consolidation Company (BCC) was established in February 1992, with initial capital of BGL933 million — 20 per cent from the BFTB and 80 per cent from the BNB in the form of the latter's interests in commercial banks. As a result, the BCC became a shareholder in many

---

17 The developing practice in western banking is to assign a risk-weighting to each of several classes of asset and to use the weighted average as the denominator in prudential reserve ratios.

18 If a bank goes over this limit because it has engaged in a debt–equity swap with a debtor-enterprise, it has three years to dispose of the excess (Article 17(3)).

commercial banks and it is envisaged that the ultimate disposal of those shares will be a part of the mechanism by which commercial banks are privatized.

The BCC's first task, as its name implies, was to organize the consolidation of the publicly owned commercial banking sector which, as already noted, comprised 67 institutions, in addition to the BFTB and SSB. Consolidation got into its stride with what, by the standards of other Bulgarian reforms, can be considered admirable expedition. In December 1992, 22 commercial banks were merged and reincorporated as the United Bulgarian Bank. Then, in April 1993 a licence was granted to an amalgamation of three regional banks under the name of Balkanbank. June of that year saw the licencing of two new banks — Expressbank (a merger of 12 commercial banks, one sectoral and 11 regional) and Hebros Bank (one sectoral and seven regional) — and in December Sofiabank (one sectoral and three regional commercial banks) was licenced. Thus, within less than two years of its establishment, the BCC had effected the grouping of 49 sectoral and regional banks into five large organizations. By the end of 1994, the main consolidation had been completed, with the original 70 commercial banks being amalgamated into eleven.

As 1994 progressed, attention became concentrated on the issue of bank privatization. The earliest policy statements indicated that a start would be made with those banks in which the state's (that is, the BCC's) stake was smallest, but the pendulum swung around completely until the programme approved by the Council of Ministers in the summer gave priority to seven banks in which the BCC holding was greatest (two sectoral banks and five amalgamated banks) and two smallish banks in which the state's holding was negligible).[19] In the latter two cases and in one of the former, it was proposed to sell the whole of the BCC stake; in two of former cases, only part of the BCC holding would be offered for sale; and in the remaining cases there would be no sale of BCC-held shares but new equity would be raised by public issue.

The proposal then became enmeshed in the kind of public squabbling between competent public authorities so familiar in the area of industrial privatization (see Chapter 8 below). One parliamentary committee and

---

19 *168 Hours BBN*, 13–19 June 1994.

the director of the BCC took the view that parliament should not be involved, whereas the chairman of another parliamentary committee and the governor of the BNB took the opposite view.[20] The process stalled and during the hiatus the First Private Bank became the largest commercial bank in the country as a result of the successful issue of shares to the value of BGL1 billion.

In the meantime, of course, parliament was dissolved and the BCC took the matter into its own hands, announcing that it intended to sell immediately part of its stake in the Bank for Agricultural Credit (the sectoral bank which the original programme had designated for complete state divestiture). It then announced the sale of its minority interest in six unamalgamated regional banks which had not been mentioned in the original programme.[21] All 11 state-owned banks have prepared privatization programmes and it is expected that quite a wide variety of procedures will be used. Most of these banks are seriously undercapitalized and priority is likely to be given to methods which increase shareholders' funds rather than merely disposing of the BCC's holdings, floating new issues or attempting to attract core investors.

THE BAD DEBT PROBLEM

The Law on the Settlement of Unserviced Credits[22]

The object of this law is to contribute to the cleaning-up of banks' balance sheets by replacing non-performing credits to enterprises with government securities. As already noted, there is a problem about the timing of such an operation. There is the related stock-flow issue: that is, should the stock of bad debts held by the banks on the collapse of the planning system be distinguished from non-performing credits granted since transition began? The answer must lie in a mixture of principle and practicality. The principle is that the banks contracted these debts in circumstances where they were not autonomous agencies and so cannot reasonably be launched onto the liberalized waters with such excess ballast. But when did they become autonomous?: after the

---

20 *168 Hours BBN*, 25–31 July 1994.

21 *168 Hours BBN*, 7–13 November 1994.

22 Passed 20 December 1993.

first elections?; after the big bang of February 1991?; after the passage of new banking legislation?; or some other date? The date could never have been the date of the bad-debt legislation because of the moral-hazard problem. The practicality is that a date must be chosen, even if there are objections on principle to any such date, and that the whole exercise does not eliminate a burden, but simply transfers it from the banks to a state budget which is anyway in serious difficulties. Bulgaria balanced these issues by choosing 31st December, 1990, which approximates to 'big-bang day', could not have been much earlier without evading the central problem at stake and could not have been much later without creating unsupportable fiscal burdens.

The scheme applies to debts of enterprises with at least 50 per cent state participation to banks with the same state participation, contracted before 31 December 1990 and which had not been serviced for the 180 days up to 30 June 1993 (Article 1(1) of the Law). It involves the swap of government bonds[23] for the debts in question. Interest accruing since 30 June 1993 has to be written off by the banks themselves (Article 2). The scheme then divides in two: one referring to domestic debts in leva and the other to debts contracted in convertible currency. The latter part also covers the amounts spent by the BFTB on foreign-debt service on behalf of clients prior to 29 March 1990 but for which it had not been reimbursed by the state by 31 December 1993, subject to a maximum of $158 million (Article 1(2)).

The lev debts will be swapped for 25-year government bonds with a redemption value of BGL32 billion. The fiscal pain, and so the value to the banks, is reduced in the short term by a sliding-scale interest rate: one-third of the basic interest rate for the first two years, one-half for the next two, two-thirds for the next two, and the full basic rate thereafter (Article 4). In the case of the debts in convertible currency, the swap will be effected by 25-year bonds of a value up to $1,808 million at an interest rate equal to the 6-months LIBOR rate, with no sliding scale. The servicing will be in leva at the central BNB rate on the relevant day (Article 5). Both sets of bonds are freely transferable,

---

23 These bonds are now known popularly as *ZUNK*-bonds, after the initials of the Bulgarian name of the Law (*Zakon za Urezhdane na Neobsluzhvani Krediti*). The similarity to the English expression 'junk-bonds' removes any disguise from this irony.

may be used as collateral and, of considerable importance, may be used as to buy shares in privatization programmes (Articles 5 and 6).

This last point is of particular interest since there are considerable incentives for the banks to use these bonds to buy shares in enterprises offered for privatization. The yield on the bonds is very low in the first few years and the offer value of shares in the privatization programme will be small compared with the redemption value of the bonds. The resulting potential excess demand from banks for these shares will drive up their value in secondary trading, with a resultant capital gain for those banks which used their bonds early in the privatization process.[24] Indeed, it appears that the effects of these incentives are already being felt. One report indicates that, as early as September 1994, BGL720 million of these bonds had been committed to privatization share purchase.[25] As already noted, there are legal restrictions on the extent to which the banks may participate in the ownership of non-financial enterprises and so a significant proportion of this figure must be represented by sales of *ZUNK*-bonds to the public, who then use them in the privatization process.

The next issue concerns the quantitative adequacy of the scheme. The only recent estimate of the scale of the bad-debt problem known to the present author is that by Dobrinsky,[26] who claims that, at mid-1992, the total bad debts of the commercial banks were of the order of BGL111 billion, The origin of this estimate is unclear but, if reasonably accurate, it suggests that bad debts represented about two-thirds of outstanding claims on non-financial institutions and about one-half of all outstanding credit by the commercial banks at that date.[27] This estimate

---

24   This issue is reviewed quantitatively in Petrov (1994).

25   *168 Hours BBN*, 3–9 October 1994.

26   Dobrinsky (1994), pp. 335–6 and 344.

27   Year-to-year changes in the way the BNB presents the consolidated balance sheet of the commercial banks hardly facilitate this analysis. 'Claims on non-financial institutions and other clients' were stated to be 37.5 per cent (*Annual Report 1993*, p. 100) of total assets (BGL509.7 billion – *Annual Report 1992*, p. 110) at the end of 1992, or BGL191 billion. If this same percentage ruled a year earlier (whether or not it did is not revealed by the data), the equivalent figure for the end of 1991 would have been BGL152 billion, a rough approximation for mid-1992 therefore being BGL170 billion. The equivalent estimate for the total including claims on financial institutions would be BGL222 billion. Hence the figures of two-thirds and one-half respectively given in the text.

is vastly in excess of that of the BNB, which suggested a total of BGL41 billion for the end of 1992.[28] For the working of the bond-loan swap, it is encouraging that Dobrinsky estimates that, of the BGL111 billion, BGL35 billion were lev credits granted before the cut-off date for the scheme (which provides BGL32 billion for this purpose) and that BGL34 billion were in convertible currencies, for which the scheme provides $1.8 billion. Much less heartening is his estimate that the remaining BGL42 billion (or 38 per cent of the total) were granted after the end of 1990 and so would not qualify under the scheme. The latter figure will certainly have grown in the meantime and so, even if the scheme is successful, there will remain a serious threat to bank solvency.

The banks are replacing non-performing assets with performing assets, but what about the debtor enterprises? They are replacing liabilities to the banks with liabilities to the state and the Law (Articles 11–13) valiantly requires enterprises to service these debts. Enterprises must submit programmes for financial restructuring which provide, *inter alia*, for the service of the new obligations under contracts with the ministry of finance. In the event of failure to honour such contracts, the state may file for bankruptcy. At the time of writing, this looks like an exercise in optimism rather than realism. It is not evident why the state would be any more successful in using these obligations to enforce enterprise restructuring than would the banks which, in a market economy (and could be done under Bulgarian law), would also require major debtors to agree a restructuring programme the failure of which could lead to the bank initiating a bankruptcy procedure. Banks are already seizing collateral and have started bankruptcy proceedings against defaulting clients. Of the approximately 1,500 enterprises whose debts to the banks were swapped for bonds, ten had had their restructuring programmes approved by the ministry up to the end of 1994: they have repaid their principal, with the accrued interest written off, but they are all small. The test will come when larger enterprises with significant employment are at stake. It is expected that perhaps 500 will look for complete forgiveness of their debts and it is accepted at the official level that the political sensitivity of hard budget constraints will

---

28 Bulgarian National Bank, *Annual Report 1992*, p. 111.

make it difficult to impose liquidation or major contraction in these cases. It is too early to judge.[29]

SECURITIES MARKETS

There are at present 18 institutions in Bulgaria describing themselves as stock exchanges, but most of these are really no more than brokerage houses. The two largest in terms of market capitalization and turnover are the Sofia Stock Exchange and the First Bulgarian Stock Exchange (FBSE). The former was the first to open for business (in January 1992 whereas the latter began trading in May of that year) and is by far the larger as regards turnover, with about 70 per cent of the total business of the two exchanges. It is, however, much less restrictive than the FBSE in its rules and, if one considers only those securities which would meet the FBSE's listing regulations, the turnover percentages are reversed.

Because it has adopted more stringent criteria for listing (there are as yet no national standards or regulatory body, each exchange being responsible for its own regulation), the FBSE is the more interesting in giving a glimpse of a future where more strict regulation is inevitable, and so the present review will be limited to that institution and attention will be concentrated on the three aspects of stock market activity which are of most significance for transition to a market economy -- as a primary market to mobilize capital for the private sector, as a primary and secondary market in shares of privatized state enterprises, and as a primary and secondary market in government securities.

The FBSE currently lists 24 issues of 16 companies, with a market capitalization in excess of BGL3 billion (approximately $50 million). Of these companies, 15 are *de novo* private companies and the sixteenth is a company which was the subject of one of the most interesting

---

29 Saunders and Sommariva (1993), who provide a very thorough review of the options for dealing with the bad-debt problem, are very negative about this: 'Even given the relatively rudimentary skills of bankers in Eastern Europe, there must be a high probability that state bureaucrats will perform even worse in managing and recapturing bad assets. Indeed, since state bureaucrats (government departments) will be dealing with other state bureaucrats (managers of state firms) sclerosis and gridlock is likely to occur in the restructuring exercise' (p. 950). A similar position is taken by van Wijnbergen (1994).

privatization deals to date — the Grand Hotel Varna which was sold off 49 per cent to a Bulgarian core investor, 20 per cent to the employees and, in stages, the remainder by public flotation. The last part is of particular interest for two reasons. First, half of these shares were sold and they are the sole example to date of secondary trading in the shares of a privatized enterprise. Secondly, the situation regarding the other half, yet to be sold, provides an insight into the attitudes of the Privatization Agency. The shares already sold were, at the time of writing, trading on the FBSE at around BGL85 per share. However, it appears that the PA are offering the remainder at a price of BG115 for cash and BGL150 for purchases using *ZUNK* bonds. This would seem to be another example of the PA paying less attention to market realities than to its own fear of selling public enterprises 'too cheaply'.

Thus, a secondary market for shares in privatized companies has begun to develop, but as yet no other privatization has involved offering on a stock exchange, though this is about the happen with the small BCC holding in the Bank for Agricultural Credit. On the other hand, the extremely low proportion of Bulgarian budget deficits financed by the non-bank public has already been noted, and of great concern for monetary policy is the lack of any true secondary market for government securities.

The problem would appear to be a mixture of conflicting incentives and institutional defects which together serve to strengthen the position of the commercial banks. At present, the monthly yield on treasury bills is approximately 7 per cent whereas that on time deposits is less than 5 per cent.[30] Such bills should therefore be attractive to the non-bank public. Furthermore, a wider market for its securities would be in the interests of a government wishing to minimize the cost of budgetary finance. On the other hand, the commercial banks have no incentive to encourage participation by their customers: a lack of choice of liquid assets for the public facilitates the maintenance of the wide and profitable spread between rates on deposits and loans. In addition, the banks seem to be in a strong position for administrative reasons. A member of the public wishing to acquire or dispose of government paper can buy or sell only through his or her bank and there seem to be

---

30 A significant gap has arisen only since late 1994 when the government removed a minimum-price constraint on treasury bill auctions.

delays in registering transactions, whereas the banks themselves can take advantage of what is now a rapid inter-bank clearing mechanism.

If this interpretation is correct and there are such impediments to non-bank transactions in government securities, an important development is being frustrated. As this is being written, the authorities are attempting to draw conclusions from the difficulties of operating monetary policy in 1994 (Chapter 3 above), and one of these lessons may be the need for institutional arrangements which encourage rather than inhibit secondary trading.

7. Fiscal Reform

THE NATURE OF FISCAL REFORM

Nowhere are the institutional differences between centrally planned and market economies more apparent than in the fiscal area. Essentially, this is because, in a market setting, the state can (with a little fuzziness at the margins) be clearly distinguished from the rest of the economy. Prices of final and intermediate goods and services, factor rewards and interest and exchange rates are not direct policy instruments. They may of course be influenced by government policy, but usually in an indirect way rather than by fiat. Therefore, resources are appropriated for public purposes through a well-defined tax system which may fail to perform as intended because the government cannot directly determine revenue — it can do no more than define the nature (but not the magnitude) of the tax base and set the nominal tax rates.

Under central planning, the fiscal system was not institutionally distinct: it was simply part of the more general structure of plan-determined financial flows. Thus, although it was normal to have tax legislation which looked similar to equivalent legislation in market economies, such legislation was no more than a description of certain aspects of the planning system. For example, the plan set levels and prices of outputs and material and factor inputs and so set profit, a proportion of which was then assigned to the state as tax revenue: this was called profits tax. This meant not only that revenue could be controlled directly but also that the transfer of resources to the government could be organized through the same administrative system which arranged payments among producers, arranged the payment of wages and assigned the payment and repayment of bank credit. In most formerly planned economies, including Bulgaria, the actual payments were effected through the banking system. When a taxable enterprise deposited its sales proceeds in the bank, the bank then debited its account with the turnover tax and credited the same amount to the government's account (there being only one bank). Or, when an enterprise drew from the bank the money to pay its wages, the bank debited the same account with the social security contributions and credited them to the government. So, there was no need for a tax administration as such, except for auditing.

Just as important as this institutional difference between a planned and market economy was that, in the former, the very notion of fiscal flows was ill-defined. Of course, in market economies, governments do things which are the exact economic equivalent of taxes or public expenditures but which do not appear in any budget. Just to take one example, suppose a government attempts to reduce pollution externalities by regulating the permitted sulphur content of smoke emissions. This procedure is in principle indistinguishable from the imposition of a tax on those generating sulphurous smoke and using the proceeds to abate the effects of the smoke, the difference being that, in the latter case, the budgetary numbers would be affected. The point being made here is that this kind of disguised taxation and subsidization was pervasive in centrally planned economies since the whole planning system was like our pollution example writ large. At the macroeconomic level, an example would be the use, in a market economy, of an increase in personal income tax to restrain private consumption. In a planned economy, this was unnecessary (in fact, personal income taxes were of minor importance) because, in the first place, wages were controlled by the plan and, secondly, the supply of consumer goods was also controlled and so households were frequently in disequilibrium. In a market economy, such a deflationary policy would show up as an increase in the budget surplus (or reduction in the deficit) but in a planned economy there would be no such effect on the budget.

Which brings us to the question of the overall budget balance. One obvious difference from market economies follows from what was said above. Since prices and quantities were susceptible to governmental manipulation, it was always possible for sufficient revenue to be raised to cover expenditure. Even essentially costless bank credit could be arranged to ensure that enterprises had sufficient liquidity to meet their predetermined tax liabilities. As a result, balanced budgets were the norm. Only if it was impossible for the system to respond to major exogenous shocks within the fiscal year would deficits arise.

More important, however, was the fact that there was no necessity to use budget deficits or surpluses as policy instruments. In market economies, state budgets may be deliberately unbalanced in order to stimulate or repress aggregate demand, depending on whether the priority is to increase capacity utilization or to reduce inflation. In a planned economy, on the other hand, there were direct methods available to prevent open unemployment or inflation from emerging or to correct disequilibrium in the balance of payments.

The fiscal challenge in transition economies is not how to change big governments into small governments: after all, there are successful market economies the scale of whose budgets, relative to GDP, are not much smaller than was typical in European centrally planned economies. The challenge is that, once prices and trade are liberalized and allocative decisions are made by non-governmental agencies in response to market signals, the existing fiscal system becomes either ineffective or economically dangerous.

The first thing which happens is that the overall budget balance can no longer be directly controlled and that, more significantly, the balance takes on an economic importance which it did not have in the past. Since, in countries such as Bulgaria, Poland and Russia, where there was a severe monetary overhang, price liberalization caused a huge increase in the general price level, the stabilization priority was to prevent this from degenerating into hyperinflation. But, with markets determining prices, budget deficits now had inflationary implications — and even more severe implications than would the same scale of deficit in, say, Western Europe since, in transition economies, the lack of personal wealth and capital markets has meant that the whole of any deficit has to be financed by the domestic banking system. Restricting budget deficits then becomes urgent, but also very difficult because the fiscal system has taken on a life of its own.

Whenever concern is expressed about the size of a budget deficit in a market economy, attention is almost invariably focused on the need to restrain public expenditure. This almost exclusive attention to the expenditure side of the budget is inappropriate in transition economies where the immediate fiscal problem is that the tax system cannot deliver enough revenue to finance levels of public expenditure which would not be regarded as excessive in most market economies. Of course, the expenditure side needs to contribute, as indeed it has been doing, especially where governments have recognized that the logic of transition to a market economy requires the elimination of most of the subsidies to enterprises which took up a sizeable part of the budget. Also, formerly planned economies would not have in the state apparatus effective systems of expenditure management and control, which need to be developed. But it is the tax system which must bear the main burden of fiscal adjustment, both in the sense of delivering revenue more effectively and in the sense of contributing to the development of a more efficient economy.

Restoring the revenue capacity of the tax system in transition economies requires two major types of reform — the design of taxes capable of generating amounts of perhaps 45 per cent of GDP in a situation where prices, and transactions generally, have been liberalized, and the construction of a system of tax administration which can effectively collect what is due. The collapse of enterprise profitability means that the single most important tax base in the old system is no longer available.[1] Old-style turnover taxes also lost revenue-effectiveness as prices were liberalized.[2] Finally, more effective personal income taxes are required as wages are liberalized, as non-wage personal incomes increase in significance and as the private sector develops.

To cope with these problems, all countries in the region have been constructing taxes and tax administrations similar to those familiar in developed markets economies (although in Bulgaria, as we shall see, these processes have been disappointingly slow). Global personal incomes taxes, profits taxes with bases defined according to western norms and value-added taxes are being put in place. What is also important is that governments in the region are, often with considerable reluctance, giving these taxes the structural features needed if the tax

---

1 Even if profitability had not declined, the adoption of western accounting practices and of western definitions of taxable profit would have reduced the tax base which, under the old system, was defined gross of certain items, notably interest, which are deductible under western-style profits taxes.

2 Of course, the collapse of real consumption in the initial stages of transition would have caused a dramatic decline in the real revenue from even a good consumption tax such as a value-added tax: the point being made here is the longer-term one that the old turnover taxes could not, in a liberalized situation, capture anywhere near the whole of their intended base.

system is not to perpetuate distortions which are inimical to the overall efficiency of the economy.

THE PRE-TRANSITION FISCAL SYSTEM IN BULGARIA[3]

Overall Fiscal Performance

Table 7.1 illustrates, for Bulgaria, some of the points made above. As a proportion of GDP, the budget grew steadily during the 1980s from around 50 per cent to nearly 60 per cent. Deficits or surpluses were very small by western standards throughout the decade, but the last year before transition began in earnest showed the fiscal implications of the breaking of the dam already identified as regards real output and inflation. In 1990, the budget deficit was of a different order of magnitude from what it had been previously. Furthermore, the deficit shown in the table is the cash deficit: in 1990 it would have been even larger but for the moratorium of foreign debt service which was in place for most of the year.

Table 7.1 State budget as percentage of GDP, 1987–90

	1987	1988	1989	1990
Revenue	59.5	56.9	58.3	54.3
Tax revenue	46.3	47.4	49.7	43.9
Expenditure	59.0	58.4	58.9	59.3
Current expenditure	52.7	53.0	53.4	56.2
Deficit	−0.5	1.5	0.6	4.9

Source: Bulgarian National Bank

---

3 The figures in this section refer to the State budget, which includes the Republican (or central) budget, regional and municipal budgets and the Social Security Fund. A brief description of budgetary organization can be found in Chand and Lorie (1993).

The Revenue System

We start by describing the tax system which Bulgaria had as it faced into transition. Table 7.2 reveals the structure of revenue from taxes.

Table 7.2 Structure of tax revenue, 1987–90

(a) Percentage of total tax revenue

	1987	1988	1989	1990
Profits tax[a]	40.9	44.7	47.0	51.9
Income tax	8.6	8.5	8.4	
Turnover tax[b]	28.6	11.7	10.2	23.5
Excises	–	12.8	12.6	
Customs duties	0.9	1.7	1.7	
Social security[c]	20.6	20.0	19.5	25.4

(b) Percentage of GDP

	1987	1988	1989	1990
Profits tax[a]	18.9	21.2	23.4	22.8
Income tax	4.0	4.0	4.2	
Turnover tax[b]	13.3	5.5	5.1	10.0
Excises	–	6.1	6.3	
Customs duties	0.4	0.8	0.8	
Social security[c]	9.5	9.5	9.7	11.2

[a] 1990 includes income tax
[b] 1990 includes excises and customs duties
[c] Net of contributions made by the government as an employer
Source: Bulgarian National Bank

The most obvious features of Table 7.2 are the significance of profits taxes, taxes on domestic consumption and social security contributions, and the relative unimportance of personal income taxes.

Profits taxes consisted (and still consist since, at the time of writing, a new profits tax law had yet to be passed, these taxes being governed by Decree 56 and its amendments) of three imposts: a state profits tax (which was at a rate of 50 per cent but is now 40 per cent in the general case, with lower rates for agriculture and tourism and higher rates for financial institutions), a municipal tax at 10 per cent, and a 2 per cent levy for the Irrigation Fund. However, the effective rate on any given enterprise could be varied downwards by the intervention of the Council of Ministers if that enterprise had liquidity difficulties. This latter provision would have had less relevance if taxable profits had been defined as is normal in market economies: it was relevant in Bulgaria because the tax base was defined to include certain expenses, notably interest, and so what in western terms would have been loss-making enterprises could find themselves with a liability to profits taxes.

Personal incomes were taxed by a schedular system with markedly different rate structures according to the source of income. Four separate taxes were in operation: a tax on wages and salaries; a tax on individual labour services and private business activity; a tax on cultural activity; and a tax on rental incomes and dividends. Personal interest incomes (from bank deposits) were not taxed. At the time of writing, this system is still in operation. In addition, social security contributions were paid at a rate of 30 per cent (now 35 per cent) on wages and salaries and 20 per cent by self-employed professionals.

The turnover tax, while having its rates expressed as percentages of the retail price, did not function in the same way as turnover taxes in the West. The retail price was set by the planners and was the sum of the producer's price, the wholesale margin, the retail margin and the turnover tax. The tax was just another administered component of the final price and was in fact collected at the producer's level. Until 1988, there were over 2,000 separate rates according to commodity. In that year, the number of rates was reduced to 43, ranging from 5 to 70 per cent of the retail price (that is, these were tax-inclusive rates). There was a substantial range of final goods exempt from the tax, and *de facto* negative rates were applied in cases where costs rose but the authorities did not wish these increases to be reflected in the retail price. This latter factor explains the relative decline in the importance of the turnover tax in the late 1980s, when material input prices rose significantly. Transactions in intermediate goods were not liable to turnover tax.

In late 1990 there was a further simplification of the rate structure to three rates: zero on basic foodstuffs. children's clothing, household energy use and public transport; 10 per cent on less basic foods; and 20 per cent on other consumer items.

The 1988 reform of the turnover tax was accompanied by the introduction of excises on a narrow range of goods such as alcoholic drinks, tobacco, coffee, petroleum products, cars and minor 'luxury' items. Excisable goods were not subject to turnover tax. It will be noted that the revenue from these excises immediately overtook that from the turnover tax.

Under the old system, customs duties were of negligible importance in revenue terms. This was partially because of defects in customs administration, but mainly because there was a device which was the economic equivalent of a tariff, was lucrative for the government, but was recorded as non-tax revenue. The revenue in question came from two main sources — what were called 'coefficient differences' and 'price differences'. They were essentially the product of arbitrage opportunities available to a government which controlled the (multiple) exchange rates and all domestic prices. The former arose because the (mono)bank's foreign assets and liabilities were valued at the official rates whereas foreign transactions by bank customers were recorded at the market rate. The resulting discrepancies were credited to the government as revenue.[4] The latter item reflected the extent to which the domestic price of import-competing goods exceeded the import price at the market exchange rate.[5]

Public Expenditure[6]

Nothing so graphically illustrates the fiscal role of governments under socialism as the structure of public expenditure, especially as regards subsidies and social security benefits. As will be seen from Table 7.3, the high figures for these items go a long way to explain the excess of

---

4 Or debited, if the lev were stronger in the market than at the official rate. In practice, in recent years there were growing credits to government.

5 This again could be negative and so result in an expenditure by government, but this happened only briefly in the mid-1980s.

6 As is normal in government accounting in most countries, the figures in this section are on a cash basis. In fact, the use of this rather than an accrual basis has little effect on the figures shown here, except for debt interest in 1990, the year the moratorium on the service of foreign debt was introduced. This failure to meet commitments had a much greater impact in later years.

the expenditure/GDP ratio over what would be more normal in
developed market economies. It is appropriate here to give a brief
description of the web of subsidization in which the Bulgarian
government was enmeshed under the old system.

Table 7.3 Structure of public expenditure, 1987–90

(a) Percentage of total public expenditure

	1987	1988	1989	1990
Current operations	40.5	39.6	41.2	40.5
Subsidies	29.1	30.2	26.4	25.0
Debt interest	2.4	3.5	5.2	8.8
Social security	17.3	17.4	17.7	20.3
Capital	10.7	9.2	9.4	5.2

(b) Percentage of GDP

	1987	1988	1989	1990
Current operations	24.0	23.1	24.2	24.1
Subsidies	17.2	17.6	15.6	14.9
Debt interest	1.4	2.1	3.1	5.3
Social security	10.2	10.2	10.4	12.0
Capital	6.3	5.4	5.5	3.1

Source: Bulgarian National Bank

As already noted, subsidies (and commodity taxes) were an inherent
part of the planning mechanism: at any stage in the process of
production and distribution, they were deliberate wedges inserted
between input and output prices. They were used to maintain a
distortion over a long period of time (for example, to provide a below-
cost price for household energy use or to resolve the conflict between
the need to set agricultural producer prices at levels consistent with
production incentives and the desire to keep retail food prices low) or
to insulate users from exogenous shocks in input prices.

Subsidies can be divided into those related to international economic
relations (trade and debt) and those relating to domestic transactions.

Perhaps the single most important distortion created by the planning mechanism was the insulation of domestic prices from international prices and, aside from the administered exchange rate, the most important mechanism for this was the pattern of subsidies on traded goods. On the import side, the subsidy was simply the negative side of the 'price differences' already mentioned in relation to non-tax revenue: if import prices exceeded domestic wholesale prices, the difference was covered by a subsidy to the importer. Similarly on the export side, where a subsidy was paid if the domestic export price exceeded the foreign price.

Subsidies relating to foreign debt became very important in the late 1980s as that debt increased rapidly to a very high level. Most of this debt was created to finance imports by enterprises: it was a liability of the BFTB who sold the foreign currency to enterprises through a domestic counterpart credit at the administered interest rate. The difference between the latter and the rate payable on the foreign debt, plus any exchange losses, were covered by a subsidy to the BFTB.

There were three main categories of domestic subsidies. First, there were subsidies to unprofitable enterprises to maintain the material balances in the plan, to underpin the planned price structure and to maintain employment. The main beneficiaries were in metallurgy, chemicals, engineering and food processing. Secondly, to improve production incentives by raising output prices without raising retail prices, subsidies were paid to agricultural producers. Thirdly, there was direct subsidization of the retail price of certain consumer items, notably foodstuffs, this being essentially a negative version of the turnover tax.

THE FISCAL SYSTEM IN TRANSITION

Movements in the overall budgetary situation have already been reviewed (Chapters 2 and 3 above): concern here is with the impact of transition on the structure of the budget.

Tax revenue as a proportion of GDP had begun to decline in 1990 (see Table 7.1 above), and from Table 7.4 it will be seen that this decline has continued steadily ever since, being in 1993 17 percentage points of GDP below the peak reached in 1989. On the other hand, expenditure fell sharply in 1991, but has recovered in the past two years until, in 1993, it was within five points of GDP of the level reached in 1990.

Table 7.4 State budget as percentage of GDP, 1991–93

	1991	1992	1993
Revenue	42.7	43.8	42.1
Tax revenue	37.1	34.7	32.6
Expenditure	47.0	48.7	55.0
Current expenditure	45.0	45.6	51.8
Deficit	4.3	5.0	12.9

Source: Ministry of Finance and Bulgarian National Bank

On the revenue side, the spectacular collapse was in revenue from profits taxation — the result, as already noted, of the financial difficulties of the enterprise sector and the move towards western methods of determining taxable profits. From Table 7.5, it can be seen that this tax, which used to be the most significant provider of state revenue, delivered a mere 9 per cent of total tax revenue and 3 per cent of GDP in 1993, compared with 47 per cent and 23 per cent respectively in its heyday in 1989. Personal income tax remains unimportant relative to GDP though of course the decline in profits tax revenue has increased the relative importance of personal tax in the revenue system. It must be expected that, as non-wage personal incomes and private-sector employment increase in significance, this tax will begin to assume the importance it has in market economies, but only if reforms in its structure and administration are effected urgently (see below).

Another revenue workhorse, the turnover tax, had, as we have already seen, declined sharply in importance after the reforms in 1988, although this decline had been balanced by the buoyant revenue from the new excises. The impact of liberalization on consumption is reflected in the reduction in the combined revenues from these taxes in 1991 and 1992, as a proportion both of total revenue and GDP. In 1993, domestic consumption taxation began to pick up in relative terms, for two reasons. First, the base of these taxes revived as a proportion of GDP, not because they grew in real terms but because the base of other taxes continued to fall rapidly. That is, there was an increase in the ratio of consumption to GDP, and there was an increase in real demand for excisable products as small groups in the population experienced an increase in real income. Secondly, the collection mechanism for turnover tax had begun to adjust to price liberalization.

Table 7.5   Structure of tax revenue, 1991–93

(a) Percentage of total tax revenue

	1991	1992	1993
Profits tax	35.6	21.9	9.2
Income tax	17.9	15.9	16.4
Turnover tax	9.4	10.9	12.4
Excises	8.9	7.4	12.3
Customs duties	2.8	6.4	9.9
Social security	22.0	30.9	32.4

(b) Percentage of GDP

	1991	1992	1993
Profits tax	13.2	7.6	3.0
Income tax	6.6	5.5	5.3
Turnover tax	3.5	3.8	4.0
Excises	3.3	2.6	4.0
Customs duties	1.0	2.2	3.2
Social security	8.2	10.7	10.5

Source: Ministry of Finance and Bulgarian National Bank

At the time of writing, detailed figures on the composition of revenue in 1994 were not available, but preliminary data indicate two favourable features. First. the decline in revenue from profits taxation as a proportion of GDP appears to have been arrested. Secondly, the new VAT, which replaced the turnover tax in April, performed markedly better than would have been expected, given the administrative difficulties which attended its introduction.

The most buoyant aspect of revenue in the past four years has, as would have been expected, been customs duties. Liberalization of trade has shifted the relative demand for imports and domestic production and, although there are perennial complaints about the efficiency of the customs service as a revenue-collector, import duties are easy to collect. As a result, by 1993 these duties had outstripped profits taxes as a source of revenue. This process cannot be expected to continue because, unless exports rise relative to GDP, the relative base of customs duties will have to be restrained by monetary measures.

Social security contributions, whose base is wages, remain important and recent movements in their contribution to revenue reflect three counterbalancing influences — the serious decline in employment in the state sector where such contributions are easy to collect, the degree of success in restraining real wage growth in the state sector, and the collapse of profits which has increased the proportion of GDP accounted for by wages. The future importance of these taxes depends on two factors. First, a completely new administrative system is required to impose the liability for these contributions on the private sector: at present it is a reasonable conjecture that they are being paid solely by the state sector. Secondly, and more fundamentally, reform of the whole social security system is urgent. The number of pensioners now approximates to the number of persons employed in the state sector (essentially, the number paying contributions), which must be the highest dependency ratio in the world. In 1993, expenditure from the Social Security Fund exceeded its income by over 30 per cent, the balance being covered by transfers from the central budget. Eligibility terms have to be reviewed (most men currently qualify for pensions at 60 years of age and women at 55 years, and in some occupations the qualifying ages are even lower) and the entire system of financing such benefits needs to be questioned.

The structure of public expenditure has been dominated by the impact of transition on subsidies and social security benefits and by the effects on interest payments of the increase in the budget deficit from 1990 onwards. The relevant figures are shown in Table 7.6. An essential part of the liberalization package was the abolition of most of the huge structure of subsidization of the enterprise sector and certain retail prices which had been such an important aspect of fiscal operations under communism. In 1990, subsidies had accounted for 25 per cent of public expenditure, or 15 per cent of GDP, and even then they had declined somewhat compared with earlier years (see Table 7.3 above). The big bang of February 1991 reduced these at a stroke, the respective 1991 figures being 9 per cent and 4 per cent respectively. There was some reversal of trend in 1993, especially because of the extreme difficulties in the energy sector, but these items now pale into insignificance compared with their earlier levels.

Table 7.6 Structure of public expenditure, 1991–93

(a) Percentage of total public expenditure

	1991	1992	1993
Current operations	43.8	46.2	39.9
Subsidies	8.8	5.9	6.9
Debt interest	13.1	14.3	19.0
Social security	27.2	28.6	28.4
Capital	4.2	6.5	5.7

(b) Percentage of GDP

	1991	1992	1993
Current operations	20.6	22.5	21.9
Subsidies	4.1	2.9	3.8
Debt interest	6.1	7.0	10.4
Social security	12.8	13.9	15.9
Capital	2.0	3.2	3.2

Source: Ministry of Finance and Bulgarian National Bank

Debt interest is growing rapidly in importance, even in cash terms, because of the need to service the domestic debt incurred in financing the greatly increased scale of budget deficits. There was also, in 1992 and 1993, some resumption of interest payments on foreign debt, but this was comparatively unimportant. In 1994, interest can be expected to increase to even higher levels as a proportion of total expenditure and GDP: the budget deficit, totally financed domestically, jumped to almost 13 per cent of GDP — or more than double the ratio in the previous year; the new *ZUNK* bonds have to be serviced; and with the London Club agreement (see Chapter 5 above) the moratorium on the servicing of foreign debt came to an end.

Social security payments are affected by two factors — the demographic profile which has produced an increasing trend in the ratio of pensioners to the labour force, and the large increase in unemployment which first became significant in 1991. The latter should prove to be a relatively declining fiscal burden, the number of persons registering for unemployment benefits having reached what may be expected to have been its peak in the early part of 1994.

What is called in the tables 'current operations' is dominated by the salaries of government and municipal employees and has remained quite stable in relative terms, for obvious reasons. It is difficult to do much about this item. There is probably still some overmanning of activities which were important to the planning system, but transition itself creates a demand for public manpower: large numbers of staff have had to be recruited for the tax administration and there is evidence that progress on privatization and land-restitution is being inhibited by a lack of staff. Nor are salary levels in the public service any more at governmental discretion than they are in existing market economies. Average levels are driven by a combination of a rigid structure with uniformity across ministries at each grade and growing competition from the private sector for both existing professionals and new, well-qualified staff.

Finally, as in all countries which have fiscal problems, capital expenditure is the one item which can technically be reduced quickly. The decline in public investment relative to GDP began in the mid-1980s and has continued, with a small revival in the past two years in an effort to arrest the serious deterioration in the quality of public infrastructure. This item will continue to be the fiscal shock-absorber, though some further increase in its relative importance can be expected because of the availability of project-based finance from international agencies.

It has already been noted that the central, structural issue for the fiscal system is tax reform and we turn to this now.

GENERAL ISSUES OF TAX REFORM

In market economies, the past two decades have seen a steady process of tax reform which has been remarkably consistent across countries in its main thrust.

Any policy change involves losers and gainers and such change is easier to effect the smaller the number of losers relative to gainers. Nonetheless, losers tend to be the more vociferous group and they rarely, in any country, lack for public representatives who seize the opportunity to gain political advantage from this discontent. This is especially the case with a change in tax policy, where it is easy to identify in advance who will gain and who lose by the change.

Politicians are also more obviously associated with tax policy than with perhaps any other aspect of economic policy. Tax policy is therefore inevitably very highly politicized. This is the case in all countries and explains why tax reform tends to be a gradual process.

However, in transition economies, such reform cannot be gradualist: the old revenue systems simply cannot deliver what is required. Such economies therefore, on the one hand, have the advantage that they have the experience of the rest of the world to guide them but, on the other, cannot afford the time which, elsewhere, has been deemed necessary as a lubricant for what is a politically difficult exercise.

Before looking at Bulgaria explicitly, we review very briefly the prescriptions which tax economists have been pressing on governments in market economies and which are now being enjoined on transition economies.[7] The analysis of tax policy is usually organized around the three principles of economic efficiency, equity and administrative efficiency and this schema will be adopted here.

Economic efficiency is the need that taxes should not interfere with the allocation of resources. Strictly speaking, this does not mean that taxes should be uniform (for instance, that sales taxes should impose the same rate on all transactions), but the information required to design non-uniform taxes which are economically superior to uniform taxes is never available and so a reasonable rule of thumb indicates the desirability of uniformity. Such a prescription is markedly different from the tax systems prevalent in formerly planned economies, even after the reforms implemented in the last days of communism.

Horizontal equity refers to the equality of treatment of those in similar situations. At a fundamental level, it is no more than the application to taxation of the principle of equality before the law, but it is of particular economic interest because it can imply the kind of non-discriminatory taxes referred to in the previous paragraph. Vertical equity is concerned with the effect of taxes on the distribution of net incomes: how should the tax treatment of persons vary with their income? Some kind of redistribution, or special treatment for the least well-off in society, is clearly desirable, but most taxes (the personal income tax being the obvious exception) are not as effective at achieving distributional

---

7 For a more thorough discussion, see Gandhi and Mihaljek (1992) and Holzmann (1992).

objectives as are other fiscal instruments and so there is here potentially yet another argument in favour of non-discriminatory taxes.

Administrative efficiency has tended to take a back seat in academic discussions of tax policy, but it takes on a special importance in countries, such as those of most interest here, whose systems of tax administration are poorly developed. There is no point in prescribing taxes which cannot be effectively administered because the incidence of such taxes then becomes arbitrary and not at all what the designers intended. Furthermore, to spend more than a small proportion of revenue on collecting that revenue is simply wasteful. Here again, non-discriminatory taxes have advantages because they are simple. For example, if a sales tax has only one rate or an income tax does not distinguish according to the source of income, it is easier for the responsible taxpayer to comply with the law, harder to avoid or evade tax, and easier for the authorities to audit tax payments.

In applying these general notions to reforming socialist economies, what we say below is broadly representative of a consensus among tax economists.[8]

Taxes on Consumption

These taxes are, in market economies, growing in importance relative to so-called direct taxes because they are in principle less distortionary than income taxes and have a high revenue capacity at comparatively low nominal tax rates. As already noted, the turnover taxes prevalent in planned economies are impracticable in a liberalized economy and have to be replaced. In economic terms, the obvious candidate is a retail sales tax, but the large number of retail outlets (and therefore taxpayers), combined with the ill-developed state of tax administration in transition economies, makes such a tax equally impracticable. Even in developed economies with sophisticated revenue-collection machinery, retail sales taxes are difficult to police. For this reason, the value-added tax (VAT), which is economically equivalent to a retail sales tax but has superior

---

8 It is only fair to mention an almost lone dissenter from this consensus, Charles McClure: see McClure (1992) and, for a statement explicitly in the context of Bulgaria, McClure (1991). McClure's arguments are directly challenged in Tait (1992).

administrative qualities, is now emerging as the dominant form of consumption taxation.[9]

A VAT operates at each stage from importation/manufacture through to retail level (for both goods and services), but avoids cascading by granting credits at each stage for the tax charged at the previous stage. This multi-stage collection, combined with the need for documentation to support claims for credits, makes the VAT less vulnerable to evasion than a purely retail tax. As long as adequate investment is made in information systems and taxpayer education, it is a very simple tax to administer.

The aforementioned criteria of a good tax imply that a VAT should have as few as possible rates — ideally only a zero rate and a single positive rate with minimal exemptions.[10] Since this is supposed to be a tax on domestic consumption, and nothing else, exports should be zero-rated and capital purchases charged to tax, with the appropriate credit given for the latter.

Governments implementing VAT have considerable difficulty with the uniformity prescription because they often insist on mitigating the regressivity of the tax by zero-rating or having special low rates on such items as food, often combined with a gradation of several rates according to the degree of 'luxury' of the good or service. Such a temptation is particularly acute in transition economies which have been used to extreme non-uniformity in turnover taxes and even negative taxation of certain consumption items. Non-uniformity of this kind is nevertheless misguided because it seriously increases administrative cost without contributing to efficient income-redistribution.

A VAT which attempted to cover all importers, manufacturers, wholesalers and retailers would clearly involve excessive administrative

---

9 See Tait (1991) for the international development of this tax and its structural and administrative characteristics.

10 Zero-rating means that no tax is payable on sales and credit is received from tax passed on from the previous stage (this usually means the payment of rebates, which is administratively cumbersome and is one reason why the ideal VAT restricts zero-rating to exports). On the other hand, an exempt transaction pays no VAT but attracts no credit. The purest recommendation is to restrict exemption to transactions, such as those by financial intermediaries, for which a credit-type VAT is unsuitable.

cost. For this reason, the tax is usually applied only to sellers above a certain threshold in size. The proportion of the potential base lost in this way is very much less than the proportion of potential taxpayers who are excluded.

Value-added taxes would typically, and justifiably, be complemented by a set of excises on the importation or domestic manufacture of a narrow range of goods such as tobacco, alcoholic drink, petroleum products and motor vehicles. If limited to these kind of products which have a relatively low price-elasticity of demand, such excises are excellent revenue-raisers and are relatively non-distortionary. They are also cheap to administer because there are few collection points.

Personal Income Tax

Personal taxes were not important under socialism but they are important in developed market economies and so major reform is to be expected in this area. The principles enunciated above suggest the desirability of a comprehensive, or global, income tax, which would be a significant departure from earlier practice which applied different schedules to different types of income. The essence of a comprehensive income tax is that all income is treated equally (that is, only the amount of income, and not its source, is relevant) and that the only deductions allowed are for expenses incurred in earning taxable income or are related to the existence of persons dependent on a taxpayer. The main issue of principle on which opinion varies concerns the unit of taxation: that is, should each person be treated individually or should the incomes of spouses be aggregated for tax purposes? Income need not be in monetary form and would include capital gains as they accrue.

No country has a comprehensive income tax (notably, for administrative reasons, capital gains are never taxed until they are realized) but the thrust of income tax reform throughout the world is in the direction of such a tax, with the removal of the schedular treatment of different types of income, improved taxation of non-monetary income and the abolition of exemptions for certain kinds of receipts and of deductions for expenditures not associated with the earning of taxable income. Such reform is sometimes called 'broadening the base' and has been associated with moves to reduce both the level of marginal rates and the number of such rates. This simplification of the rate structure has not, in general, resulted in the income tax becoming less progressive since the base-broadening has usually involved the abolition of deductions or exemptions the benefit from which had been concentrated in the hands of those with higher incomes. This is a very important consideration for transition economies, where there is typically greater concern than in traditional market economies to have a redistributive fiscal system.

For transition economies, the speed with which a global income tax can be implemented depends upon administrative capacity. The most effective way of administering a personal tax is to make maximum use of withholding at source and there is no doubt that this is simpler to do with a schedular system since the determination of tax liability does not then require that an individual's income from various sources be aggregated. But this need not be a serious problem. As long as the schedules have common definitions of income, deductions and nominal rate structures, the lower the degree of progressivity the nearer a schedular tax becomes to a global tax in its incidence — another argument for a simple rate structure with a fairly low top marginal rate.

Taxation of Enterprise Profits

Of course, profits taxation will inevitably become less important than it has been to the revenue systems of formerly planned economies: in OECD countries it accounts for less than 10 per cent of tax revenue on average. However, nowhere is there greater opportunity to introduce complexity and distortion into a tax system than in the treatment of profits: not only did the old systems contain seriously arbitrary elements where enterprises bargained over their tax liabilities, but the formal structure was excessively complex and was riddled with inter-enterprise discrimination.[11] Nowhere is there a greater temptation (not resisted in many market economies) to introduce discriminatory 'incentives' to reward behaviour deemed to be especially desirable. Tax holidays for foreign investors have to be paid for by domestic taxpayers; exemptions or other special concessions for certain sectors create the need for higher taxation on other sectors than would otherwise be necessary; and

---

11 It is taken for granted here that western accounting systems have been implemented before tax reform takes place, and so the appropriate definition of profit can also be taken as read.

— on the principle that what is termed an incentive could equally well be called a loophole — discrimination not only distorts behaviour but creates opportunities for avoidance (or evasion, by falsifying accounts) which are expensive for the administration to police.

What this implies is the need for a single nominal rate, for simple depreciation rules which do not discriminate between activities, for no tax holidays for foreign investment,[12] and for no sectoral exemptions or other concessions.

Customs Duties

These were, even formally, unnecessary under planning: they were not needed for protection because of the existence of quantitative restrictions on imports and because the exchange rate was administered, and were not needed for revenue because — as was noted for Bulgaria — they had an exact revenue equivalent in the 'price differences'. The removal of quantitative restrictions and the liberalization of the exchange rate has changed all this.

The economic issue here concerns the optimal level and structure of protection but a discussion of this would lead too far afield. There is certainly little point in liberalizing trade in order to introduce competition into the domestic economy and then imposing tariffs high enough to protect domestic activity from such competition. Some protection is surely justified to give a breathing space for restructuring, but of most interest here is the contribution of tariffs to revenue. As long as they are reasonably uniform and easy to operate, they have the admirable characteristic that there are very few points of collection compared with other taxes — an advantage which should not be overlooked where tax administrations are rudimentary.

---

12 This is probably a counsel of perfection in a region where competition to attract western investment is intense, notwithstanding the lack of evidence that such holidays are of any lasting benefit to the country receiving the investment.

Tax Administration[13]

From this large subject, just two items need be emphasized here. First, governments need to recognize that investment in effective tax administrations will pay good dividends especially since it is probably true that administrative improvements will have a greater pay-off in terms of additional revenue than any feasible change in tax structure. This is particularly true in transition economies, where governments probably think they already had tax administrations, whereas they did not. Major reorganization, personnel training and taxpayer education is required.

Secondly, a significant cultural shift is required, not so much on the part of taxpayers (whose degree of civic sense over taxes varies greatly among countries), but on the part of tax collectors. Under the old system, the relationship between payers and collectors was both too antagonistic and too close. The modern approach to tax collection is to assist compliance and encourage responsible taxpayers rather assuming that all clients are criminally inclined. It was too close in that those responsible for assessment and audit were essentially part of the same bureaucracy as those liable for turnover or profits taxes: bargaining, while to a degree an inescapable part of any user-friendly system of administration, was central to the procedure. This has implications for the form of organization, with the need to change from one where the same official exercises all functions (assessment, collection and audit) relating to one tax paid by a particular set of enterprises to one where an official is responsible for only one of these functions but exercises that function with respect to a range of taxes. This eases the problem of the informational flows needed to cross-check returns for various taxes and minimizes the likelihood of the abuse of an excessively close relationship between the payer and the collector.

TAX REFORM IN BULGARIA

A cynic would expect this section to be very short since one of the most disappointing, and harmful, aspects of Bulgaria's transition policies has been the slow progress on tax reform. The VAT was long delayed and

---

13 For a more thorough treatment, see Casanegra de Jantscher et al. (1992).

there is still no new income or profits tax. Nonetheless, a basic tax administration code has been enacted, as have laws on excises and VAT, and we now review these items.

Value-Added Tax

Bulgaria's VAT went through a prolonged and tortuous design and legislative process before it came into operation on 1 April 1994. The first steps were taken as long ago as May 1991 and, at that stage, an implementation date of July 1992 was envisaged. This was never realistic since hardly any country in the world has taken so little time to implement a VAT. By early 1992 the target date had been set back to January 1993. In June 1992 draft VAT and excise laws were sent for consideration by the Assembly but they did not pass the first reading until March 1993, at which time it was declared that VAT-Day would be 1 July 1993. This was in any case unrealistic since the vital administrative developments had been delayed but, be that as it may, final parliamentary approval was not given until October 1993.

The VAT was designed in accordance with the EU's Sixth Directive and, indeed, is in many respects superior in structure to the equivalent taxes currently prevailing in several EU member states, the latter engaging in excessive zero-rating and multiple rates. Western European VATs were the pioneers and still carry the relics of the political concerns of the time of their institution, and Bulgaria has had the good sense to learn from the experience of others.

The new tax is admirably simple in structure, with zero-rating restricted to exports and a single rate of 18 per cent. The main structural complexities arise from the rather large number of exemptions. As is necessary, financial intermediation is exempt and, as might be expected, so are education and health services and transactions under a privatization programme. Gambling is exempt and so are land transfers and the rental of land and buildings, but the transfer of buildings, including housing, is not exempt (though, of course, most sales by owner-occupiers would be effectively exempt as a result of the turnover threshold — see below). The tax is rather confused in its relative treatment of rented and owner-occupied buildings and this reflects a more general confusion over the treatment of second-hand goods.

The main concession to distributional concerns over the replacement of the turnover tax by VAT is that certain goods which attracted zero or low rates under the latter are exempt from VAT for three years. These are bread, staple dairy products, energy for domestic use, school textbooks and medicines. Household energy (electricity, heating and solid fuel) is particularly sensitive because, as we have seen, the movement towards world prices has, since 1990, caused a dramatic increase in the real price of this item and so, given the general apprehension about the introduction of VAT, this attempt to sugar the pill is understandable. However, these exemptions should not be allowed to become permanent and the political challenge will have to be met in 1997.

In a medium-income country with a reasonably effective administration, a VAT with a rate in the high 'teens might be expected to generate revenue equivalent to about 8 per cent of GDP. In a transition economy where, because of the depression of investment, consumption (the base of the VAT) represents an above-average proportion of GDP, one might expect the revenue capacity of this tax to be somewhat higher than this, but this is probably offset by a below-average administrative capability in such countries in the short term. If the 8 per cent target were achieved immediately in Bulgaria, the VAT would bring in more than has been achieved by the turnover tax in the past three years. In fact, as already noted (see Chapter 3 above), VAT in 1994, when it was in operation for only nine months, generated revenue equal to 7.4 per cent of GDP, an achievement which reflects either the fact that consumption is a higher proportion of GDP than one would have estimated or administrative efficiency greater than one would have been expected. Whichever is the explanation, this result is a tribute to the revenue capacity of this tax.

A universal concern is over the effect on inflation when a VAT is introduced. In this context a distinction must be drawn between a once-for-all increase in the general price level and the perpetuation of that increase through, for example, a wage–price spiral. In general, one might expect that a revenue-neutral substitution of VAT for an existing sales tax would have no major impact on prices (though there may be some if there is a significant change in the relative taxation of different goods). If the substitution is revenue-enhancing (as it would be expected to be in Bulgaria), then there are two offsetting effects: an initial price increase accompanied by a reduction in the budget deficit, which is counter-inflationary. In a study of 35 countries which had introduced VAT, it was found that in 22 there were no overall price effects, in eight there was a once-for-all shift in the price level, and in the remaining six VAT contributed to inflation but in all such cases wage and monetary policies were not counter-inflationary.[14] In the Bulgarian case, we have already noted that the large nominal devaluation of the lev would account for the major proportion of the jump in prices in April, 1994. However, it is likely that the introduction of VAT did cause a shift in the price level, primarily because of consumer expectations that it would have that effect and because sellers exercised monopoly power to take the opportunity to increase prices to a greater extent than the tax-substitution itself warranted. In any case, the substitution was meant to be revenue-enhancing to some degree and so a price shift would be expected. Thus, the introduction of VAT was probably slightly inflationary but it pales into insignificance when compared with the effect of the almost simultaneous devaluation.

The compulsory registration threshold is a turnover of BGL1.5 million in the previous year, with voluntary registration for smaller traders. This made sense when it was first thought of in 1991, but subsequent inflation almost certainly makes this threshold too low and will increase the costs of administration by increasing the number of taxpayers. The law makes no provision for indexing the threshold to the consumer price index, or even for periodic, discretionary increases through the issue of regulations. This issue will have to be addressed if inflation continues at a high level.

Excises

As already noted, excises had been introduced in 1989 when the turnover tax was simplified, but they were put on a firmer footing by a new law passed in March 1994 which repealed not only past excise legislation, but also the turnover tax, thus paving the way for VAT. The base of the VAT, as is universal practice, includes any excises (and customs duties) payable on the relevant transaction. Excises are chargeable on the producer of dutiable items when they are sold or on the importer at the time of importation.

If the structure of indirect taxation reveals something about a country's culture, then the excise duty law shows Bulgaria to be a mixture of

---

14 Tait (1991), pp. 7–9.

liberalism and puritanism. As to the former, the specific duty rates on alcohol and tobacco are low, even as a percentage of the retail price — 1.5 leva on a litre of beer, six leva on a litre of wine and between two and 20 leva on a packet of cigarettes.[15] This may reflect not so much social attitudes to drinking and smoking as the fact that the country is a major producer of tobacco and alcoholic drink, but the puritanism is less ambiguous. Gambling, while exempt from VAT, is subject to heavy excises: lotteries pay duty at 50 per cent and it costs the operator BGL3 million per quarter (at the time of writing nearly $50,000) to run a roulette table. Entrance to a night club carries a duty of 50 per cent and so-called 'erotic' products pay 70 per cent. The latter is certainly a sop to those who complained that 'decent' literature and pornography were treated equally under the VAT (they are both liable). This is the kind of foolishness which tax-designers get into when they try to use taxation to reward and penalise what they approve and disapprove of respectively. The remainder of the duty schedule is fairly typical, covering coffee, tea, petroleum products, cars, and certain more luxurious products at a range of *ad valorem* rates, although here again the system has been complicated administratively, and to no revenue purpose, by a desire to appease envy over consumption of items such as VCRs, fur coats and jewellery.

The most important economic point relates to the use of specific rates (for alcohol, tobacco and some gambling) in times of high inflation. These rates were introduced at a time when inflation was running at an annual rate of around 100 per cent and the consequent erosion of the real value of excises is a serious defect in a system where these imposts are an important part of the revenue structure. Again, the law makes no provision for the regulatory increase of these rates and so, if they are to be increased in line with inflation, they have to run the gauntlet of parliamentary review. As with the VAT threshold, indexation or quite frequent regulatory adjustment would be desirable.

---

15 For instance, the excise on a packet of high-quality, imported cigarettes is less than one-third of the typical retail price, or a tax-exclusive rate of less than 50 per cent.

Personal Income Tax

At the time of writing, a reformed income tax had not been enacted, though draft laws have been circulating, and supposedly under parliamentary consideration, for several years. What follows in based on a recent draft, though it may have been overtaken. For this reason, a detailed critique would be inappropriate.

The most important point is that it is proposed to substitute a global tax, with aggregation across sources (with certain exceptions), for the current schedular system. The main exception relates to interest and dividend income which is to be charged at a flat rate and not included in the aggregation. This is certainly a simple, though imperfect, way of dealing with the possibility of the double taxation of dividends (see below) but is not appropriate for, for example, interest received on government securities (interest received on loans made is not treated in this way).

The tax base includes almost all incomes as usually defined, both monetary and in kind, and includes realized capital gains. One major exemption is of receipts under social insurance (which presumably includes public pensions), which is either unnecessary or inequitable. It is unnecessary if a person receives all or most of his income from such a source, and that income is lower than the personal allowance (which is proposed to be the minimum wage). It is inequitable if a person's income, including social benefits, exceeds that allowance since there is no reason to treat pensions or unemployment compensation more favourably than wages of the same amount. It is furthermore proposed to exempt farmers' incomes for five years after they gained possession of their land (or eight years for young families). Undoubtedly, the stimulation of agricultural productivity is an important policy objective in Bulgaria, but tax exemption is an inefficient way of doing this. The authorities do not know the value of the implicit subsidy and the scale of the subsidy rises as agricultural income rises, which is inequitable and inefficient. This kind of stimulus is better provided, if at all, through the expenditure side of the budget. However, a most welcome feature is that it is not proposed to favour other sectors or sub-sectors in this way.

As regards deductions, the draft law is fairly standard although it is confusing, and potentially unwise, as regards depreciation for unincorporated businesses. It suggests that the expense of acquiring fixed assets shall be written off for tax over two years and then says that depreciation will be in accordance with the provisions for the profits tax: it cannot be both. The proposed rate structure is as follows. The first part of income (which will equal the minimum wage — or 1.5 minimum wages for those with dependents,[16] or two minimum wages for single parents without alimony) is not taxed; the next slice represented by six minimum wages bears 15 per cent; the next slice, also of six minimum wages, pays at 30 per cent; and the remainder pays 40 per cent. This proposal is commendable in four respects. First, it is simple in having only three marginal rates: the 15 per cent is rather low and a structure of, perhaps, 25 and 40 per cent would have been even simpler to administer, but the proposed structure would be regarded as acceptable in a tax-reforming market economy. It is a great improvement over the current structure, which has eight rates above the exemption level, rising in steps of a mere four percentage points. Secondly, the top rate is not high by international standards and should not create severe disincentives to saving or work. Thirdly, the rate brackets are quite broad and so the top rate should not become effective for more than a small proportion of taxpayers. Finally, and very importantly in these inflationary times, the basic allowance and the rate brackets are not expressed in fixed, nominal terms, but in terms of the minimum wage which is revised upwards periodically (though not automatically) in response to inflation. This is most welcome as an antidote to the 'bracket creep' which can cause effective, real tax rates to move up in an unlegislated way when nominal incomes rise simply as a response to inflation. Again, this would be an improvement over the present tax, which defines the rate bands in leva.

With the VAT, a personal income tax capable of capturing a good base and contributing to efficiency in a market economy is an urgent requirement in a reformed fiscal system, and the failure, after four years of debate and redrafting, to put such a tax in place represents a policy failure of some magnitude.

---

16 The tax unit is the individual.

Taxation of Profits

Again, there is no reformed law in place (profits being taxed under Decree 56) and the discussion is based on a draft. In this case, however, a shorter discussion would be appropriate because in fact successive amendments to Decree 56 have produced a system of profits taxation quite similar to the draft new law. In any case, profits taxation is, if the experience of developed market economies is anything to go by, not going to have the same significance in the revenue system as VAT or personal income tax.

Profits taxation is everywhere extremely complex and the discussion here will be restricted to those aspects of most economic importance. Both the amended Decree 56 and the draft law impose a tax which is commendably uniform across sectors. There are no sectoral exemptions and only a minor difference in rates applies: currently, banks pay 50 per cent and all others 40 per cent, a distinction which is maintained in the draft law. Currently, private companies with a taxable profit less than BGL1 million are taxed at 30 per cent, but this concession, very sensibly, is not retained in the draft law.

Inter-sectoral discrimination used to exist as regards depreciation provisions, there being several thousand different rates according to the type of asset and the sector of use. This was typical of a planning mechanism disguised as a tax and has been radically reformed already. Decree 56 now allows seven rates, as does the draft law, with no distinction by sector.[17] The rates for plant are somewhat generous, but this kind of accelerated depreciation is reasonable at a time when technological improvement is crucial, and any distortion of factor choice will be minimal.

In an effort to preserve some of the base of the profits tax when western accounting methods were adopted, in 1991 state enterprises were permitted to deduct only 25 per cent of interest when computing taxable profit. This was increased to 50 per cent in 1992 and then to 75 per cent in 1993, a level it still retains. As is appropriate, the draft law

---

17 A quaint relic of old Marxian distinctions is preserved in a minor difference in the permitted rate on buildings, with those for 'production' treated slightly more favourably.

permits (with some restrictions relating to avoidance opportunities) the total deductibility of interest.

The treatment of dividends varies considerably in market economies. The US still uses the classical system in which the personal income tax as applied to shareholders takes no account of the profits tax already paid by the coroporation: this is economically inefficient and seriously distortionary as regards corporate finance. In Western Europe, most countries are moving towards an imputation system under which the shareholder, in being assessed for personal tax on dividends, receives credit for corporate tax paid on those dividends — a system which, if it works perfectly (which it rarely does) removes the aforementioned distortions. Bulgaria, according to the draft law, is adopting an intermediate measure which eliminates most of the defects of the classical system without involving the administrative complexities of the imputation system: a flat-rate withholding tax will be applied to dividends and no further liability will reside with the shareholder. It is not perfect, but is sensible.

Thus, despite the delays in passing the legislation for a completely new tax, Bulgaria has by stages transformed its old tax into something very near to what is required. With the depressed state of enterprise activity, it cannot be expected to generate a great deal of revenue in the near future, the main challenge being to ensure its effective applicability to the growing profits of the private sector.

8. Privatization

GENERAL ISSUES

One of the main characteristics of a market economy is that a very high proportion of GDP is generated by agencies which are privately owned, whereas one of the defining features of a transition economy is that most of GDP is generated by public agencies. It is therefore no wonder that privatization is seen as one of the core components of the transformation process. Its very centrality to the reorganization of whole economies makes privatization both complex and controversial and, before turning to Bulgarian experience, we need to review briefly the major general issues.[1]

Efficiency and Ownership

The issue here concerns the quest for profit. For various reasons to do with market failure, profit maximization is not a sufficient condition for either enterprise-level or overall economic efficiency. None the less, market failures are best dealt with by specific policies, such as regulation or taxation and the best starting point for improving efficiency in the allocation of resources is to encourage profitability at the enterprise level. On the very plausible assumption that an objective is most effectively pursued by those who will gain from its achievement, efficiency at the enterprise level is most likely to be achieved if those who would benefit from increased profitability have

---

1 Our review here is necessarily brief and therefore oversimplifies issues which are not only complex and controversial but on which there is very little relevant experience. For a discussion of the limits of knowledge on the dynamics of privatization, see Frydman and Rapaczynski (1994), Chapter 6.

a critical influence on the operations of the enterprise. Since profit is the return to ownership, this in turn implies that ownership matters.

Owners may be the state, private shareholders or employees (either because they are the beneficiaries of a shareholding scheme or, although they are not technically owners, because they have a collective agreement which gives them wage bonuses linked to the level of profit). Clearly, owners whose *only* interest in the enterprise is as a receiver of profit will, other things being equal, be more concerned to influence the enterprise's practices in the direction of increased profitability. Thus, workers will have a conflict of interest, their objective function having at least three possible arguments — the level of employment, the average wage level and the level of profit. Whether or not they will give primacy to profit-maximization therefore depends on, first, the way they trade off these objectives and, secondly, the way these factors interact.

The state also faces this kind of conflict. It has a two-fold interest in profitability, as shareholder (and dividend-receiver) and tax-collector, but this may be more than counterbalanced by the fact that it may attract political opprobrium if the profit-increasing policies of state enterprises raise output prices, reduce employment or reduce average wages below what they would have been. Furthermore, ministers or public officials charged with the oversight of such enterprises are agents of an amorphous public which is the real owner: their own wealth is not improved by an increase in profit.

This leaves the private shareholder as the only potential owner with an unambiguous interest in profitability and herein lies the kernel of the case for privatization. However, it will be noted that private ownership is not sufficient: the owners must have effective influence over the operating policies of the enterprise, and this is something not easy to achieve, especially if ownership is highly dispersed. First, with highly dispersed ownership, it is less likely that the wealth of any individual shareholder would be significantly affected by the financial performance of the enterprise and so no-one has the incentive to do the work necessary to influence the firm's policies. Secondly, with dispersed ownership, it is much more difficult to organize opposition to the policies of the existing board. This is of great consequence to the question of mass privatization schemes.

So, the efficiency argument for privatization is that only private owners have a clear incentive to push for increased profitability, but that this point is seriously weakened if owners have inadequate power to influence the firm's operations. It is also the case that monopoly power not only weakens the efficiency argument for profit-maximization but weakens the incentive for firm-level efficiency. However, *a priori* arguments generating hypotheses are a poor basis for a policy as dramatic as a major privatization programme. Is there any *evidence* regarding the relative efficiency of private and public enterprise? There is some,[2] but it is far from conclusive. It seems that efficiency is influenced more by the degree of competition than by the form of ownership. This last point indicates that the introduction of a competitive environment may be just as important as privatization in transition economies.

The research on which this tentative conclusion is based involved comparisons of activities in market economies and one must confess that it has limited relevance to the situation facing transition economies. It suggests that state or municipal authorities are, on occasion anyway, capable of enforcing satisfactory efficiency requirements on enterprises, but in these cases the public authority in question (a ministry or a local authority) would have only one or two enterprises under its aegis. This is quite different from the situation in Central and Eastern Europe, where a ministry could find itself responsible for several hundred enterprises and simply not have the administrative capacity to exercise effective oversight. Furthermore, although ministries in the West have been criticized for developing excessively close and supportive relationships with any public enterprises under their control, the line between the state bureaucracy and the enterprise management is usually reasonably clear. In formerly planned economies, however, the bi-directional information flows and negotiation on operational detail required by the planning mechanism meant that bureaucrats became in many respects part of the enterprise management. The planning mechanism itself also made endogenous many of the things which, in a market economy, are exogenous to the enterprise, such as input prices. Whether such officials could now develop the kind of ethos needed if they are to exercise an ownership function to stimulate efficiency in an environment where decision-making means responding to forces outside one's control is questionable.

---

2 See, for example, Vickers and Yarrow (1991), pp. 117–8.

The Irrelevance of Western Experience

It must be stressed that western experience of privatization is of dubious relevance to what is needed in transition economies. First, the British privatization boom of the 1980s involved only about 5 per cent of GDP. Secondly, privatization in market economies takes place in a situation where there exists considerable private wealth in sufficiently liquid form to be used to buy the state assets in question. Thirdly, the fact that the enterprises to be privatized in market economies have already been operating in a market environment makes judgements about their prospects acceptably certain and so makes their shares an acceptably risky investment. It is all so different in formerly centrally planned economies.

In Bulgaria, for instance, one is talking about the need to privatize or liquidate almost the whole of the industrial sector and, in total, assets which generate perhaps 95 per cent of GDP. The task is of such a different order of magnitude from what has been attempted in the West that little can be learned from the methods used to privatize public enterprises in market economies, where the process for privatizing a single enterprise could take several years and, usually, only perhaps three or four enterprises were in the privatization pipeline at any time.

Then, typically the median stock of household savings in transition economies is low, having been eroded by rapid inflation and the decline in real incomes, and there is considerable suspicion of the sources of wealth of the small proportion of the population who can afford to participate in commercially-based share issues. Apart from Bulgarians who have been living abroad for some time, the only nationals with a significant stock of liquid capital are likely to be those who were strategically placed under the old regime — including those who have engaged in 'informal' privatization — and those doing well from crime. In these circumstances, foreign investors will inevitably be in an especially favourable position and, although no sensible government places impediments on inward foreign investment, the idea of major portions of the capital stock of the country passing into foreign ownership is bound to be politically sensitive.

Finally, western privatization has invariably involved the public issue of shares at a price decided by the government, this price being strongly influenced by the government's objectives. In Britain, for example, most privatizations were immediately followed by a significant appreciation in the share value, indicating (on the assumption that the professional advice regarding the offer price was competent) that the primary objective was not to maximize fiscal revenue through setting a market-clearing share price. The inferred major objectives were, first, to avoid the embarrassment and loss of credibility which undersubscription would have created and, secondly, to create a large constituency which, as a result of the immediate capital gain accruing from the initial undervaluation, benefitted personally from privatization. These considerations have some applicability in transition economies but there is a huge difficulty in establishing an offer price, regardless of whether the objective is to clear the market or to create excess demand for a share. This is that, in the West, the market value of an enterprise due for privatization can be established within reasonably close limits. It has been subject to market forces (even if it has received overt or covert assistance or has been subject to politically motivated constraints, the impact of these factors on market performance can be reasonably well estimated) and the market environment in which it will operate after privatization is known with some certainty. This is not the case in Central and Eastern Europe, where corporate valuations are extremely difficult to establish. Balance sheet values are no guide since they are based on historic costs and nothing in the accounts gives a clue to the expected profitability of an enterprise which will be operating in a totally new environment, with competition from abroad, loss of major markets and non-administered prices for inputs and outputs. Valuations conducted to determine an offer price are therefore often little better than random numbers.[3] The wide divergence between the 'official' valuation and the valuation placed on assets by potential buyers is an important part of the explanation as to why privatization of large enterprises has turned out to be a long drawn-out process.

Methods of Privatization

As already noted, the simple western approach of commercial share issues is unlikely to be sufficient to effect privatization on the necessary scale in transition economies. In fact, a wide range of methods has been

---

3 Frydman and Rapaczynski (1994), pp. 41–3, present a case study illustrating some of the difficulties in generating objective valuations.

tried in Central and Eastern Europe and the former Soviet Union, with some difference in emphasis from country to country.[4]

The central objective of privatization is to provide an operating and control environment for enterprises which is conducive to improvements in economic efficiency. However, there are sub-objectives, the potential conflicts among which explain the heterogeneity of privatization practice and experience within the region. Among these other objectives are a desire to halt informal privatization by which enterprise managers are using state assets for their private purposes; a desire to use the proceeds of asset sales to support the state budget or to redeem public debt; the desire to attract foreign investment while countering political fears that foreign economic influence will become excessive; a desire to use privatization as a means of achieving a more uniform distribution of private wealth; and a desire to give privileges to existing employees of an enterprise (either for the quasi-political reason of giving them some influence over their own job prospects or because of a belief that worker participation in ownership is conducive to profitability).

Privatization methods can be grouped into three major categories according to the extent to which it is important to the government to receive what it considers a fair market value. At one end of the spectrum are asset sales and at the other is the free (or nearly free) distribution of shares to the citizenry at large — usually called mass privatization. An intermediate category is the employee or management buy-out (EBO or MBO) which involves sale but with less concern to obtain value for money. It will be noted that western privatization has fallen almost entirely into the first category, with some elements of the third, whereas the second of these methods is a transition-economy invention.

The most commercially oriented method — asset sales — cannot be implemented in the standard western way because of the absence of well developed stock markets, and in Central and Eastern Europe comes in a variety of forms. There may be a public invitation for tenders or a public auction or there may be direct negotiation with an individual potential buyer, the last of these being particularly suitable when a foreign investor is interested. Typically, the reserve price for tender or auction, or the opening official position in the case of direct

---

4 Estrin (1994) and Frydman, Rapaczynski, Earle et al. (1993a and 1993b).

negotiations, is set by reference to a professional valuation of the enterprise.

The EBO or MBO may be used, for a given enterprise, on its own or in conjunction with more public asset sales. It would typically give special concessions to employees, by giving them first option on a proportion of the shares, an option which may be taken up at a discount and sometimes by taking advantage of specially designed credit facilities.

The difficulty with commercial methods is that they are very slow — too slow if several thousand enterprises are to be privatized within a reasonably short period. The urgency arises because of the dangers of de-capitalization and informal privatization. The whole region has seen enterprise managers in essence defrauding the state by the use of various strategies designed to divert profits from the use of state assets into their own pockets. If these strategies are used or the state is unwilling or unable to impose hard budget constraints on enterprises, those enterprises sink rapidly into bankruptcy, thus magnifying the difficulties of ultimate privatization. To dispose of a large number of enterprises with reasonable expedition is the objective of mass privatization, first employed in what was Czechoslovakia and now being implemented or considered in several countries, including Bulgaria (see below).

Under such schemes, all adult citizens receive an endowment (free or at a nominal price) in the form of privatization vouchers which may be used to buy shares in enterprises listed for privatization or shares in intermediaries which will take up enterprise shares. These intermediaries (mutual funds) may be established from the beginning as part of the scheme (as happened in Poland) or may grow spontaneously by purchasing vouchers from citizens and using them to buy enterprise shares (as in the former Czechoslovakia).

Issues Regarding the Choice of Method

The virtues of mass privatization are five-fold. First, the capital enshrined in the assets of enterprises was derived from the enforced denial of consumption, and free distribution of those assets is a recognition that citizens have already paid for them: in other words, equity demands free distribution. Secondly, but less abstractly, other methods give an advantage to groups who were favourably placed under the old regime and so could accumulate the wealth needed to participate in commercial privatization. If EBOs on concessionary terms were used at all extensively, there would be a further inequity in that those who were lucky enough to work in enterprises with good prospects in the new environment would be advantaged compared with others, no less deserving, whose firms have no such prospects. Thirdly, and very importantly, the success of the whole transition process requires there to be a large enough constituency with a personal interest in that success. The adverse effects of the early stages of transition on the living standards of most people is being politically felt throughout the region, where it is almost universally now proving difficult to push through the legislation needed for institutional reform (including privatization) or to sustain tough monetary and fiscal policies. Mass privatization is designed to give everyone a clear stake in the new order. Fourthly, these schemes avoid the charge that privatization gives too much opportunity to foreigners. Fifthly, mass privatization should be quicker than the case-by-case approach required by more commercially oriented methods.

The disadvantages are, however, serious. In the first place, mass privatization is a denial of the very principles of market economics — that only a person who puts up his own money for a venture has a serious interest in the success of that venture. People may treat their vouchers like free lottery tickets — it is nice if you win, but you have lost nothing if you do not. Then, privatization proceeds are an important potential source of support for fiscal systems whose revenue capacity has been seriously harmed by the collapse of the planning mechanisms. Mass privatization may enable governments to shed actual or potential liabilities, but contributes nothing to the revenue side of the budget. Furthermore, free distribution offers nothing more than transfer of ownership whereas sale to genuinely interested parties offers valuable opportunities for restructuring: the new owners, especially if they are foreign, are likely to bring with them capital to finance technological upgrading, markets, marketing expertise and new managerial capability.

The most widely debated difficulty with mass privatization concerns corporate governance. The whole point of privatization is to have owners who have a real interest in efficiency and profitability, but this interest will be ineffective unless the owners can actually influence the activities of the enterprise. If ownership is widely dispersed, it is practically impossible to organize effective oversight of the management. This is the significance of the intermediaries already mentioned, although other solutions to this dilemma have been mooted. If the shares of enterprises are vested in a relatively small number of mutual funds or holding companies and citizens use their vouchers to buy shares in these intermediaries, ownership will be dispersed but control can be concentrated.

Semi-commercial EBOs offer certain advantages.[5] They are likely to be reasonably fast to effect, especially if the state is prepared to dispose of assets without too much concern for the price; and they win over what is likely to be the most vocal source of opposition to the privatization of a given enterprise — the workforce. However, they are likely to be feasible only if the assets are sold at a very substantial discount, in which case there are dangers that the employees' ownership interest will be weak compared to their interest as employees. Only if the state and the banking system impose hard budget constraints immediately, and bankruptcy is a genuine threat from the beginning, is it likely that worker-owners will have an immediate interest in profitability strong enough to overcome their interest in sustaining employment levels and real wages.

From all this, it should be clear that no single method has obvious advantages compared with other methods and so it is not surprising that most countries in the region have privatization programmes which utilize a mixture of methods.

Other Issues

One of the major sources of inefficiency under the old system was the banks' profligacy in providing credit and a result is that the great majority of enterprises are burdened with debts which they are unable to service in present circumstances. Also, in an effort to minimize their demands for bank credit in the recent past, they have typically built up large debts to each other. Thus, there is a severe problem when it comes to trying to sell such debt-ridden enterprises. Two major possibilities suggest themselves. First, the debt could be taken into account in determining the net sale price or, secondly, the creditors banks may be

---

5 For a review of the economic and political issues relating to the participation of employees in privatization programmes, see Bogetic (1993).

encouraged to participate in privatization through debt–equity swaps. The latter raises the well-debated issue of the proper role of banks in enterprise ownership.[6]

Finally, there is a question which has received remarkably little consideration in the vast literature on privatization in transition economies: since privatization will take much longer than was at first realized, what should be done with enterprises which have yet to be privatized? A simplistic economic answer would be approximately as follows: establish a competitive environment, impose hard budget constraints (that is, remove budgetary subsidies and impose commercial criteria for bank credit), implement strict bankruptcy provisions, and then leave enterprises to sink or swim. If they swim, they will be easy to privatize eventually. However, even in pure economic terms, this is inadequate since such a severe regime would kill off activities which could have long-term prospects of survival in a market environment but which in the meantime need substantial restructuring which cannot be financed because of capital market failures. But exactly how are such activities to be identified, would the authorities have the political will to distinguish them from other enterprises who should be allowed to go to the wall, and could the state muster the resources necessary to overcome the relevant market failures?

This is a far from comprehensive survey of the enormous range of issues raised by the theory and practice of privatization, but it is sufficient as background to our review of Bulgarian experience, to which we now turn.

EARLY PRIVATIZATION AND THE DEVELOPMENT OF LEGISLATION[7]

The transformation of the economy from one dominated by state agencies towards one dominated by private activity involves two

---

6 The effect on the banks of non-performing credits to enterprises and the issue of banks' participation in enterprise ownership were discussed in Chapter 6 above.

7 A review of the Bulgarian legal system and legislation as they apply to business (with the exception of privatization legislation) can be found in Gray and associates (1993), pp. 23–45.

separate but related process — the disposal of state assets to private interests and the development of private activity *de novo* — and we shall deal with both aspects. The former naturally receives more emphasis since it is so directly concerned with government policy. Nonetheless, important policy requirements exist for both processes. The development of private enterprises from the ground up requires a liberal and supportive legal, fiscal and monetary environment and so it is important to review, for instance, the legal framework which is being put in place to provide that environment.

To avoid terminological confusion, we here restrict the use of the word 'privatization' to the disposal of state assets (whether by sale or other means) to new owners other than in cases where pre-nationalization owners of particular assets have specified first-option rights to receive back their old property. The latter, which is really just one method of transferring assets from the state to private interests, is termed 'restitution'.

General Commercial Legislation

A landmark was created by the passing in January 1989 of Decree 56 on Economic Activity.[8] This was of course intended as the next, and most radical, stage in the reform of the system of central planning and state ownership and can be thought of as a general law covering the following main areas: the organization of businesses, public and private; foreign investment; bankruptcy; and business taxation. Of these four, the first three have been replaced by subsequent legislation (The Commercial Code and the Foreign Investment Law — see below) and all that remains is that Decree 56 is still the law for business taxation. As a commercial code it set out various forms of organization and prescribed the control structures to be adopted by the different types of organization and, which is what made it a landmark, established the legality of private business activity. In its original form, it was somewhat restrictive as regards the ability of private business to hire labour and engage in foreign trade, but amending regulations subsequently relaxed these restrictions. Within a year 14,000 private

---

8 *Dürzhaven vestnik*, No. 4, January 1989. For a survey of its major provisions, see Wyzan (1991), pp. 85–89.

businesses had been registered,[9] although the vast majority of these were essentially part-time activities by the owner, had no employees or were not active at all.

Nonetheless, it was Decree 56 which provided the basis for the first attempts, in 1991, to sell off state assets, an activity which was a central part of the policy package adopted by the government established under Dimitur Popov in December 1990. At the time, the programme was quite ambitious, the 1991 Budget actually allowing for privatization proceeds of BGL214 million[10] (almost $10 million at the exchange rate prevailing at the time). But ambition was not realised by experience, this embryo programme being aborted within a few months. The first phase was to involve the auctioning of around 300 petrol stations and a number of other small establishments in the service sector. Only four petrol stations were actually sold, along with about 60 other establishments, realising about $1 million.[11] The problems were essentially of a legal nature in that the activities which it was intended to privatize had not been transformed into entities recognized under the newly enacted Commercial Code[12] which required that such sales be conducted within the framework of an explicit programme of privatization.

An immediate problem facing transition economies wishing to pass economic activity from public to private hands was that the very concept of ownership as applied to enterprises was itself ill-defined and so a first step had to be to transform enterprises into a legal form which would make the transfer of ownership possible: this is the relevance of the Commercial Code to both the privatization of state assets and the development of a private sector *de novo*. Any commercial activity except those by farmers, self-employed craftsmen and professionals such as lawyers and accountants operating on their own must be registered and take one of six prescribed legal forms.

A *sole owner* is in effect a single-person partnership with unlimited liability. A *general partnership* has two or more owners, each with

---

9 Jones and Rock (1994), p. 312.

10 Frydman, Rapaczynski, Earle et al. (1993a), p. 25.

11 Jones and Rock (1994), p. 322.

12 Law on Commerce, *Dŭrzhaven vestnik*, No. 48, June 1991.

unlimited liability. Under a *limited partnership* there must be at least one person (general partner) who contributes at least 10 per cent of the capital and bears unlimited liability, the other partners (limited partners) having liability limited to their financial contribution to the partnership. A *public limited partnership* is a hybrid between a limited partnership and a joint-stock company. It must have at least three limited partners who subscribed under a public offer. A *limited-liability company*, which must have an initial capital of at least BGL50,000, is identical to what is known in other jurisdictions as a private company: its capital is provided by shareholders who are granted limited liability but the capital cannot be raised by public offer and the shares cannot be traded or passed in any other way except with the agreement of all shareholders. Finally, a *joint-stock company* is a public company whose capital may be raised by public offer, whose shares may be traded and whose shareholders have limited liability. There is a minimum size, depending on the activity and how the capital was raised. The idea is not only that new private activities must be organized in one of these forms, but also that a public enterprise should transformed into one of these before it is privatized.

The Commercial Code has been amended several times, most significantly to introduce modern bankruptcy provisions. This large piece of legislation, adding over 150 articles to the Code, was passed, after a long process, by the National Assembly in July 1994.[13] Bankruptcy law is extremely technical and the details are of no concern here. Its importance is that it now exists: only time will tell whether or not it will be implemented in such a way that its potentially vital role in economic restructuring is actually fulfilled.

The Commercial Code applies to foreign persons or companies operating in Bulgaria, but in this case there are further provisions as enshrined in the Law on Economic Activity of Foreign Persons and Protection of Foreign Investment.[14] It is this law which governs foreign participation in privatization, foreign *de novo* activity and the operation of joint ventures between Bulgarian and foreign partners.

---

13 *Dŭrzhaven vestnik*, No. 63, August 1994.

14 Usually known as the Foreign Investment Law. *Dŭrzhaven vestnik*, No. 8, January 1992

Under this law, a foreign investment is any investment made by a foreign person or a company with more than 50 per cent foreign participation. There are no general restrictions on activity but government permission is required for some activities: manufacture of arms and military equipment; banking and insurance; acquisition of immovable property in certain regions; exploration and exploitation of minerals under the sea. A foreign company may not own land but a company registered in Bulgaria, even if wholly foreign-owned, may acquire non-agricultural land. There are no restrictions on repatriation of profit and only minor restrictions on repatriation of money by foreign employees in Bulgaria. Companies with at least 50 per cent foreign participation pay state profits tax at 30 per cent rather than 40 per cent and are exempt from the 10 per cent municipal profits tax payable by other companies.

The final piece of legislation deserving mention in the present discussion is the Law on the Protection of Competition, passed in May 1991 during the tenure of the first post-communist government.[15] This law bans the creation of monopolies and a range of activities which are in restraint of trade or constitute unfair competition. It establishes a Commission for the Protection of Competition, whose permission is required if certain activities of a potentially monopolistic nature are to be carried on and which is empowered to take action against offenders. Whilst perhaps not a dead letter, this legislation is a decidedly quiescent one. The Commission was established but appears to have had no effect on any activity. This is not really surprising. The passage of this law was no more than the making of reformist noises: no-one could seriously expect it to be effective in an economy dominated by vast state-owned agencies whose very existence contravened the law. Nor does any present constituency have an interest in the implementation of anti-trust legislation. Only when the private sector becomes significant, and a large number of people have an interest in fair competition, will this law become of effective relevance.

It will be recalled that the small-scale privatization efforts of 1991 had to be abandoned because of the inadequacy of the legal framework and so it became a matter of urgency to put in place a proper, comprehensive code for the sale of state enterprises. It proved to be a

---

15 *Dŭrzhaven vestnik*, No. 39, May 1991.

difficult legislative process because, first, the construction of privatization rules is an inherently contentious process and, secondly, because the situation in parliament was unstable, thus impeding the passage of any legislation which was even remotely controversial.

The second post-communist general election took place in October 1991 and brought to power a coalition consisting of the UDF and MRF led by Filip Dimitrov. For the UDF anyway, privatization was an earnest of its radical intentions. Its problems in giving legislative form to its policies were exacerbated by the fact that the UDF, despite having just attained its primary goal of government, seemed unable to act with any semblance of party discipline. The government, in attempting to construct a privatization law, therefore found itself facing not only the BSP in opposition but also dissention within its own ranks. Initial debate within the Assembly focused on two proposals, one from the government and the other also from within the UDF submitted by a small group including the chairman of the influential economic committee.

The government's proposal was the less radical, with complete reliance on public auctions, no special concessions to workers and leaving the whole process in the hands of the relevant ministries and enterprise management. The alternative proposal envisaged a programme administered by a quasi-autonomous privatization agency and extremely generous provisions for share-acquisition by workers. The government's position was further undermined when the *Podkrepa* trade union, itself a member of the UDF group, backed the alternative proposals and criticized the government for its failure to take account of the position of workers in any privatization. Further pressure came from the IMF and the World Bank who, while not taking a position on details, had from the beginning (that is, late 1990 and early 1991) insisted on a Bulgarian commitment to comprehensive and rapid privatization.

The government had, if it wanted to survive, no option but to compromise and in early 1992 presented a new draft law which provided for a privatization agency and for concessionary participation by workers, though on a considerably less generous scale than had been indicated by the alternative proposals. The result was the passage of a privatization law in April 1992 — a law which bore all the marks of hasty drafting and compromise. It turned out to be less than satisfactory as the basis for practical privatization and was significantly amended after two years. We now review this legislation.

Legislation on Privatization

The two main laws dealing with privatization *per se* are The Law for
the Transformation and Privatization of State-Owned and Municipal
Enterprises, passed by the Assembly on 23 April 1992[16] and an Act
with the same title passed on 9 June 1994.[17] The second Act makes
very significant changes, the need for such changes being the result of
three factors. First, the earlier Act was drafted in conditions of complete
inexperience and major confusion about underlying policy issues and,
furthermore, was changed during its contentious and extended passage
through parliament. Secondly, experience in attempting to implement the
1992 Act showed up its defects and made amendments essential if the
objectives of that Act were to be achieved. Thirdly, in the meantime
there had been two policy shifts — a desire to facilitate EBOs and,
potentially of the greatest significance, a desire to institute a mass
privatization scheme based on the distribution of vouchers.

Privatization institutions
The decision to privatize an enterprise and the operation of the actual
privatization process are the responsibility of one of three agencies,
depending on the size and current status of the enterprise. State-owned
enterprises whose long-term gross assets do not exceed BGL70 million
(BGL10 million under the earlier legislation) have their fate decided by
'a government body specified by the Council of Ministers' (Article 3(1)
in each Act), which in practice means the sectoral ministry responsible
for the enterprise in question. State-owned enterprises larger than that
are the province of the Privatization Agency (PA), except that the
approval of the Council of Ministers is required with respect to
enterprises which the Council designates in advance.[18] In the case of
municipally-owned enterprises, the owning municipality is the competent
body.

---

16 *Dŭrzhaven vestnik*, No. 38, May 1992.

17 *Dŭrzhaven vestnik*, No. 51, June 1994.

18 This explicit designation of enterprises where the final decision is reserved
to the Council of Ministers replaced a provision in the 1992 Act whereby all
enterprises with assets in excess of BGL200 million were in this category.

Proposals to privatize an enterprise do not have to originate in these agencies, but the consent of the latter must be obtained before action can proceed. There is some cross-competence among the agencies (for example, a proposal may be initiated by a municipality for an enterprise in its region, even if is not municipally owned and the Privatization Agency may make proposals for any enterprise), but the main item of interest here is that the managing board or a majority of the employees of an enterprise can initiate a privatization proposal.

The PA reports directly to the Council of Ministers. It has an 11 member board, five of whom are appointed by the Council and the other six by the National Assembly, all members serving for an unlimited period.[19] The lack of limit on board service must be regarded as a potential weakness in what is a politically highly-charged area of government. The 1992 legislation lists the grounds on which the then limited-term members could be dismissed, but the abolition of the limit under the 1994 Act was accompanied by the granting of an open-ended power by the appointing body (Council of Ministers or Assembly) to dismiss a member. In all countries, appointment to quasi-governmental organizations involves the balancing of two requirements: that the body must implement governmental policy and that it should be as far as possible insulated from the continual confrontations of political life. One of the problems with policy formulation and implementation in Bulgaria at the moment is that everything seems to be subject to adversarial politics between the BSP and UDF and even within those groupings. The long-term restructuring of the economy and society requires policy to be implemented by agencies with some immunity from this syndrome, but the PA is now vulnerable to being even more politicized than it has been.[20] A member may be dismissed at any time and the legislation does not require any reasons to be established. It would have been better to have kept the limitation on board service under the 1992

---

19 Under the 1992 Act, the members served for four years, but this limit was removed by the 1994 Act.

20 Although the facts of the case are impossible to determine objectively, there is a widespread opinion that the dismissal of the first executive director of the PA in August 1993 was the result of his being regarded as politically uncomfortable to a government which relied completely on BSP support in the Assembly. The man in question is now a UDF member of the Assembly.

Act. If the Cabinet or Assembly wished to replace one of its members, it need then only wait until that member's normal term of office expired and then decline to re-appoint him or her. This is a widespread practice among quasi-governmental bodies in other countries and permits a turnover of membership without any scandal or suspicion of political motivation.

The board elects its own chairman and appoints an executive director to run the Agency. Officials and Board members, and their relatives, may not own shares in enterprises being privatized during their term of office or within a year of leaving office.

The privatization process

At the time of the original legislation, the position of the Bulgarian authorities was very definitely that the state should get value for money for the assets of which it was divesting itself: it intended to be more like Hungary than Czechoslovakia. The reasons for this stance were partly the result of experience, partly fiscal and partly a matter of principle.

The experiential aspect represented a desire to put an end to the 'informal' privatization which had been going on at least since 1991 by which managers made use of state assets for their private purposes.[21] The fiscal aspect is obvious: the virtual collapse of the capacity of the tax system to deliver revenue (see Chapter 7 above) made the prospects of revenue in the form of privatization proceeds particularly urgent. The argument from principle was simply that it is wrong to give away, or sell at bargain-basement prices, to private interests assets which had been created through the enforced denial of consumption to previous generations.[22] The authorities may also have been influenced by the view that, unless they paid good money for the privatized assets, the

---

21 The legislation has attempted to address this problem retrospectively. 'Any disposal transaction in state or municipal property, as well as any contract for partnership at civil law, concluded under obviously disadvantageous terms since 1 January 1990 may be rendered null and void' (Clause 8, Supplementary Provisions, 1994 Act).

22 The counter-argument, that if these assets belonged to the people through state ownership it would be wrong to sell them to the people, does not seem to have had much influence.

new owners would have little interest in the subsequent performance of those assets and the major point of privatization would have been lost.

So, the system established by the 1992 Act, and which has been the basis for all privatization deals to date, has been based on sales. The original Act provided for shares to be sold (i) by open sale, (ii) by public auction, (iii) by public tender and (iv) by direct negotiations with potential buyers. The 1994 Act added a fifth method — EBOs or MBOs). In respect of any given enterprise, a mixture of these methods can be used. These methods can also be used to dispose of the assets of an enterprise which has not yet been transformed into an entity under the Commercial Code or of the residual assets of an enterprise which is being wound up. The law requires that the offer price for public sale, the reserve price for auctions and tenders and the price basis for direct negotiations shall be determined as the result of an independent valuation of the enterprise. This valuation is conducted by an accountancy firm licensed for the purpose by the PA. Rather quaintly, valuation methods are to be determined by the Council of Ministers, though their expertise in this area must, to put it mildly, be open to question.

Special provisions for employees to acquire shares

Throughout the region, employees are given special privileges in the acquisition of shares when the enterprise in which they work is to be privatized. These were provided for in the 1992 Act and significantly extended in the 1994 Act.

Preferential treatment can be claimed by current employees who have been with the enterprise for at least two years, those who left the enterprise within the previous eight years (five years under the 1992 Act, extended by the 1994 Act), those who retired from the enterprise within the previous ten years, and those who have been members of the management team of the enterprise for at least a year (the last group being added by the 1994 Act).

Aside from EBOs, any of these persons has the first option on 20 per cent of the shares of an enterprise being privatized, at a price half that applying to other buyers, subject to the limitation that the total value of such a discount must not exceed his or her gross wage over the previous two years, that wage being adjusted for inflation and, for these purposes, being calculated such that it is not less than the average national wage.[23]

The 1994 legislation made an important change with respect to the rights attaching to shares acquired on these concessionary terms. Under the original law, such shares could be resold without restriction but carried no voting rights for three years. The more recent law reverses this: such shares carry voting rights but cannot be sold for three years. This change must be judged unfortunate and seems to show a lack of faith in the virtues of a market mechanism. In general, there ought to be no restriction on voting rights, but the framers of the 1992 Act had a valuable insight into the capacity of a workers' bloc to impede restructuring. A workers' bloc can be expected to be the most conservative grouping among the new shareholders and their power could be significant if the remainder of the shareholding is dispersed. If another bloc is in a position to out-vote the workers, then of course this danger is less acute. Certainly, one cannot help wondering whether the granting of such rights from the beginning will inhibit private, and especially foreign, investors in taking up shares in an enterprise in which workers exercise their full 20 per cent option.

The restriction on sale could be regarded as a denial to workers of the opportunity to realize the immediate capital gain available as a result of their acquiring the shares at a 50 per cent discount but, if this is the rationale, one must doubt the point of giving the discount in the first place. The worry is that the restriction on resale could produce perverse incentives among worker-shareholders. Shareholding offers a return in the form of a dividend or a capital gain. Since it is extremely unlikely that any privatized enterprises will offer dividends in the foreseeable future (they will either be insufficiently profitable in the short run or will retain any net income for urgent investment purposes), the only financial incentive to shareholding lies in the possibility of a capital gain. How worker-shareholders will react then depends on their personal rates of time preference. If they are looking for immediate rewards, their inability to realize an early gain will mean that they will have no interest in the profitability of the enterprise strong enough to offset their interests as employees (that is, their interest in high wages and the

---

23 This refers to the 1994 Act, which considerably simplifies the provisions of the 1992 Act in this respect (see Article 22 in each Act).

maintenance of employment). On the other hand, if they are longer-sighted, they will have an interest in profitability in the first three years since this will increase the gain which they will eventually be able to realize.

Although the introduction of EBOs into the list of methods is unobjectionable in itself, the terms of such buy-outs could also create perverse incentives. The Act (Article 25(1).5) provides that EBOs shall be effected by instalments involving the transfer of successive blocks of shares over a period of ten years. Although this is covered by the general provision stating that the initial share price shall be in accordance with the independent valuation, the law is silent as to the pricing of the subsequent blocks of shares. If, as would seem appropriate, the price of these subsequent blocks is to be adjusted to take account of both inflation and the performance of the enterprise since the buy-out was initiated, there will be perverse incentives. The new owners' concern for profitability in the early stages will be severely reduced if such profitability raises the price at which they can buy the next block of shares. Of course, it is recognized that workers would not have access to sufficient liquid funds of their own to buy all the shares at once, but this kind of instalment plan is not the best solution. A better, though not the only, alternative would be to leverage the buy-out by means of bank debt, possibly with some state support (for instance in the form of a partial guarantee) to offset the fact that the banks are likely to be severely risk-averse in these situations. In such a scenario, the worker-shareholders would have an unambiguous personal financial incentive to maximize profitability.

For enterprises with a book value of long-term gross assets not exceeding BGL10 million in the case of industry and BGL5 million in the case of trading and service activities, the 1994 Act introduced major new provisions for employees and those holding leasing contracts with an enterprise. For these smaller enterprises, there need be no public offering, auction or tendering (which there can be with respect to the EBOs referred to already) and the whole of the shares can be offered to the workers or lessees on an instalment basis. For industry and services, the instalments are spread over six years with a one-year grace period and a downpayment of 10 per cent; for trading activities the period is five years, with no grace period, and the downpayment is 30 per cent. The outstanding part is increased by half the inflation rate, but apparently by nothing else, thus avoiding the problem already referred to. Employees participating in this scheme get their shares at a 20 per cent discount, again with the two-year salary limitation.

In case foreigners regard the special concessions to employees or lessees as an opportunity for a bargain, all concessions described in this section are restricted to Bulgarian resident citizens and, in the case of lessees, to Bulgarian entities with no foreign participation.

Restitution

The restitution of formerly private property nationalized under communism is given priority over privatization *per se* and the privatization legislation takes account of this as regards real estate. The former owners of land or buildings which physically exist and now form part of the assets of a state-owned or municipal enterprise have the right to receive free a proportion of the shares equal to the proportion which that real estate forms of the total privatization value of the enterprise.[24]

Restitution has proceeded much faster than privatization, even in the agricultural sector where, as was seen in Chapter 4 above, there have been serious legal and administrative difficulties. Indeed, Bulgaria has been criticized for devoting so much effort to restitution, but such criticism is unreasonable. First, restitution is politically the easy side of privatization and it makes sense to progress as rapidly as possible with any policy which passes state or municipal assets into private hands. Secondly, at the central level restitution efforts have not impeded the sale of assets since most of the former (with the exception of land) has not been the responsibility of central agencies and, where it was, the administrative mechanism has been quite different. Non-agricultural restitution has been significant primarily in the distributive and other service sectors and has related to small businesses whose public owners were municipalities rather than ministries.

---

24 Aside from the Privatization Act itself, other legislation governing restitution is the Law on Re-establishment of Ownership of Shops, Workshops and Warehouses, the Law on Re-establishment of Ownership of the Catholic Church, the Law on Re-establishment of Ownership of Land, and the Law on Re-establishment of Ownership of Nationalized Immovable Property. The extremely sensitive issue of the restitution of agricultural land is governed by the Law on the Ownership and Use of Farm Land of 1991 (see Chapter 4 above).

Regrettably, it has been impossible to quantify the scale of non-agricultural restitution because of the primary role of municipalities and because there appears to be no central source of data on this subject. Casual observation and anecdotal evidence indicate that a high proportion of smaller shops are now in private hands (and official data do indicate the increasing dominance of the private sector in the field of distribution) and this must be to a large measure the result of the restitution programme.

Mass privatization
By far the most significant feature of the 1994 Act is that it provides, if only in outline, for a mass privatization scheme based on the distribution of vouchers. As already stated, this represented a dramatic change in policy orientation in that, until then, the Bulgarian authorities have seemed wedded to the principle of value for money combined with concessions for workers. However, the fact that the Act is silent on important details — explicitly leaving them to be determined by the Council of Ministers — creates the danger that the design of the scheme will be highly politicized. Its incorporation into legislative form with so many loose ends suggests that someone was in a hurry, perhaps because of the possible imminence of elections. It was from the outset the subject of very public disagreement within the former government, with different schemes being promoted by prime minister Berov and deputy prime minister Karabashev (who eventually resigned over this and other policy disagreements).

The scheme, to be administered by a newly created Centre for Mass Privatization under the Council of Ministers, will operate as follows. Each resident citizen aged at least 18 will receive, for a fee of BGL500, a book of vouchers with a face value of BGL25,000 and will have the right to buy at face value an additional voucher of BGL5,000. The vouchers can be used to buy shares in the enterprises designated under the mass privatization programme or to exercise the concessionary rights of employees under the normal privatization programme. The price at which shares will be traded under the mass privatization scheme is not precisely specified, except that it will be through an auction the procedure for which is yet to be determined and will not involve the kind of independent valuation prescribed under the normal programme. The vouchers may be transferred by inheritance or by gift to close relatives but they may not be sold or used as collateral for credit.

This non-negotiability of vouchers is controversial. In the first place, unless the vouchers are printed with the owner's name, the ban on sale would be impossible to police. Secondly, it is not obvious why those (perhaps the majority of citizens) who have no real interest in owning shares in an as yet unidentified enterprise should not be allowed to sell to someone who is interested in such activity. Otherwise, what is likely to happen is that the number of vouchers offered in exchange for shares will be much lower than expected (if people do not take up their vouchers or if they take up their allocation but then lose interest) and so the auction-clearing price of shares will be lower than expected and those who do participate will make a windfall gain. Permitting the sale of vouchers would be an incentive to people to take up their allocation and would remove this last problem.

On the other hand, non-negotiability is consistent with at least part of the logic of a mass privatization programme in that it maximizes equality of participation. Also, and something which could be of great significance, the unrestricted negotiability of almost-free vouchers makes them quasi-money. The total face value of almost-free vouchers will exceed BGL100 billion — around 25 per cent of the present broad money supply. Of course, they would not be traded at their face value but, even if they traded at an average 50 per cent discount and half of them were traded, their issue would represent a major monetary expansion.

Another controversial matter — and an important difference between the Berov and Karabashev schemes[25] — concerns the use of intermediaries in a mass privatization programme. The issues here — primarily as regards corporate governance — have already been reviewed. The scheme outlined in the current legislation does not establish investment funds but permits them to be established under rules yet to be determined and permits voucher-holders to use their vouchers to buy enterprise shares directly or to deposit them at face value in an investment fund so established. Thus, in this respect, the

---

25 See the article by Berov in *Bulgarian Economic Review*, 18 June–1 July 1993 and that by Karabashev in the same newspaper, 30 July–13 August 1993. The former's scheme allowed for the establishment of investment funds, but apparently as a negotiable option, whereas for the latter such funds (to be state-owned) appeared to be an essential part of the scheme.

Bulgarian scheme has more in common with the Czech experience, where funds grew up as a response to market forces, than with what happened in Poland, where the authorities established such funds as part of the scheme.

When the new legislation was passed, the government was full of optimism, the prime minister stating that 500 enterprises, representing 36 per cent of total state-enterprise capital, would be disposed of under the mass privatization scheme, that the vouchers would be distributed by October 1994 and the first stage of the scheme completed by December.[26] By August, this optimism had been given a precise timetable, with the prime minister reporting that vouchers would be distributed by 14 October, share sales completed by mid-December, and general meetings of the new shareholders being convened by 28 April 1995.[27] One of the last acts of the Berov government was to approve a bill, to be submitted to the Assembly in September, governing the new investment funds.

With the fall of the government, everything came to a halt. The director of the Centre for Mass Privatization was dismissed by the interim government and it could not be expected that a mass privatization scheme would be accelerated by a government whose head was the former director of the Privatization Agency, which was jealous of its lack of a role in mass privatization and which was the public embodiment of the 'value for money' school of privatization. More important, the new BSP government, while making encouraging noises on taking up office, has yet to be tested when it comes to the difficult decisions. It is still too early to judge.

The finances of privatization
The way the expenses of privatization are to be covered and the disbursement of the proceeds of privatization changed considerably between the two Acts, but since nothing much happened in the meantime attention can be concentrated on the most recent piece of

---

26 *168 Hours BBN*, 13–19 June 1994.

27 *168 Hours BBN*, 8–14 August 1994. The first cracks began to appear in that the original 500 companies had by now been reduced to 340.

legislation.[28] A mutual fund operated by the ministry of finance is to receive 20 per cent of the proceeds of the sale of state-owned (but not municipal) enterprises. The main purpose of this fund is to feed the social security funds. The remainder is divided as follows: 7 per cent to the PA to help cover its expenses (it also gets a grant from the State Budget); and 93 per cent to three extra-budgetary funds operated by the Ministry of Finance — the National Fund for Environmental Protection (5 per cent), the Fund for the Support of the Development of Agriculture (15 per cent) and the State Fund for Reconstruction and Development (73 per cent). The municipalities may keep all the proceeds of the privatization of municipal enterprises (this was not the case under the 1992 Act), though the use of these funds is restricted by the legislation: 7 per cent goes to covering privatization expenses, 5 per cent to the Municipal Fund for the Preservation of the Environment and the remaining 88 per cent to a fund whose priority use is the redemption of municipal enterprise debt and which may not be used for current purposes.

PROGRESS ON PRIVATIZATION

Bulgarian privatization has been journalistically described as a 'sad circus'.[29] The noun is too harsh, but one has some sympathy with the use of the adjective. No observer can fail to be disappointed with the slow pace of privatization so far and the purpose of this section is to document what has happened by looking at the general picture and by reference to a number of high-profile cases.

Tables 8.1–8.5 present some statistics on the progress of privatization activity governed by the 1992 and 1994 Laws.

Table 8.1 may appear to indicate a reasonable level of activity on the part of the responsible agencies, but quite a different picture is shown by the figures on the number of deals closed (Table 8.2).

---

28 An example of the inaction is that the 1992 Act required the establishment of a mutual fund to receive privatization proceeds 'within three months after this Act comes into force' (Article 8(1)) whereas in the 1994 Act those words are replaced by 'by 30 June 1994'.

29 *Business Central Europe*, September 1994, p. 28. The following words were 'Bulgarians deserve better'.

Table 8.1 Privatization process commenced (cumulative number of cases), 1992–94

	PA	Minis-tries	Munic-ipal	Total
Dec 92	5	35	43	93
Dec 93	53	282	389	724
Mar 94	76	351	445	872
Jun 94	87	439	495	1021
Sep 94	135	527	730	1392
Dec 94	196	676	956	1828

Source: National Statistical Institute

Table 8.2 Privatization process completed (cumulative number of cases), 1992–94

	PA	Minis-tries	Munic-ipal	Total
Dec 92	–	–	5	5
Dec 93	2	39	72	113
Mar 94	12	51	116	179
Jun 94	12	57	157	226
Sep 94	12	61	205	278
Dec 94	26	71	353	450

Source: National Statistical Institute

The terminal date in Table 8.2 is over two and a half years after the passage of the relevant legislation and the figures reveal a disappointing performance. The fact that there are, according to varying estimates, 3–4,000 enterprises under the aegis of the PA or the Ministries shows how little progress has been made. Of course, the number of cases tells one only part of the story since they vary so much in size. There appear to be no available data on the size of enterprises actually sold, but Tables 8.3 and 8.4 below indicate the value of gross assets and the level of employment in enterprises where the privatization process has been initiated. They refer solely to state (that is, excluding municipal) enterprises since the relevant data are not available for municipal enterprises privatized. The same restriction applies to Table 8.5 which shows the amounts received by the extra-budgetary funds from privatization.

Table 8.3 Gross   assets   in   cases   where   privatization   process   commenced (cumulative BGL bn), 1992–94

	PA	Minis-tries	Total
Dec 92	1.2	0.4	1.6
Dec 93	13.0	4.9	17.9
Mar 94	21.9	5.8	27.7
Jun 94	23.1	6.4	29.5
Sep 94	41.4	9.3	50.7
Dec 94	63.1	15.8	78.9

Source: National Statistical Institute

Aside from what they show about progress, these figures reveal the huge disparity in the size of the organizations for which the various agencies are responsible. Thus, the average size of enterprises for which the process had begun by the end of 1994 was, in terms of gross assets BGL322 million and BGL23 million and, in terms of employment, 534 and 118 for the PA and the ministries respectively. In the light of the average size of Bulgarian state enterprises, this demonstrates the difficulties of privatizing those firms which dominate their sectors: the large (and therefore more typical) enterprises by and large still remain in state hands. The average size of municipal privatizations is of course very much smaller even than for the ministries.

If the Bulgarian authorities had any hope that privatization proceeds would make a meaningful contribution to budgetary revenue, that hope has been disappointed. As Table 8.5 shows, after almost three years, the total net receipts represented less than one per cent of merely the domestic debt of the government.

Table 8.4 Employment in cases where privatization process commenced (cumulative '000), 1992–94

	PA	Minis-tries	Total
Dec 92	1.3	3.2	4.5
Dec 93	29.2	24.7	53.9
Mar 94	32.1	28.2	60.3
Jun 94	34.6	30.8	65.4
Sep 94	67.5	63.6	130.8
Dec 94	104.8	79.9	184.7

Source: National Statistical Institute

Table 8.5 Net receipts from privatization (cumulative BGL mn), 1992–94

	PA	Minis-tries	Total
Dec 92	–	–	–
Dec 93	148	169	317
Mar 94	422	218	640
June 94	422	256	678
Sep 94	422	258	680
Dec 94	2066	300	2366

Source: National Statistical Institute

We now turn our attention to the history behind the figures.

Privatization Experience

The first sale of a state enterprise did not occur until February 1993 when the ministry of trade disposed of a vehicle workshop and the first sale by the PA — of a maize processing plant in Razgrad for $45 million to a Belgian company and the United Bulgarian Bank — waited until May of that year — over a year after the passage of the legislation. The only other major deals closed in 1993 were the purchase of a chocolate factory by Kraft Jacobs Suchard in December and the sale in June to US interests of an electronics company. The latter became a *cause célèbre*. The agreed purchase price for this moribund operation was $1.6 million but the buyer delayed paying. The PA persevered because of the lack of alternative buyers, but in the meantime accepted that the value of the assets had fallen to the value of the company's debts. The deal was finally closed in May 1994 at a nominal price of $1, the debts to be paid by the buyer.[30]

Towards the end of 1993, only 3 per cent of planned transactions had been finalized and only the PA and three ministries had sold any state enterprises. Even the executive director of the PA was disappointed, describing the year's privatization as a 'disastrous performance'.[31]

The pace quickened somewhat in 1994, but the operation has been bedeviled by controversy over a number of well publicized cases.

SOMAT[32] is the largest trucking company in Europe, with over 3,000 vehicles and 6,000 employees. Once one of Bulgaria's most important earners of foreign currency, its fortunes declined with the demise of the CMEA, the Gulf War and the UN embargo on trade with Serbia. When the privatization process began in August 1993 it was planned to deny any private investor a controlling stake but, very sensibly, this constraint was removed and it was decided to sell 55 per cent of the company by negotiation to a core investor. Two interested parties emerged, one French and the other German, both of whom had business associations with SOMAT but by July 1994 it had been decided to offer the stake to the German company. The French company publicly complained that it had not been given a fair chance and the unions complained that the expected price was too low, as well as claiming that the management had already sold off trucks worth around BGL70 million to private interests.[33] The parliamentary transport committee added more fuel to

30 At the time of writing, it appears that this deal is unravelling in that the American buyer has failed to observe the contracted programme for repaying the company's debts (*168 Hours BBN*, 14–20 November 1994).

31 *Bulgarian Economic Review*, 24 September–7 October 1993.

32 *Stopanska organizatsiya mezhdunaroden avtomobilen transport.*

33 *168 Hours BBN*, 4–10 July 1994.

the fire[34] but the contract was signed on 22 July under which the German company agreed to pay $55 million for 55 per cent of the shares (the state will retain a 25 per cent holding, with the normal 20 per cent being available to the employees), with responsibility for debts of $16 million and a promise to invest a further $48 million. It was the largest privatization deal so far, but the story may not end there, with continuing uncertainty about the scale of the company's debt.

The process concerning Balkan Bulgarian Airlines began in early 1993, when a total value of almost $80 million was placed on the company and it was decided that foreign interests were to be canvassed but would not be sold a controlling stake. The field was soon reduced to Austrian Airlines and a British bank, neither of whom were interested in more than a 20 per cent holding, with Austrian wanting equity in exchange for expertise rather than money. This is a test of the Bulgarian authorities' enthusiasm for market forces and their realism over privatization. Balkan has an overblown route network and a large, obsolete, Russian fleet. It makes large operating losses and has major hard-currency debts over the leasing of new, western aircraft. It really has very little to sell. Foreign investors see this, but for the authorities Balkan is the national flag-carrier with fixed assets with a high book value. Paradoxically, the airline's management and the ministry of transport seem to be more realistic about this than does the PA who, while insisting on considerable secrecy, has entered into acerbic, public conflict with the other Bulgarian parties over this case. Everyone now accepts that, as Balkan's net worth steadily declines, there are only three options: privatization at the best price available quickly; huge budgetary subsidies; or bankruptcy. Although no subsidies have been received since 1989, unsustainable operating losses have just recently produced a claim for assistance in the form of a state loan (which would realistically mean a subsidy) of $67 million.[35] Other countries may be able to afford that kind of help to a decrepit airline: Bulgaria cannot.

The country's six cement producers were put up for privatization in early 1993 and considerable foreign interest was reported, despite technological and financial weakness in the industry. Some financial restructuring was undertaken in that some debts were taken over by the

---

34 *168 Hours BBN*, 1–7 August 1994.
35 *OMRI Daily Digest*, 2 February 1995.

state and some, to energy producers, rescheduled, all of which was designed to increase the attractiveness of these operations. However, there were ominous signs from the beginning in that the scheme involved the government's retaining a 51 per cent share, and suspicions on this score were confirmed when in September 1994 the process was suspended *sine die* by the Council of Ministers. A report of this decision stated that the minister of construction, on whose proposal the Cabinet took this action, 'argued that Bulgaria still lacks adequate experience in the privatization of an entire subsector and the State's interests may thus be impaired. He lobbies for a definite participating interest to stay in the hands of the State which will allow it to keep its regulatory functions on the cement market and prices'.[36]

Finally, we consider the large hotels in Sofia, which are noteworthy for being the subject of extraordinary warfare between the PA and the Committee for Tourism (equivalent to a ministry for privatization purposes). The PA initiated the procedure for the five best known state-owned hotels in the capital in February 1994, only to be met by the Committee petitioning the Supreme Court that the PA was acting *ultra vires* — a move reflecting not so much a legal issue as a fundamental conflict between the agencies as to the sequencing and timing of hotel privatization. The Council of Ministers joined in on the side of the Committee[37] in circumstances where the Cabinet's competence was dubious. Again, one suspects that the root of the problem was that, for most of these hotels, the only realistic interest came from foreigners and the Committee on Tourism saw itself as representing the local industry. This suspicion is supported by the fact that a large Black Sea hotel privatization (Grand Hotel Varna) went through without a hitch in an imaginative deal combining public offering, employees and a 49 per cent core investor: the latter was Bulgarian. It is further supported by the evidence of the first sale, at the end of 1994, of a major Sofia hotel, the Vitosha. Eighty per cent of the shares were sold for $41 million to an expatriate Bulgarian (the other 20 per cent being reserved for the employees). One especially interesting feature of this transaction was

36 *168 Hours BBN*, 5–11 September 1994.
37 *168 Hours BBN*, 14–20 March 1994.

that it was effected by the use of the Brady bonds issued in support of the London Club agreement (see Chapter 5 above).[38] The merits or otherwise of the arguments in individual cases is of little concern here: the purpose of describing these episodes is that they reveal attitudes which will continue to be significant influences on the privatization programme.

First, although the liberal Foreign Investment Law would seem to indicate a welcome to foreign investors, when it comes to privatizing high-profile projects different attitudes emerge. In the trucking, airline and cement cases, in all of which potential foreign investors were to the fore, fear of giving bargains to foreigners has been central to the controversies. That rapid privatization, even on bargain terms, may be better than the available alternatives — that is, a continuing decline in net worth with imminent bankruptcy or heavy subsidization — is not a position which has dominated policy in any of these cases.

Secondly, in the cement and airline cases, there has been a failure to grasp the meaning of transition to a market economy. For the Council of Ministers to halt the privatization of the cement industry for the reasons suggested by the above-quoted views of the relevant minister shows how far there is still to go to gain freedom from old attitudes. Cement is an important infrastructural input and, if supply is monopolistic, there is a case for some regulation. But this is no argument against privatization, especially since it was never proposed to sell the existing enterprises to a single buyer. The state's interest should lie in ensuring a competitive environment and in the industry's attracting the capital needed for restructuring, and nothing else.

The Balkan case is a difficult one because its current status and underlying problems are remarkably similar to those of state-owned airlines in Western Europe. With the exception of Britain, all members of the European Union have state-owned airlines which make losses and are supported by direct or indirect subsidies and illiberal regulation. They all have unprofitable intercontinental networks, excess capacity and over-manning. The problem of Balkan is not merely the familiar one of how to sequence privatization and restructuring, but that the fate of the national flag-carrier is seen to involve national prestige. The authorities approved the initiation of the privatization process before

38 *168 Hours BBN*, 19 December 1994–2 January 1995.

they had developed any kind of realistic airline policy. It is not our purpose here to propose such a policy, but a very brief review of the central issues would help to understand why this case has degenerated to such an extent that it is internationally notorious.

An airline policy for Bulgaria involves taking a position on two polar cases and deciding towards which end of the spectrum one envisages Balkan's lying in, say, five years time. One polar case is to attempt to serve approximately the present network; the other is to see Balkan as providing regional services and operating feeders to intercontinental services from major European hubs. Exactly the same question is confronting the governments responsible for Olympic, Alitalia, Iberia and TAP (to mention but a few) but, unlike Bulgaria, they have not attempted to sell their flag-carriers before taking a position on this strategic question. Potential buyers are certain to see Balkan's future as nearer the second polar case whereas the authorities seem inclined to the first polar case but do not appear to have recognized the budgetary consequences of such a stance. When the object to be traded is seen so differently by the seller and potential buyers, is it any wonder that there is no sale?

The case of the Sofia hotels is remarkable as an illustration of the rancour which can be generated when public authorities in a fledgling democracy attempt to deal with a politically sensitive issue which also involves significant private, commercial interests. That one of the parties should resort to the courts at such an early stage in the argument is a comment not only on the quality of the drafting of the legislation but, more importantly, on the quite inappropriate effort to use judicial reference to resolve what was fundamentally a policy difference between two public agencies.

There is a common element in all these cases, and it concerns the degree of commitment to privatization when the going gets tough. Some comment on this is offered in the next chapter.

THE PRIVATE SECTOR

Estimates of the size of the public sector must be treated with considerable caution. The registration of a business brings with it the attentions of tax collectors and it must be expected that official statistics underestimate the number of private businesses and the level of activity in the private sector. With that *caveat* we now look briefly at what is known about the scale of private commercial activity in Bulgaria.

Estimates of the number of private firms vary considerably, but there were probably about 400,000 at the end of 1993. A statistical profile of 147,000 of them suggested that 60 per cent of them were in trade, 16 per cent in industry and 9 per cent in transport.[39] Average net receipts during the year were BGL663,000, but this disguises the fact that most of these firms were very small: 20 per cent of them had receipts of less than BGL10,000 and the median was only BGL 61,000. They were also small in terms of employment, 40 per cent of them having less than 5 employees and 98 per cent having less than 100 employees.

Official estimates of the contribution of the private sector to GDP suggest considerable growth, with real growth in all parts of the economy at a time when public sector activity has been declining markedly. Thus, in 1993, real output in private industry was estimated to have grown by 29 per cent, in private construction by 16 per cent, and in private trade by 20 per cent, giving private activity's share of sectoral output of 4, 34 and 57 per cent respectively. Estimates of the overall share of private activity in GDP are shown in Table 8.6.

Table 8.6 Share of private sector in GDP (%), 1990–93

	1990	*1991*	*1992*	*1993*
Total[a]	9.1	11.8	15.3	19.4
Agriculture, forestry[b]	32.8	39.0	50.9	57.0
Industry, construction[b]	3.7	6.4	9.1	11.6
Services[b]	3.9	8.4	12.4	19.0

[a] % of total GDP
[b] % of sectoral value added
Source: Derived from Bulgarian National Bank

The figure for services disguises a very large variance within that group and, especially, does not reveal the dominance of the private

---

39 The doubts surrounding the reliability of such figures are not relieved by the fact that among the sectors shown as containing private firms is 'Government'! (National Statistical Institute, *Current Economic Business*, June 1994).

212 The Bulgarian Economy in Transition

sector in distributive activities, where it is estimated that the private share in total trade turnover reached 60 per cent in 1993.[40] At the broad sectoral level, the most spectacular growth has been in agriculture, reflecting the pace of land restitution. By late 1994, around 60 per cent of agricultural land was in private hands, and private farming in 1993 accounted for 97 per cent of potato production, 69 per cent of fruit, 79 per cent of sheep, 59 per cent of cattle and 70 per cent of milk.

40 National Statistical Institute, reported in *168 Hours BBN*, 20–26 June 1994.

9. Some Reflections

Bulgaria began its transition to a market economy with severe disadvantages. Some were shared with other reforming economies in the region, but no other country had all of them. First, domestic monetary disequilibrium created a severe overhang which, with the implementation of the big-bang liberalization package, caused prices to jump dramatically. Secondly, the existence of a large foreign debt which could not be serviced from 1990 onwards meant that the country was denied access to foreign capital except from the official multilateral agencies. Thirdly, and most fundamentally, Bulgaria suffered grievously because of the overwhelming dominance of the CMEA in its foreign trade. The institution itself collapsed; the real import demand of its members declined; there was a severe deterioration in the terms of trade as transactions among members began to take place at international prices; and trade with members outside the former Soviet Union began to be transacted in hard currencies. Allied to all this is that, as noted in Chapter 1, communism distorted the economy more than that of any other country in the region, bequeathing a structure of activity which bore little resemblance to comparative advantage and so creating especially difficult challenges as regards international competitiveness. Bulgaria suffered more than any country outside the Soviet Union itself from the long-term strategy of the latter to achieve military parity with the United States while having only a fraction of the American *per capita* income.

In addition to these legacies of the old regime, the country has been an innocent sufferer from the policies of the United Nations with regard to Iraq and Serbia–Montenegro. The embargo on Iraqi oil sales denied to Bulgaria major debt repayments in kind and the embargo on non-humanitarian sales to Iraq deprived the country of a what had been its largest non-CMEA market. Even worse, sanctions against the rump of Yugoslavia not only eliminated a traditional hard-currency market and lucrative transportation activity but has physically isolated Bulgaria from

213

Central and Western Europe at a time when the reorientation of trade is a central transition requirement.

This book has attempted to describe how Bulgaria has coped with the problems of transition in the face of these crippling handicaps. Westerners seem unable to write about formerly communist economies without offering advice, and the inhabitants of such economies are now less interested than they were in receiving such advice, but it is appropriate to venture, if only diffidently, an overview of the progress which has been made in the half-decade since the fall of Zhivkov. Transition has become a spectator sport, even to the extent that scores are awarded. It is reported[1] that the European Bank for Reconstruction and Development scored Bulgaria as follows (the scale 1–4 indicating increasing degrees of progress towards a market economy): privatization 2; restructuring 2; prices and competition 3; trade and foreign exchange 4; banking reform 2. This represented the lowest aggregate score for any reforming country of Central and Eastern Europe outside the former Soviet Union and in this chapter we consider whether such scores are appropriate, note the successes and suggest reasons why there have been significant disappointments.

MACROECONOMICS

With only the not very encouraging example of Poland to follow,[2] Bulgaria took a leap in the dark in February 1991, removing almost all price controls and trade restrictions, reducing subsidies and liberalizing the foreign exchange market. Subsequent macroeconomic history has been dominated by that event.

For the first three years, things went quite well. The initial price explosion was somewhat greater than expected, but appeared under control, with annual inflation, while remaining high, at least moving in the right direction. Output fell sharply, and continued to fall, with a consequent increase in unemployment, just as would have been

---

1 *The Economist*, 3–9 December 1994.

2 Czechoslovakia's first major step took place only a month prior to Bulgaria's and in any case was less relevant since the initial conditions were much more favourable.

expected, given the initial conditions. The balance of payments performed quite well for much of the period.

However, two time-bombs lay at the heart of the macroeconomy and they began to detonate in late 1993. First, the fiscal situation was never under control, making monetary restraint difficult to impose and generating persistent and increasing inflationary pressures. This was exacerbated by a combination of slow progress on banking reform and the willingness of the BNB, at negative real interest rates, to sustain the liquidity of an increasingly insolvent commercial banking system. Secondly, the real exchange value of the lev appreciated to such an extent that the effects of the spectacular devaluation accompanying the big bang were dissipated over a period of two years or so during which little had happened to provide a basis for long-term competitiveness. Admittedly, the BNB was faced with an exceptionally difficult dilemma. The interests of the real economy required that any market pressures for nominal devaluation should not be resisted whereas such depreciation would have increased the lev value of the foreign debt and its servicing during a period of extreme fiscal difficulty because of the collapse of state revenue. Market stability is obviously necessary but a managed devaluation, or crawling peg, would have been superior to a policy whose essence was to resist devaluation until the situation became hopeless.

The great disappointment was that, unlike for instance Poland and the Czech Republic, Bulgarian policy failed to dampen inflationary expectations to any significant extent and all roads seem to lead back to the fiscal situation, which did much to drive inflation, contributed nothing but confusion and conflict to the design of exchange-rate policy, and ensured that the burdens of monetary restrictions were borne entirely by the enterprise sector, public and private. In contrast to similar episodes in developed market economies, the root of the fiscal problem lay less with expenditure than with revenue. Any country going through the kind of contraction in real activity experienced by Bulgaria for five years would see real budget revenue declining. But this was entirely predictable, at least qualitatively, from 1990 — not only from an *a priori* examination of the effects of liberalization on the capacity of the tax system to deliver the required proportion of GDP as state revenue, but from what was happening in, for instance, Poland where, after an initial increase in revenue resulting from the impact of inflation on inventory profits, a steady reduction set in. The unwillingness, or incapacity, to respond quickly to a situation where reliance on profits tax was no longer realistic and to put in place systems which could capture a reasonable proportion of non-wage personal incomes, of growing private-sector profits and, above all, personal consumption was an example of real governmental failure.

Stabilization has been more difficult in Bulgaria than in any other country of the region because of the exceptionally severe initial conditions. Output began falling in 1989, primarily because of supply difficulties, and the decline accelerated in the following two years as, first, the CMEA went into terminal collapse and, secondly, domestic demand fell as a result of the big bang. According to official statistics, real GDP produced fell by 25 per cent between 1989 and 1994, only in the latter year showing any signs of recovery. Real household consumption, which in all countries is difficult to measure, is estimated to have fallen by something over 20 per cent during the same period. If one takes one's starting point as the end of 1990 (a year during which prices rose by something in excess of 50 percent) the official index of consumer prices increased 37-fold by the end of 1994, or by 10-fold if one ignores the immediate effects of the big bang of February 1991. Of course, these figures are to a degree misleading: private sector activity has grown sharply and has been inadequately represented in the national income accounts; aggregate consumption is measured residually and so subject to considerable estimation errors; and the consumer prices index overstates inflation. Nonetheless, by any measure what has happened in the past five years adds up to serious macroeconomic trauma.

Was it all necessary? The difficulty with this question stems from the relationship between macroeconomic stabilization and microeconomic reform. Some of the real depression could have been avoided if trade liberalization had not been instituted so suddenly and if monetary policy had given a lower priority to the control of inflation. Inflation would have been less explosive in the early stages if a more gradual approach had been taken to the liberalization of prices. However, if macroeconomic reform had been more gradual and if monetary policy had been concerned more with the fall in output than the increase in prices, restructuring would have been delayed even more than it has been. Competition from imports is the most effective form of competition available in Bulgaria and can constitute a major stimulus to efficiency improvements at home. The most that can be argued is that the dismantling of quantity restrictions on imports could have been accompanied by somewhat higher tariffs than were put in place. This would have contributed much needed revenue as well as introducing competition less abruptly. But then the extent of foreign competition would have become yet another political issue, the political incentives being to maintain excessive protection for too long.

If price controls had been relaxed gradually, the same problem would have arisen: all the pressures would have been to maintain the distortions which transformation to a market economy is designed to eliminate. Finally, if monetary policy had been more relaxed in an effort to maintain output, inflation would have been even worse. The problem with this is that rapid inflation, and the inevitable, accompanying depreciation in the foreign value of the currency, has real effects. In particular, it creates an environment so uncertain as to generate severe disincentives for investment, which had already collapsed and which is essential for enterprise restructuring.

There is thus no real trade-off between macroeconomic and microeconomic objectives. Those who claim that 'shock therapy' is all shock and no therapy fail to recognize that the therapeutic results do not inevitably follow from the shock. The unpleasant macroeconomic medicine is designed to assist economic reform: the latter is not something which happens automatically if one takes the medicine. Bulgaria's problem is not so much that there has been a dramatic decline in living standards, but that the suffering will have been in vain if reforms at the more microeconomic level do not take place. This is the difficult part of transition policy and we now offer some comment on this issue.

PRIVATIZATION AND RESTRUCTURING

The more hawkish of western commentators would give Bulgaria low marks in this area. First mooted in 1991, the basic privatization legislation was not passed until April 1992 and then it was poorly drafted and had to be extensively revised within two years. Worse, privatization strategy was incoherent, with the authorities at loggerheads with each other over individual cases, no articulated fallback position in negotiations and no clear idea as to how to deal with enterprises not yet privatized.

The latter defect is particularly serious, not because of an abstract conclusion that the state cannot be trusted to be an effective agent of restructuring and so should privatize or liquidate with all speed, but because the practicalities of privatization ensure that very many enterprises — potential successes as well as candidates for liquidation — will remain in state hands for a long time to come. Since soft budget constraints by default are recognized by all as a recipe for disaster, the state cannot avoid an exercise in what those who disapprove of discriminatory industrial policies disdainfully describe as 'picking winners'.

In the previous chapter, the difficulties attending attempts to privatize large enterprises were illustrated with examples from the trucking, airline, cement and hotel industries. What do these examples reveal about attitudes to and procedures for privatization in Bulgaria?

What appears to have gone wrong is in part a policy failure and in part an institutional failure. The policy failure arises because, once it has been decided to privatize an enterprise, none of the relevant public agencies has a clear picture of what will be done if that goal is not achieved: the Bulgarian authorities appear to have no coherent policy as regards enterprises which have yet to be privatized. As a result, large-scale privatization efforts too easily turn into a trial of strength among public institutions instead of there being defined criteria by which the options can be evaluated.

Suppose an auction or tender process produces a highest bid which is judged insufficient by reference to the prior valuation, or negotiations with buyers are generating offers significantly below that valuation. What is then to be done? The privatizing authority may start the process again, with as much optimism as it can muster, but in the meantime it comes under attack from other political, official or commercial interests who whip up opposition with the cry that that authority is proposing to dispose of state assets at giveaway prices. This is because no decision has been made in advance as to the second-best strategy, something which could be built in to the privatization programme for an enterprise. With all respect to the prestigious accounting firms involved, the valuations which play a central role in these dramas are subject to huge margins of error because of the great uncertainties involved. What is much less subject to error is an estimate of the cost to the state over the next few years if an enterprise is not privatized. The present value of that cost could be incorporated into the privatization strategy to determine the acceptable limits of any selling price, and this could be done just as formally as the asset valuation.

After all, selling an enterprise for $20 million when the valuation says $30 million is in fact a good deal for the state if the cost of the alternative, in terms of subsidization or state investment to maintain the capital value of the enterprise, exceeds $10 million. On top of this is the fact that there will be a systematic tendency for all parties involved (privatizing authority, enterprise management, sectoral association, sectoral ministry and members of the Assembly) to over-value any enterprise in their own minds.

Other indicators of alternative action could similarly be built in. The point is that the present process is too vulnerable to politicization if a privatization project is not immediately successful, because the pre-defined parameters of action are too limited. The objective is not to privatize at any price, but to give privatization a chance by forcing all parties to recognize publicly that non-privatization is not costless. At present, it is too easy for objectors: the system does not force them to state that their objection carries with it a demand for extra taxes or a dramatic reduction in an enterprise's level of employment.

The institutional failure is one which has bedevilled many of Bulgaria's reform efforts. At the simplest and most general level, radical reform is impossible in any society without the creation and empowerment of constituencies committed to that reform. If we apply this general point to privatization, what do we find? The only organ of the state with an unambiguous interest in privatization is the PA, but it is politically vulnerable: it is far from inconceivable that its board would be replaced if its policy in relation to a particular enterprise (as opposed to its general policies) met with government disapproval. The ministries have conflicting interests: they have privatization responsibilities but they are under direct political control, they have close relations with the managements of enterprises for whose privatization they are responsible and, because they are responsible for sectors, they have developed an inclination to act as the representative of 'their' sectors. The same considerations apply to the municipalities.

The Council of Ministers, the Assembly and its committees have no particular interest in privatization and they involve themselves in individual cases in circumstances where neither the Constitution nor the Privatization Law gives them explicit competence. Apart from a case involving an employee buyout, it is difficult to think of any realistic circumstances in which a politician could accumulate political capital by being in favour of a privatization. There will always be a section of society which sees itself as losing in any privatization deal and there will always be a deputy willing to express its objections. These problems are exacerbated by the contentiousness of politics in Bulgaria and the instability of parliamentary coalitions.

Among the populace at large there is no significant pro-privatization constituency. One may develop if mass privatization is initially successful or if there is progress in privatization by public share offerings, but at present most people probably regard privatization as a mixture of a threat and a conspiracy. Aside from public officials, the main constituent of what, in a market economy, would be called a middle class is enterprise management and its attitude to privatization will be at best ambiguous and at worst hostile. This also is likely to change as the management of an increasing number of enterprises is forced to recognize that the old easy options are no longer available, but this in turn requires hard choices for government and the state of politics at present gives no grounds for optimism in the short term.

There is no obvious solution to these institutional and political problems: it is in the nature of democracy that what may seem to be technical problems become politicized. In addition, the problems are made worse by the absence of an executive which can be confident of the support of the legislature. A further difficulty, which is inherent in a process involving the large-scale disposal of state assets in a situation where there is little competition, is that authorities have access to economic rents: to put it simply, they are in a position, in cases where competitive bidding is ineffective, to dispense large favours. There will always be rumours of pay-offs to strategically placed officials or politicians — rumours which are impossible to confirm — and it is obviously desirable to minimize the opportunities for public corruption of this kind. However, it is not clear what kind of institutional arrangement would achieve this objective. Concentration of privatization authority (for instance, by giving the PA exclusive jurisdiction) would reduce the number of persons with access to these rents but would increase the average value of the rents at the disposal of such persons. One might concentrate power and give the relevant officials very high salaries (or, better, a share in the proceeds of privatization) to reduce the temptations they face, but then any infection would spread to the recruitment policies of this all-powerful agency. This point may appear to cast aspersions on the integrity of officials, but it is not a comment on the state of public administration in Bulgaria: all countries have their scandals when officials and politicians are in a position to do large favours to commercial interests.

One will never get politics out of the privatization process, but some institutional re-design could help to avoid the disintegration of that process in major cases. The lead should be taken by the politicians, who have been guilty of sins of both commission and omission. The Council of Ministers and the Assembly interfere at the wrong stage in the process. The legislation clearly envisages, by requiring parliamentary approval of the PA's annual programme and requiring the Cabinet's approval in very large cases, that political consent will be given at the initiation of the process for any given enterprise: it does not envisage political authorities' intervening later. These authorities have neglected their responsibilities in laying down the strategic parameters for an enterprise at the beginning of the process and have substituted tactical interference during the process itself. This division of competence between political and administrative organs is something which has to be learned by experience but, if Bulgaria does not learn it quickly, every major privatization will be a SOMAT, a Balkan or a Sunny Beach.

There is nothing in principle wrong with the ministries having privatization responsibility for their smaller enterprises, but the Cabinet needs to support the PA in a firmer line on issues where ministries behave as representatives of sectoral interests. The time for the minister of construction to argue about cement or the Committee on Tourism to argue about resorts is when they appear on the list submitted by the PA. Once that list is agreed, privatization of the relevant enterprises should be treated as an administrative matter for the competent administrative authority.

Many of these problems are related to the absence of any strategy as to what to do with enterprises which have yet to be privatized. Privatization is conducted in a vacuum and not within the context of a more general industrial policy. This issue is also germane to the more general question: how important is it that privatization should be conducted swiftly?

This is an extremely complex question which goes to the very heart of transition strategies and, appropriately, has generated a large literature.[3] The reason it is so complex is that, even if it could be

---

3 For a recent summary, see Roland (1994).

established that privatization is a necessary condition for effective transition, no-one argues that it is sufficient. Many other institutional changes have to be made if the potential benefits of privatization are to be reaped and, what is more, if privatization is not to turn into a poisoned chalice. After all, there is no clear evidence that the rapid and widespread Czech privatization has done much to date to improve the efficiency of that economy and it could be argued that the other allegedly star performer in this area — Russia — has, through privatization which turned out to be insider ownership, created an even less efficient system of corporate control than existed under state ownership.

It turns out that the strongest arguments both for and against rapid privatization are political, not economic. In favour are the points that, first, widespread private ownership creates a pro-market constituency which is large enough to influence policies promoting further reform and, secondly, that widespread state ownership gives governments — for whom economic efficiency is not a primary objective — too much opportunity to intervene at the microeconomic level. Against these points are the contentions that extensive privatization leads to politically unacceptable distributions of wealth and to socially unrestrained restructuring of enterprises which generates widespread hardship. Such privatization thus provokes an anti-reform backlash (as evidence for which some, though not the present author, would cite the resurgence of former/reformed communists in Bulgaria, Hungary, Lithuania and Poland).

Those who have paid most attention to the political economy of transition tend to conclude that gradualism — that is, phased restructuring of enterprises before privatization, rather than having privatization as the first step to restructuring — will on balance minimize the risk that reform will be frustrated for many years because, with restructuring, the pain comes before the benefit.

However, a suggestion that it may actually be desirable to delay privatization should provide no consolation to Bulgarian politicians and officials who, as we have seen, have not exactly been in the vanguard in promoting privatization. The reason is that the debate has not been about whether privatization should be pursued: hardly any commentator on transition economies would argue that it should not. The debate has in fact been about sequencing: is it better to effect at least some restructuring (that is, efficiency-raising changes in enterprise practices, which is the whole point of the exercise) before privatization. A dogmatic view that politicians and bureaucrats are incapable of overseeing any kind of painful restructuring is simply not convincing since, not only have suggestions been made as to how this can be done in the light of the relevant political constraints,[4] but there is evidence that it can be and has been done.[5]

This brings us back to the point about the absence in Bulgaria of any kind of industrial policy. Not only is such a policy necessary so that, in individual cases, the alternative to privatization can be evaluated (this is the point made earlier), but it is essential as a (possibly superior) alternative to immediate privatization. This is a major policy failure — in the longer term more serious than the defects regarding fiscal and exchange-rate policy already noted. This failure to put together anything remotely resembling a coherent strategy for enterprise restructuring, and so any policy for weeding out those who obviously have poor survival prospects in a market environment, has been possible because of the continuing use of the banking system to subsidise the enterprise sector. In broad terms, the banks appear to be in no better shape, even after the *ZUNK* operation, than they were on the eve of transition. Their claims for BNB assistance in the face of new non-performing credits to enterprises have been a major constraint on monetary policy and, what is worse, the continuing accumulation of such assets in their balance sheets has meant that a vital part of the required institutional structure is fundamentally weak. Some good work has been done on bank consolidation, but there are now strong arguments that bank privatization is more urgent than industrial privatization, since this may be the only realistic way of hardening the budget constraints faced by the banks. Stock exchanges, quite apart from the instability they experience as a result of the quotation of fraudulent ventures such as pyramid schemes (of which Bulgaria already has its share), cannot carry to any significant extent in the foreseeable future the responsibility to be an important channel of finance for industrial investment and so the banks will continue to be much more important in this respect than they would be in a typical, developed market economy.

---

4 See, for example, Aghion, Blanchard and Burgess (1994).

5 Pinto, Belka and Krajewski (1993), which reports efficiency improvements in Polish enterprises still in state ownership.

There is no easy way out of these dilemmas: restructuring is painful but essential. The failure to grasp these nettles could be put down to the cowardice or incompetence on the part of politicians, but that would be too simple. We now consider briefly the political context within which the difficult decisions on transition policy have to be worked out.

POLITICS

Macroeconomic policy is politically asymmetrical: in all countries, anti-inflationary policies are unpopular whereas policies designed to stimulate domestic demand are popular. Unfortunately for transition economies, their first recent experience of democracy coincided with the need for seriously depressive policies on top of the dramatic exogenous shocks produced by the collapse of planning systems throughout the region.

Then, at the microeconomic level, transition involves great uncertainty as to employment prospects. Even in market economies, privatization tends to be resisted by the workforce[6] who see the likely short-term effect to be job insecurity. Restructuring of public enterprises encounters similar resistance. In transition economies, this adds up to a formidable coalition which, quite rationally, sees no personal short-run advantage in privatization or restructuring. Workers may recognize in the abstract that past practices cannot continue, but it takes a very considerable exercise of faith for a worker to sustain that recognition when his or her own job is under threat.

This is only one dimension of the most important impact which the abandonment of planning has had on the economic and social life of the populace at large: the replacement of security by uncertainty. Some commentators (especially those who do not live in the region) pass this off as no more than the need to grow up — to replace the security of the child with the insecurity of the adult — but this is facile in the extreme. No electorate in a western democracy would tolerate a government which presided over the kind of collapse in living standards experienced in the past few years. Regardless of any statistical difficulties in

---

6 But less so by the management who, in public, look forward to escape from what they call 'the dead hand of bureaucracy' and, in private, welcome freedom from public sector salary restrictions.

measuring the scale of this collapse, no-one can deny that the mass of the population has suffered severely. Particularly acute is the situation of pensioners, who account for almost one-third of the population and who have least opportunity to supplement their incomes (which have declined relative to average wages), and the several hundred thousand who are at least partially unemployed and all of whom had jobs five years ago.

Under the old system, an important component of household living standards was represented by access to social services provided by employers or public authorities. Such provision has declined significantly (and is not captured in aggregate consumption statistics) as the financial situation of enterprises and the budgetary situation of the public authorities has deteriorated. In the west, decline in the quality of publicly provided social services threatens governments, as the current situation in Britain illustrates: in Bulgaria, that decline has been much more dramatic.

These conditions have generated a deep and widespread discontent, made worse by a recognition that no alleviation is in prospect in the immediate future, even with the best of policies. Some quantitative indication of this discontent can be derived from annual surveys of public opinion in Central and Eastern Europe conducted by the Austrian-sponsored New Democracies Barometer project. Table 9.1 extracts from the vast wealth of information collected in those surveys just two indicators of Bulgarian attitudes to what has been happening, politically and economically, since 1989. Survey I was conducted in late 1991, Survey II in late 1992 and early 1993 and Survey III in late 1993 and early 1994.

What is shown is progressive disillusionment with the new political and economic regimes. In 1991, Bulgarians had strong preferences for the political changes, with 76 per cent liking the new system and only 33 per cent approving of the old regime (the excess above 100 per cent is accounted for by the fact that the question referred to approval, not preference) and were very optimistic about the political future, at least in the sense that over 90 per cent said that they expected to approve of the new system in five years' time. They were less enthusiastic regarding the changes from a command to a liberalized economy. More than half approved of the old economic regime, whereas under 30 per cent approved of the new system, but again there was optimism, with

226   *The Bulgarian Economy in Transition*

almost 90 per cent expecting to approve of a market economy in the future.

However, the hardships of transition have wrought significant changes in public opinion, the later surveys indicating a very clear increase in approval of the old regimes (both political and economic), diminishing approval of the new systems and, not surprisingly but somewhat dishearteningly, declining expectations that the new regimes would be approved of in five years' time.

Table 9.1 Indicators of public opinion (%)

	I	II	III
Political			
Approving old system	33	42	51
Approving new system now	76	55	59
Approving new system in 5 years time	92	72	70
Economic			
Approving old system	55	59	66
Approving new system now	29	24	14
Approving new system in 5 years time	87	63	56

Source: Rose and Haerpfer (1992), pp. 36 and 47; Rose and Haerpfer (1993), Appendix Tables 16–18 and 23–25; Rose and Haerpfer (1994), Appendix Tables 22–24 and 32–34.

Table 9.2 Reaction to statements (%)

	A	B	C
Strongly agree	9	23	41
Somewhat agree	16	22	25
Somewhat disagree	25	21	16
Strongly disagree	50	33	17

Source: Rose and Haerpfer (1994), Appendix Tables 43, 45, 46.

It would be wrong to infer from these figures that there really are serious reservations about democracy itself. Attitudes to this issue are revealed by the answers to questions in the 1993/94 survey designed to test agreement with certain anti-democratic statements. Table 9.2 gives these answers. The columns in the table are statements as follows: A — we should return to communist rule; B — best to get rid of parliament and elections and have a strong leader who can quickly decide things; C — the most important decisions about the economy should be made by experts and not the government and parliament. What this indicates is that, even after several years of hardship, three-quarters of Bulgarians have no wish to see a return of communist rule. They do, however, have serious doubts about the ability of the parliamentary system to be effective in the making of policy: they are divided approximately equally in this respect. They have a particularly jaundiced view concerning the capacity of representative government to deliver effective economic policies (where two-thirds think that economic policy should be left to technocrats), but this is not even a transition, let alone a particularly Bulgarian, opinion: long-standing democracies do not want for those who prescribe 'a government of businessmen' as a cure for economic ills.

More generally, there is a very low level of identification with major socio-political institutions. More than two-thirds stated that they do not trust any of the following: parties, the courts, the police, civil servants, government, parliament, and trade unions. The same proportion mistrust private enterprises, which is somewhat discouraging.[7]

It is against this background that political activity is conducted. No politician promises (or threatens, according to one's viewpoint) a return to the old days: that at least is a small compliment to the realism of the electorate. Whether or not they would welcome such a return is beside the point: they know it is not on the menu. Also, Bulgarians claim that stoicism is a defining national characteristic, developed to cope with the long Ottoman occupation and proving valuable during the communist decades. If this trait were in fact prevalent, it would help to explain the apparent passivity and fatalism in the face of present difficulties.

We have noted definite governmental failures manifested by delays in legislation, tardiness in tax reform and inadequate progress on such matters as privatization and bank reform. The extreme cynic would say that it is only the country's reliance on the IMF and the World Bank,

---

7 Rose and Haerpfer (1994), Appendix Tables 48–62. Westerners should note that 71 per cent of respondents indicated mistrust of 'foreign organizations and experts advising our government'.

and those institutions' insistence on the observation of the conditions attached to their assistance, which has produced any structural reform at all. It must be left to Bulgarians to pass judgement on the quality of their own politicians, but some observations on the working of political processes would be in order.

In the first place, the communist regime was overturned with none of the drama of Czechoslovakia, Romania or, over a more extended period, Poland. One aspect of this is the failure of any dominant personality to emerge: no-one equivalent to, for example, the pairing of Havel and Klaus in Prague materialized as the personification of the new era, with the charisma to excite the public imagination for reform and the political legitimacy to effect such reform. President Zhelev has performed sterling, non-partisan service in ensuring some continuity of government in the face of repeated parliamentary fragmentation, but his is a non-executive post and he rose to prominence as an academic opponent of communism, not as an economic reformer.

Nor has any effective pro-reform political grouping emerged. This role could have been performed by the UDF: over the years it has published quite fervent protestations in favour of privatization, monetary and fiscal rectitude and the need for the rapid adoption of market institutions, attitudes and practices. However, it is barely a party in the American sense, let alone the Western European sense. It began as a grouping of organizations (if that is not too flattering a word) with nothing in common but opposition to the old regime. By its political naivety it snatched defeat from the jaws of victory at the first elections. Its opportunity came after the second elections in 1991 when it formed the government with the MRF, but government requires discipline and parliamentary coherence, and the UDF's inability to maintain unity, or to accept the need for compromise with actual or potential partners, ensured that it remained in power for barely a year. The seal was set on its ineffectiveness by the results of the elections of December 1994, in which it polled less than one-quarter of the votes.

Opposition is always easier than government and the situation in Bulgaria is so depressed that few deputies are comfortable supporting current policies. The upshot is that policy formation and parliamentary activity are detached from each other. Between the first free elections and the end of 1994, Bulgaria had five governments, only two of which were formed directly from the Assembly and involved major figures in the parliamentary parties. These both followed elections but were short-lived. For three of the past four-and-a-half years, the country has been governed by administrations with no parliamentary roots, comprising essentially non-party figures whose survival depended on majorities in the Assembly whose support was perennially insecure. There has as yet been no government constructed on the basis of anything more than the vaguest platform, even on the two (or, since January 1995, three) occasions when governments were created following elections.

The fundamental problem has been the failure to create, in the country and the Assembly, anything resembling a significant constituency in favour of even parts of a reform programme — or even coherently against reform. This difficulty cannot be laid at the door of the electoral system, despite the hankering of some Bulgarians for a first-past-the-post procedure. There is extreme fragmentation, but the fact that 49 parties were registered for the elections held on 18 December 1994 is not evidence of that: the existence of a party whose sole membership is its leader and her brother is not a peculiarly Bulgarian phenomenon and the requirement of a minimum of 4 per cent of the popular vote to achieve parliamentary representation ensures that the number of parties in the Assembly is small. Nor does the failure of any party, until the most recent elections, to achieve a majority of seats make Bulgaria unusual among European polities.

One source of the failure at the parliamentary level, which is perhaps unsurprising in a fledgling democracy, is a belief that democracy is enough. Behaviour on the floor of the Assembly and in its committees has the flavour of a university faculty meeting, with little feeling that an important purpose is to create policy — which requires cohesion and compromise — rather than merely to express opinions.[8] It is true that the construction of log-rolling coalitions — and the very notion that any party is itself a coalition which must be disciplined if it is to be effective — are ideas and skills which took a long time to learn in western democracies, and they still fail from time to time in countries which have practised representative government for two or three centuries. However, serious policy making cannot take place without a

---

8 When the author commented to the chairman of a parliamentary committee that he and his colleagues seemed to behave like a group of professors, his reply was 'Actually, many of us are'.

belief that parliaments should properly play a role in the formation of policy as well as providing a forum for the expression of diverse views. Of course, policy always exists: if the politicians fail to take a leading role, policy is made by default. In this case, it is made by functionaries — officials and enterprise managers. The first example of this in post-communist Bulgaria was the growth of informal privatization which, by all reports, continues still and will go on as long as formal privatization is slow, commercial law is ineffectively implemented and serious budget constraints are not placed on state-owned enterprises. The close-knit nature of the old *nomenklatura* makes it comparatively simple for transactions to take place which ensure that profits accrue to private interests, balanced by losses in public enterprises.

More generally, the pace of reform, in the absence of political leadership, is set at the administrative level. This has already been noted with respect to privatization, which can proceed no faster than is permitted by the wishes of the Privatization Agency or the relevant ministries, the latter being constrained by the attitudes of the management of the enterprises to be privatized. But the same issues arise everywhere, from tax reform to banking policy: the absence of a strong commitment at the political level has inhibited those officials who are anxious for reform but, on the other hand, has allowed more conservative officials ample opportunity to make their conservatism effective.

Equally pervasive — and again an example of this was seen in the case of privatization — is that reform which requires governmental power gives rise to scarcity rents: a price can be, and possibly is, attached to both the granting of permission and the withholding of permission. Perhaps the strongest constitutional argument in favour of a full-blown market economy is that it minimizes such rents and, in particular, reduces the opportunities for personal gain from the exercise of political and administrative power granted by the law. Corruption of politicians and bureaucrats exists in all societies, but in many ways it is like tax evasion. One may hope that an honest culture may develop, or one may institute severe penalties for malefactors, but the best method is to minimize the incentives for such behaviour. This is of special significance in transition economies, which are not only attempting to create a market economy but are also struggling to establish a civil society. Popular cynicism that politicians and bureaucrats abuse their positions for personal gain in exactly the same way as they did under the old regime is not conducive to support for either a civil society or a market economy. In the game of a market economy, politicians are supposed to set the rules and bureaucrats are supposed to be the referees: neither group is supposed to be numbered among the players. Just why there have been major policy failures and why the political process is held in such deservedly low esteem would provide rich fields for research. Perhaps it is simply that the sheer scale of the economic, social and political transformation required is beyond the short-term capacity of any polity. Certainly, Bulgaria is far from unique as regards the disillusionment of its population: the surveys cited above generated qualitatively similar results for most transition countries for most of the aspects of public opinion investigated. Political leadership is an elusive concept and it is pointless just wringing one's hands over its apparent absence. In mature democracies, most politicians most of the time choose their profession for reasons which are rather remote from any notion of leadership. They may have vague ideas of duty, and even vaguer ideas that they may actually be able to effect major change, but by and large they enter politics for the same kinds of reasons why anyone else chooses a job — material considerations, social status and, more generally, because they are attracted by what they see as the day-to-day activities of that job. One could, however, perhaps have expected that, in transition societies, politics would have been more attractive than elsewhere to those who want to change the world. In Western Europe and North America, policy-making is most of the time incremental: no policy change does more than effect a marginal change to the *status quo*. No-one wants radical changes and there is great inertia in the policy system. In former communist countries, on the other hand, major change is accepted as inevitable and so one might have expected that politics would have attracted persons who would like to participate in that change. Furthermore, the opinion surveys seem to suggest that strong leadership would be welcomed by the voters. Perhaps politicians have yet to learn what leadership can mean in a parliamentary democracy, which is so different from what it meant when a ruling elite, or even a dominant individual, could use a repressive state machine to enforce its will. The only politicians who have experience of any of the relevant skills for exercising non-coercive leadership are those who operated within the old communist party, but most of those have now departed from the scene. In any case, that experience is of limited value since it involved essentially what could be called committee work with a comparatively small group of colleagues. No-one has yet developed skill in holding together a large group (that is, a parliamentary party) in an intensely dynamic environment. Until those skills are acquired, inactivity on the policy front is the rational behaviour for a party leader. It is also the rational behaviour for a party since a good rule of thumb is that elections are lost, not won. In the absence of a significant constituency in favour of identifiable change (and not simply 'anything is better than what we have now'), elections are least likely to be lost if the electorate cannot identify a party with a specific set of policies.

THE FUTURE

It was noted in the Preface that a writer on contemporary Eastern Europe can never be sure that he or she knows even what is happening today. Looking forward is even more hazardous, but it is expected of an author.

Some effort has been made by Bulgarian economists to provide medium-term forecasts of macroeconomic developments[9] but it is difficult to rate the results as much better than guesswork. Not only is the current situation so unstable, but the quality of many of the available data is enough to induce despair in any forecaster. Serious defects in the official statistics for GDP, unemployment and the balance of payments have been noted above and so, with such doubts surrounding measurement of the present, how much more doubt must attend any attempt to make quantitative predictions. When writing in 1993, the authors cited expected negative real growth in 1994 and zero growth in 1995. However, their later forecasts suggests that the bottom of the output trough will have been reached in 1994, with some real growth in 1995 (and the official estimates for 1994 indicate just this — see Chapter 3 above). Nor did they predict the acceleration in the inflation rate in 1994, though they did forecast a nominal depreciation in the exchange rate (but not the scale of that depreciation). This shows how difficult macroeconomic forecasting is.

Even if it is accepted that aggregate output has turned up and will, in

---

9 Angelov et al. (1993) and an update by the same team reported in *Bulgarian Business News*, 9–15 January 1995.

the absence of new exogenous shocks, continue to increase, it is impossible to predict the growth rate: it depends upon so many interrelated structural factors, perhaps the most important of which are international competitiveness and the climate for investment. These in turn depend upon attitudes to and the pace of restructuring and privatization, exchange-rate policy and fiscal and monetary policy. This book has been repeatedly critical of policy failures in these regards, and it is impossible to be optimistic until more coherent policy formation materializes. There has been so much drift on the policy front that one is tempted to conclude that *any* policy package, even if is not the best one as long as it is cogent and consistently pursued, would contribute to the creation of an environment encouraging socially useful enterprise and foreign investment. Nor should the role of international suppliers of capital be underestimated. Effective management of the monetary system requires the IMF and the appalling state of the country's infrastructure necessitates the support of such agencies as the World Bank. Access to such assistance has already been jeopardized by domestic policy failures.

The monetary upheavals of 1993–94 seem, at the time of writing, to have passed. If the inflation rate prevailing in the early part of 1995 were to be maintained throughout the year, the level for the year as a whole would be less than 40 per cent — by far the lowest since 1989. Associated with this is restored stability in the exchange rate. Whether or not this is false dawn will depend upon the ability of the new government to restrain its fiscal urges and to make genuine progress on banking reform and privatization.

As regards that government, the early signs were mixed. Encouraging were statements by the new minister for economic development that there would be strict control of the budget deficit[10] and by the prime minister that the mass privatization programme would get under way during 1995.[11] Less encouraging was the appointment to the education ministry of the man who had held the same post in the 1980s and had been a leader of the anti-Turkish policies at that time.[12] There is some game-playing over actions taken by earlier governments to keep former

---

10 *OMRI Daily Digest*, 24 January 1995.
11 *OMRI Daily Digest*, 30 January 1995.
12 *OMRI Daily Digest*, 24 and 27 January 1995.

communists out of high office in universities and to recover public money allegedly appropriated by the communist party. Least encouraging of all were signs that certain economic reform processes were to be reversed. The government introduced legislation to restore some of the overriding powers of the state in relation to agricultural land, by limiting private sales of land and giving the state first option to buy.[13] This was certainly a bad omen.

Casual observation may suggest that things are getting better. The shops in the cities now look more like western shops, with a good range of goods, including luxury items. Private cars exist in much greater numbers and one notices a fair proportion of Volvos and BMWs. However, this reflects primarily what has happened to the distribution of income and reveals nothing about general living standards. The regular economy has failed, and continues to fail, a large proportion of the population who cope by resort to stratagems long since redundant in Western Europe.[14] The quality of access to education and health care has noticeably declined and public services are manifestly crumbling.

This is the reality of Bulgarian transition and how long it will be tolerated is anyone's guess. All one can hope is that some sense of urgency can be instilled into a political process which has to date been noteworthy mainly for its failures. The political success has been that the feared spill-over of the Yugoslav conflict has not occurred and that, so far anyway, there have been no signs of dissatisfaction being channelled into a revival of the ethnic conflict which scarred the country as late as the 1980s. This non-sociologist observer gains some comfort from the following judgement:[15]

The Bulgarians pride themselves on sustaining a ... work culture, in contrast to the Serbs' ... hero culture or the Romanians' and Greeks' alleged mercantile-ingenuity culture ... The Bulgarians are, on balance, rather impressively utilitarian and hard-headed, with little of the romanticism or mysticism of other Slav peoples.

---

13 *OMRI Daily Digest*, 8 March 1995. This legislation was vetoed by President Zhelev and, at the time of writing, was the subject of constitutional dispute.

14 For an analysis of coping tactics, see Rose (1993).

15 Quoted in Glenny (1993), p. 182.

Bibliography

Aghion, P., Blanchard, O. and Burgess, R. (1994), 'The behaviour of state firms in Eastern Europe, pre-privatisation', *European Economic Review*, 38(6), 1327–49.

Angelov, I., Doulev, S., Houbenova-Delissivkova, T., Yotzov, V. and Konsoulov, V. (1993), *Economic Outlook of Bulgaria 1994–1996*, Bulgarian Academy of Sciences, Sofia.

Aroio, Z. (1989), 'The enterprise in the People's Republic of Bulgaria' in United Nations Commission for Europe, *Economic Reforms in the European Centrally Planned Economies*, New York.

Beleva, I., Bobeva, D., Dilova, S. and Mitchkovski, A. (1993), 'Labour market trends and policies — Bulgaria' in Fischer, G. and Standing, G. (eds), *Structural Change in Central and Eastern Europe: Labour Market and Social Policy Implications*, Organisation for Economic Cooperation and Development, Paris.

Berov, L. (1993), 'Demonopolization and international competition in Bulgaria 1990–1992', *Russian and East European Finance and Trade*, 29(1), 87–100.

Bleaney, M. (1988), *Do Socialist Economies Work?*, Blackwell, Oxford.

Blommestein, H.J. and Spencer, M.G. (1994), 'The role of financial institutions in the transition to a market economy' in Caprio, G., Folkerts-Landau, D. and Jane T.D. (eds), *Building Sound Finance in Emerging Market Economies*, International Monetary Fund and World Bank, Washington D.C.

Bogetic, Z. (1993), 'The role of employee ownership in privatisation of state enterprises in Eastern and Central Europe', *Europe-Asia Studies*, 45(3), 463–82.

Bogetic, Z. and Fox, L. (1993), 'Incomes policies during stabilization: a review and lessons from Bulgaria and Romania', *Comparative Economic Studies*, 35(1), 39–57.

Borensztein, E., Demekas, D.G. and Ostry, J.D. (1993), 'An empirical analysis of the output declines in three Eastern European countries', *International Monetary Fund Staff Papers*, 40(1), 1–31.

Bruno, M. (1992), 'Stabilization and reform in Eastern Europe — a preliminary evaluation', *International Monetary Fund Staff Papers*, 39(4), 741–77.

Burda, M. (1993), 'Unemployment, labour markets and structural change in eastern Europe', *Economic Policy*, 16, 101–37.

Calvo, G.A. and Coricelli, F. (1993), 'Output collapse in Eastern Europe — the role of credit', *International Monetary Fund Staff Papers*, 40(1), 32–52.

Caprio, G. Jr. and Levine, R. (1994), 'Reforming finance in transitional socialist economies', *World Bank Research Observer*, 9(1), 1–24.

Casanegra de Jantscher, M., Silvani, C. and Vehorn, C.L. (1992), 'Modernizing tax administration' in Tanzi, V. (ed.), *Fiscal Policies in Economies in Transition*, International Monetary Fund, Washington D.C.

Chand, S.K. and Lorie, H.R. (1993), 'Bulgaria's transition to a market economy: fiscal aspects' in Tanzi, V. (ed.), *Transition to Market — Studies in Fiscal Reform*, International Monetary Fund, Washington D.C.

Chary, F.B. (1972), *The Bulgarian Jews and the Final Solution 1940–1944*, University of Pittsburgh Press, Pittsburgh.

Cochrane, J.H. and Ickes, B.W. (1991), 'Inflation stabilization in reforming socialist economies: the myth of the monetary overhang', *Comparative Economic Studies*, 33(2), 97–122.

Commission of the European Communities (1991), *Bulgaria's Agriculture: Situation, Trends and Prospects*, Luxembourg.

Corbett, J. and Mayer, C. (1991), 'Financial reform in Eastern Europe: progress with the wrong model', *Oxford Review of Economic Policy*, 7(4), 57–75.

Cottarelli, C. and Blejer, M.I. (1992), 'Forced saving and repressed inflation in the Soviet Union, 1986–90: some empirical results', *International Monetary Fund Staff Papers*, 39(2), 256–86.

Crampton, R.J. (1987), *A Short History of Modern Bulgaria*, Cambridge University Press, Cambridge.

Daviddi, R. (1989), 'Monetary reforms in Bulgaria' in Kessides, C., King, T., Nuti, M. and Sokil, K. (eds), *Financial Reform in Socialist Economies*, World Bank, Washington D.C.

Dobrin, B. (1973), *Bulgarian Economic Development since World War II*, Praeger, New York.

Dobrinsky, R. (1994), 'Reform of the financial system in Bulgaria' in Bonin, J.P. and Szekely, I.P. (eds), *The Development and Reform of Financial Systems in Central and Eastern Europe*, Edward Elgar, Aldershot.

East, R. (1992), *Revolutions in Eastern Europe*, Pinter, London.

Estrin, S. (ed.) (1994), *Privatization in Central and Eastern Europe*, Longmans, London.

Frydman, R., Rapaczynski, A., Earle, J.S. et al. (1993a), *The Privatization Process in Central Europe*, Central European University Press, Budapest, London and New York.

Frydman, R., Rapaczynski, A., Earle, J.S. et al. (1993b), *The Privatization Process in Russia, Ukraine and the Baltic States*, Central European University Press, Budapest, London and New York.

Frydman, R. and Rapaczynski, A. (1994), *Privatization in Eastern Europe: Is the State Withering Away?*, Central European University Press, Budapest, London and New York.

Ganchev, G. (1992), 'Bulgaria's foreign debt in freely convertible currency: structural problems', *Russian and East European Finance and Trade*, 28(1), 41–61.

Gandhi, V.P. and Mihaljek, D. (1992), 'Scope for reform of socialist tax systems' in Tanzi, V. (ed.), *Fiscal Policies in Economies in Transition*, International Monetary Fund, Washington D.C.

Glenny, M. (1993), *The Rebirth of History: Eastern Europe in the Age of Democracy*, 2nd ed., Penguin Books, London.

Gocheva, R., Stoyanova, K., Boicheva, M. and Tsanov, V. (1992), 'The reflection of the freeing of prices on the standard of living', *Bulgarian Quarterly*, II(2), 53–61.

Gray, C.W. and associates (1993), *Evolving Legal Frameworks for Private Sector Development in Central and Eastern Europe*, Discussion Paper 209, World Bank, Washington D.C.

Grosser, I. (1989), 'Economic reforms in Bulgaria' in Gabrisch, H. (ed.), *Economic Reforms in Eastern Europe and the Soviet Union*, Westview Press, Boulder and London.

Grosser, I. (1991), 'Bulgaria: delayed transition exacerbates economic crisis' in Havlik, P. (ed.), *Dismantling the Command Economy in Eastern Europe*, Westview Press, Boulder and Oxford.

Grosser, I. (1992), 'Economic transition in Bulgaria' in Richter, S. (ed.), *The Transition from Command to Market Economies in East-Central Europe*, Westview Press, Boulder and London.

Hexter, D., Coricelli, F., Thorne, A., Begg, D., Portes, R. and van Wijnbergen, S. (1993), 'Round table on banking', *Economics of Transition*, 1(1), 111–21.

Holzmann, R. (1992), 'Tax reform in countries in transition: central policy issues', *Public Finance/Finances Publiques*, 47, Supplement, 233–55.

Hughes, G.A. (1991), 'Foreign exchange, prices and economic activity in Bulgaria', *European Economy*, Special Edition No 2, 157–75.

Hughes, G. and Hare, P. (1992a), 'Trade policy and restructuring in Eastern Europe' in Flemming, J. and Rollo, J.M.C. (eds), *Trade, Payments and Adjustment in Central and Eastern Europe*, Royal Institute of International Affairs, London.

Hughes, G. and Hare, P. (1992b), 'Industrial restructuring in Eastern Europe', *European Economic Review*, 36(2–3), 670–76.

Hughes, G. and Hare, P. (1994), 'The international competitiveness of industries in Bulgaria, Czechoslovakia, Hungary and Poland', *Oxford Economic Papers*, 46, 200–21.

Hunter, W.C. (1993), 'Banking reform and the transition to a market economy in Bulgaria: problems and prospects', *Federal Reserve Bank of Atlanta Economic Review*, 78(1), 15–22.

Ickes, B.W. and Ryterman, R. (1993), 'Roadblock to economic reform: interenterprise debt and the transition to markets', *Post-Soviet Affairs*, 9(3), 231–52.

Ivanova, N. (1994), *Impact of Agricultural Policy in Bulgaria in Transition*, mimeo.

Izvorski, I. (1993), 'Economic reform in Bulgaria 1989–93', *Communist Economies and Economic Transformation*, 5(4), 519–31.

Jackson, M. and Kopeva, D. (1994), *Land Markets in Transition Economies: the Case of Bulgaria's 'Radical' Reform*, mimeo.

Jeffries, I. (1993), *Socialist Economies and the Transition to the Market — a Guide*, Routledge, London.

Jones, D.C. (1991), 'The Bulgarian labour market in transition', *International Labour Review*, 130(2), 211–26.

Jones, D.C. (1993), *The Nature and Performance of Small Firms in Bulgaria*, mimeo.

Jones, D.C. and Kato, T. (1993), *The Nature and Determinants of Labor Market Transitions in Former Socialist Economies: Evidence from Bulgaria*, mimeo.

Jones, D.C. and Meurs, M. (1991), 'On the entry of new firms in socialist economies — evidence from Bulgaria', *Soviet Studies*, 43(2), 311–28.

Jones, D.C. and Rock, C. (1994), 'Privatization in Bulgaria' in Estrin, S. (ed.), *Privatization in Central and Eastern Europe*, Longmans, London.

Kostov, V. (1992), 'The export structure and expansion of participation of the Bulgarian machinery-construction industry in the world market', *Russian and East European Finance and Trade*, 28(2), 80–92.

Koves, A. (1992), *Central and East European Economies in Transition: the International Dimension*, Westview Press, Boulder and Oxford.

Lampe, J.R. (1986), *The Bulgarian Economy in the Twentieth Century*, Croom Helm, London.

Lazarova, D. and Harsev, E. (1994), 'Clearing between Russia and Bulgaria in 1991–1992', Bulgarian National Bank, *Bank Review*, 2, 14–21.

Marer, P., Arvay, J., O'Connor, J., Schrenk, M. and Swanson, D. (1992), *Historically Planned Economies: a Guide to the Data*, World Bank, Washington D.C.

McClure, C.E. Jr. (1991), 'Tax policy for Bulgaria', *Bulletin for International Fiscal Documentation*, 45(5), 235–47.

McClure, C.E. Jr. (1992), 'A simpler consumption-based alternative to the income tax for socialist economies in transition', *World Bank Research Observer*, 7(2), 221–37.

McIntyre, R.J. (1988), *Bulgaria: Politics, Economics and Society*, Pinter, London.

McIntyre, R.J. (1992), 'Innovation with an unchanging core: no path to the market in Bulgaria?' in Jeffries, I. (ed.), *Industrial Reform in Socialist Countries — from Restructuring to Reform*, Edward Elgar, Aldershot.

Mileva, N. (1994), 'Bulgarian agriculture in the period of transition', Bulgarian National Bank, *Bank Review*, 1, 34–44.

Miller, J.B. (1994), 'The price index gap: a window to understanding the Bulgarian economy', Bulgarian National Bank, *Bank Review*, 3, 12–22.

Minassian, G. (1992), 'Bulgarian industrial growth and structure 1970–89', *Soviet Studies*, 44(4), 699–738.

Minassian, G. (1994), 'The Bulgarian economy in transition: is there anything wrong with macroeconomic policy?', *Europe-Asia Studies*, 46(2), 337–51.

Minassian, G. and Totev, S. (1992), 'The Bulgarian economy in the early 1990s — will the way down lead up?', *Russian and East European Finance and Trade*, 28(4), 74–88.

Minkov, P. (1993), 'Banks and banking reform in Bulgaria', *Russian and East European Finance and Trade*, 29(2), 22–43.

Mladenov, M. (1992), 'Money, banking and credit: the case of Bulgaria' in Kemme, D.W. and Rudka, A. (eds), *Monetary and Banking Reform in Postcommunist Economies*, Westview Press, New York.

Nenova, M. (1993), 'Wage controls: the Bulgarian experience', Bulgarian National Bank, *Bank Review*, 3, 24–31.

Organisation for Economic Cooperation and Development (1992), *Bulgaria: an Economic Assessment*, Paris.

Osband, K. (1992), 'Index number biases during price liberalization', *International Monetary Fund Staff Papers*, 39(2), 287–309.

Paunov, M. (1993), 'Labour market transformation in Bulgaria', *Communist Economies and Economic Transformation*, 5(2), 213–28.

Petrov, G. (1994), 'State commercial banks at a major crossroads', Bulgarian National Bank, *Bank Review*, 1, 1–7.

Phelps, E.S., Frydman, R., Rapaczynski, A. and Shleifer, A. (1993), *Needed Mechanisms of Corporate Governance and Finance in Eastern Europe*, Working Paper 1, European Bank for Reconstruction and Development, London.

Pinto, B., Belka, M. and Krajewski, S. (1993), 'Transforming state enterprises in Poland: evidence on adjustment by manufacturing firms', *Brookings Papers on Economic Activity*, 1, 213–70.

Portes, R. (1994), 'Transformation traps', *Economic Journal*, 104, 1178–89.

Poulton, H. (1993), *The Balkans: Minorities and States in Conflict*, Minority Rights Publications, London.

Poznanski, K.Z. (1993), 'Pricing practices in the CMEA trade regime — a reappraisal', *Europe-Asia Studies*, 45(5), 923–30.

Pundeff, M. (1992), 'Bulgaria' in Held, J. (ed.), *The Columbia History of Eastern Europe in the Twentieth Century*, Columbia University Press, New York.

Roland, G. (1994), 'On the speed and sequencing of privatisation and restructuring', *Economic Journal*, 104, 1158–68.

Rollo, J. and Smith, A. (1993), 'The political economy of Eastern Europe's trade with the European Community: why so sensitive?', *Economic Policy*, 16, 140–81.

Rosati, D.K. (1992), 'The CMEA demise, trade restructuring and trade destruction in Central and Eastern Europe', *Oxford Review of Economic Policy*, 8(1), 58–81.

Rosati, D.K. (1994), 'Endogenous budget deficits during transition: the mechanism and policy response' in Herr, H., Tober, S. and Westphal, A. (eds), *Macroeconomic Problems of Transformation: Stabilization Policies and Economic Restructuring*, Edward Elgar, Aldershot.

Rose, R. (1993), 'Contradictions between micro- and macro-economic goals in post-communist societies', *Europe-Asia Studies*, 45(3), 419–44.

Rose, R. and Haerpfer, C. (1992), *New Democracies between State and Market: a Baseline Report of Public Opinion*, Studies in Public Policy 204, University of Strathclyde, Glasgow.

Rose, R. and Haerpfer, C. (1993), *Adapting to Transformation in Eastern Europe*, Studies in Public Policy 212, University of Strathclyde, Glasgow.

Rose, R. and Haerpfer, C. (1994), *New Democracies Barometer III: Learning from What is Happening*, Studies in Public Policy 230, University of Strathclyde, Glasgow.

Rostowski, J. (1993), 'Creating stable monetary systems in post-communist economies', *Europe-Asia Studies*, 45(3), 445–62.

Saunders, A. and Sommariva, A. (1993), 'Banking sector and restructuring in Eastern Europe', *Journal of Banking and Finance*, 17(5), 931–57.

Schrenk, M. (1992), 'The CMEA system of trade and payments: initial conditions for institutional change' in Hillman, A.L. and Milanovic, B. (eds), *The Transition from Socialism in Eastern Europe: Domestic Restructuring and Foreign Trade*, World Bank, Washington D.C.

Sokolovsky, J. (1990), *Peasants and Power: State Autonomy and the Collectivization of Agriculture in Eastern Europe*, Westview Press, Boulder and Oxford.

Solimano, A. (1991), 'Central and Eastern Europe: an historical background' in Corbo, V., Coricelli, F. and Bossak, J. (eds), *Reforming Central and Eastern European Economies: Initial Results and Challenges*, World Bank, Washington D.C.

Sturgess, I. (1994), *Credit and Marketing in Bulgarian Agriculture during the Transition Period*, mimeo.

Tait, A.A. (ed.) (1991), *Value-Added Tax: Administrative and Policy Issues*, Occasional Paper 88, International Monetary Fund, Washington D.C.

Tait, A.A. (1992), 'A not-so-simple alternative to the income tax for socialist economies in transition', *World Bank Research Observer*, 7(2), 239–48.

Tchukov, V. (1990), *Still in the Queue: Bulgaria Waits for Democracy*, Institute for European Defence and Strategic Studies, London.

Thirkell, J.E.M. and Tseneva, E.A. (1992), 'Bulgarian labour relations in transition: tripartism and collective bargaining, *International Labour Review*, 131(3), 355–66.

Thorne, A. (1992), Reforming financial systems in Eastern Europe: the case of Bulgaria' in Lampe, J.R. (ed.), *Creating Capital Markets in Eastern Europe*, Woodrow Wilson Centre, Washington D.C.

Thorne, A. (1993), 'Eastern Europe's experience with banking reform: is there a role for banks in the transition?', *Journal of Banking and Finance*, 17(5), 959–1000.

van Wijnbergen, S. (1994), *On the Role of Banks in Enterprise Restructuring: the Polish Example*, Discussion Paper 898, Centre for Economic Policy Research, London.

Vickers, J. and Yarrow, G. (1991), 'Economic perspectives on privatization', *Journal of Economic Perspectives*, 5(2), 111–132.

Vidinova, A. (1993), 'Bulgaria – tripartism in industrial relations', *Policy Studies*, 14(4), 31–39.

Wädekin, K.-E. (1993), 'Bulgaria, Czechoslovakia and the GDR' in Braverman, A., Brooks, K.M. and Csaki, C. (eds), *The Agricultural Transition in Central and Eastern Europe and the Former USSR*, World Bank, Washington D.C.

Wendel, H. and Manchev, T. (1994), 'The international value of the lev and its effect on domestic prices', Bulgarian National Bank, *Bank Review*, 1, 16–20.

Williamson, J. (1994), 'In search of a manual for technopols' in Williamson, J. (ed.), *The Political Economy of Policy Reform*, Institute for International Economics, Washington D.C.

Winiecki, J. (1991), 'The inevitability of a fall in output in the early stages of transition to the market – theoretical underpinnings', *Soviet Studies*, 43(4), 669–76.

Winters, L.A. (1992), 'The Europe agreements: with a little help from our friends' in *The Association Process: Making It Work – Central Europe and the European Community*, Centre for Economic Policy Research, Occasional Paper 11, London.

World Bank (1991), *Bulgaria: Crisis and Transition to a Market Economy*, 2 vols, Washington D.C.

Wyzan, M.L. (1990), 'Bulgarian agriculture: sweeping reform, mediocre performance' in Wädekin, K.-E. (ed.), *Communist Agriculture — Farming in the Soviet Union and Eastern Europe*, Routledge, London.

Wyzan, M.L. (1991), 'The Bulgarian economy in the post-Zhivkov era' in Sjoberg, O. and Wyzan, M.L. (eds), *Economic Change in the Balkan States: Albania, Bulgaria, Romania and Yugoslavia*, Pinter, London.

Wyzan, M.L. (1993), 'Stabilisation policy in post-communist Bulgaria' in Somogyi, L. (ed.), *The Political Economy of the Transition Process in Eastern Europe*, Edward Elgar, Aldershot.

News media and statistical publications

168 Hours BBN/Bulgarian Business News
Bulgarian Economic Review
Bulgarian National Bank, *Annual Reports*
Bulgarian National Bank, *News Bulletin*
Bulgarian National Bank, *Monthly Bulletin*
Business Central Europe
Dŭrzhaven vestnik
National Statistical Institute, *Finansovo sŭstoyanie na predpriyatiyata*
National Statistical Insitute, *Iznos i vnos, Export and Import*
National Statistical Institute, *Privatizatsiyata v Republika Bŭlgariya*
National Statistical Institute, *Statisticheski izvestiya, Statistical News*
National Statistical Institute, *Tekushta stopanska konyunktura, Current Economic Business*
National Statistical Institute, *Tseni i inflatsiya*
OMRI Daily Digest
The Economist

Index

Bulgarian Socialist Party 24–7,
63–4, 82–3, 95, 191, 201
Bundesbank 124

cement industry 207–9, 218, 221
Centre for Mass Privatization 199,
201
Chervenkov, V. 4–5
Club for *Glasnost* and Democracy
24
CMEA
organization 9, 54, 106–8
trade with x, 28, 32, 35, 49, 56,
58, 74, 84, 90–1, 94, 104–14,
118–9, 126, 206, 213, 216
Comecon *see* CMEA
Commission for Protection of
Competition 190
Committee for Tourism 208, 221
Confederation of Independent
Trade Unions in Bulgaria 34, 67
see also trade unions
constitution 3, 5, 22, 63, 82, 219
Construction Bank 131
consumption 32, 35, 38–41, 58,
75, 148, 150, 157–8, 170, 216,
225
credit 51–2, 59, 68–70, 86–7, 89,
99–100, 102, 123–5, 127, 129,
131–4, 136, 148, 185–6, 197,
199
see also money supply
Czechoslovakia
economy x, 19, 34, 39–40, 53,
84, 121–2, 127, 214–5
history ix
politics, 26, 228
privatization 183, 194, 222

debt, foreign xi, 16, 28–9, 48–9,
54, 68, 73, 107, 114–20, 141,
156, 160, 213, 215
moratorium 29, 32, 48, 114, 117,

151, 154, 160
see also London Club; Brady
bonds
debts, bad 68–9, 87, 89, 102, 119,
126–30, 134–5, 140–4, 160, 185,
223
see also laws, bad debts
debts, inter-enterprise 52, 86–90,
185
Decree 56 11, 152, 175, 187–8
Democratic Party 82
demonopolization 85–6, 89, 100
Dimitrov, F. 63–64, 83, 191
Dimitrov, G. x, 3–5
Dimitrova, B. 63

Economic Bank 132–4
Ekoglasnost 24, 82–3
elections x, 3–4, 21, 24–7, 33–4,
63, 81–3, 141, 191, 199, 227–9,
232
Electronic Bank 131
embargos *see* Iraq; Serbia
employment 9, 19, 33, 47–8,
59–60, 77, 80–1, 159, 178, 185,
197, 205, 211, 219, 224
see also agriculture, employment;
industry, employment
European Bank for Reconstruction
and Development 55, 214
European Union 54–5, 57, 110,
118, 121–2, 169
exchange rate 17, 19, 29, 35,
41, 44–5, 52–7, 65, 67, 69–75,
79, 92, 105, 111, 154, 156, 167,
171, 215, 217, 232–3
exports 54, 56–7, 72, 94, 101, 105,
107–9, 110–6, 120, 156, 159,
164
Expressbank 139

Fatherland Front 2–4, 21, 82
Federal Reserve Board 124